RWANDA

RWANDA

From Genocide
to Precarious Peace

SUSAN THOMSON

YALE UNIVERSITY PRESS
NEW HAVEN AND LONDON

For information about this and other Yale University Press publications, please contact:
US Office: sales.press@yale.edu   yalebooks.com
Europe Office: sales@yaleup.co.uk   yalebooks.co.uk

Set in Adobe Caslon Pro by IDSUK (DataConnection) Ltd
Printed in Great Britain by Gomer Press Ltd, Llandysul, Ceredigion, Wales

Library of Congress Control Number: 2017958709

ISBN 978-0-300-19739-6

A catalogue record for this book is available from the British Library.

10 9 8 7 6 5 4 3 2 1

CONTENTS

CONTENTS

PLATES, MAPS AND TABLES

Plates

1. Belgian paratroopers guard a group of alleged Hutu arsonists during Rwanda's Social Revolution, September 1960. © René Lemarchand.
2. A patron and his clients, Goma, 1961. © René Lemarchand.
3. Rwandans in makeshift grass homes, Byumba prefecture, 1992. Courtesy of Jim Lavery.
4. Civilians listen to a member of the security services in the Sainte-Famille Catholic church, May 1994. © Corinne Dufka.
5. Rwandan children after the destruction of their orphanage, Kigali, May 1994. © Corinne Dufka.
6. Hutu men accused of participating in the genocide line up at a detention center in Kabuga, June 1994. © Corinne Dufka.
7. Major-General Guy Tousignant of the United Nations Assistance Mission for Rwanda discusses prison conditions with the RPF warden in Kirambo, April 1995. © Thomas Roach.

Maps

Tables

ACKNOWLEDGMENTS

You would not be holding this book in your hands if it were not for my formidable (and female) editorial team at Yale University Press. Phoebe Clapham encouraged me to start the project. Heather McCallum, Marika Lysandrou, Rachael Lonsdale and Samantha Cross brought it to the finish line. A special thank you to Marika and Rachael for supporting this work in large and small ways.

Marie-Eve Desrosiers and Rosalind Raddatz deserve special thanks for their constructive criticism and fierce belief in my project. Among my many cheerleaders are colleagues who are also friends. Throughout the course of writing Jennie Burnet, Marie-Eve Desrosiers and Noel Twagiramungu fielded my many questions to help me better understand the beautiful, complex and troubled country we all love. Catharine Newbury offered helpful advice in the final stage of writing, for which I am appreciative. I also benefited from email exchanges with journalists, academics, students and military men, Rwandan and foreign, who generously answered all of my questions about this or that event they had witnessed or researched.

ACKNOWLEDGMENTS

Hearty thanks go to all who so graciously shared their photography with me. Aubrey Graham, PhD (Copyright 2012) deserves special mention for her stunning cover image of two young men pushing a bicycle towards the top of a hill just outside of Rubavu. In the background, Mount Nyiragongo, an active volcano located across the border near Goma in the DRC, smokes.

For their boundless support and bedrock of friendship: Antonio Berrera, Marie-Eve Desrosiers, Rosalind Raddatz, Cassie Taylor, Kim Taylor and Tammy Wilks. And to Monica Costa, Heather Dockstader and the crew at Hamilton Whole Foods for keeping my desk in the back quiet and ready for my bursts of writing.

Many, many thanks to my first readers Becky Gough, Jamie Gagliano, Shannon Staley and Steve Terrill for encouraging me to keep writing, even when the book was in its messy first iterations.

Colgate University students in two of my undergraduate courses deserve enormous thanks. My 300 Level spring 2013 and spring 2015 *Rwanda since the 1994 Genocide* classes helped me to think about balancing the relationship between human rights and economic development. Students in my spring 2017 first-year course *Rwanda, 1860 to present* asked smart questions and offered important advice on drafts of various chapters that I assigned them. I am grateful for the chance to nurture their affection for Rwanda.

Colgate University's Research Council generously provided financial support, for which I am also grateful. This funding supported my team of exceptional research assistants: Amanda Brown, Kristi Carey, Kevin Costello, Michelle Sagalchik and Hannah Sosland.

I am especially thankful for the care that each of my three anonymous reviewers put into improving my text. For an academic, pages and pages of criticism are never easy to swallow—except in this case. It was a privilege to have my work read so carefully and so constructively.

Good peer review reminds me that I have also had the good fortune of having teachers and mentors who have taught me so much about reading and writing. Those Rwanda scholars who came before provided a sturdy bedrock of articles and books that I consulted in the course of writing. In addition to the work of scholars mentioned earlier, I hold dear the analyses of An Ansoms, Anu Chakravarty, Alison Des Forges, Lee Ann Fujii, André Guichaoua, Bert Ingelaere, Villia Jefremovas, René Lemarchand, Timothy Longman, Catharine Newbury, David Newbury, Filip Reyntjens, Marc Sommers, Scott Straus and Lars Waldorf.

Thanks too to my boys, Evan and Riley. You are simply the best.

Finally, my deepest and most urgent thanks go to Rwandans, who gave so much of themselves to help me explain their country to you. In this regard, David Himbara, Alice Gatebuke, Etienne Mashuli, Revi Mfizi, Willy Rangira and Joseph Sebarenzi deserve special mention. Many chose not to be acknowledged by name. I know why. Let me simply say: your generosity and intelligence are the beating heart of this book. *Murakoze cyane.*

ABBREVIATIONS

AgDF	Agaciro [dignity] Development Fund
ADL	Rwandan Association for the Defense of Human Rights and Public Liberties (Association rwandaise pour la défense des droits de la personne et des libertés publiques)
AFDL	Alliance of Democratic Forces for the Liberation of Congo (Alliance des forces démocratiques pour la libération du Congo)
AIDS	Acquired Immunodeficiency Syndrome
ALiR	Army for the Liberation of Rwanda (Armée pour la libération du Rwanda)
APROMOSA	Association for the Social Promotion of the Masses (Association pour la promotion sociale de la masse)
CDR	Coalition for the Defense of the Republic (Coalition pour la défense de la République)
CIA	Central Intelligence Agency (United States)

CNDP	National Congress for the Defense of the People (Congrès national pour la défense du peuple)
CNLG	National Commission for the Fight against Genocide (Commission nationale de lutte contre le génocide)
DANIDA	Danish Development Cooperation Agency
DFID	British Department for International Development
DGPR	Democratic Green Party of Rwanda
DMI	Department of Military Intelligence
DRC	Democratic Republic of Congo
EDPRS	Economic Development and Poverty Reduction Strategy of the World Bank
FAO	Food and Agriculture Organization of the United Nations
FAR	Rwandan Armed Forces (Forces armées rwandaises)
FDLR	Democratic Forces for the Liberation of Rwanda (Forces démocratiques pour la libération du Rwanda)
FDU–Inkingi	United Democratic Forces–Inkingi
FEWS	Famine Early Warning Systems Network
GDP	Gross Domestic Product
GNI	Gross National Income
HIV	Human Immunodeficiency Virus
ICTR	International Criminal Tribunal for Rwanda
IDP	Internally displaced persons
IMF	International Monetary Fund
IOC	Integrated Operations Centre
LIPRODHOR	Rwandan League for the Promotion and Defense of Human Rights (Ligue rwandaise pour la promotion et la défense des droits de l'homme)
MDR	Republican Democratic Movement (Mouvement démocratique républicain)
MINAGRI	Ministry of Agriculture
MINALOC	Ministry of Local Government

MINECOFIN	Ministry of Finance and Economic Planning
MINEDUC	Ministry of Education, Science, Technology and Scientific Research
MINITERRE	Ministry of Lands, Environment, Forestry, Water and Natural Resources
MoH	Ministry of Health
MRND	National Republican Movement for Democracy (Mouvement républicain national pour la démocratie)
MSF	Doctors without Borders (Médecins sans frontières)
NEC	National Electoral Commission
NGO	Non-governmental organization
NRA	National Resistance Army (Uganda)
NRM	National Resistance Movement (Uganda)
NURC	National Unity and Reconciliation Commission
OAU	Organisation of African Unity
ORINFOR	Rwandan Information Office (Office rwandais d'information)
OtP	Office of the Prosecutor (at the International Criminal Tribunal for Rwanda)
PARMEHUTU	Hutu Emancipation Movement Party (Parti du mouvement de l'émancipation Hutu)
PL	Liberal Party (Parti libéral)
PRSP	Poverty Reduction Strategy Plan
PSD	Social Democratic Party (Parti social démocrate)
PS-Imberakuri	Social Party Imberakuri (Parti social imberakuri)
RANU	Rwandese Alliance for National Unity
RCD	Congolese Rally for Democracy (Rassemblement congolais pour la démocratie)
RCS	Rwandan Correctional Services
RDF	Rwanda Defense Force (replaced the RPA as Rwanda's national army in 2002)
RISD	Rwanda Initiative for Sustainable Development

RNC	Rwandan National Congress
RPA	Rwandan Patriotic Army (also called RPA-Inkotanyi)
RPF	Rwandan Patriotic Front (also called RPF-Inkotanyi)
RWF	Rwandan francs
TIG	Works in the public interest (Travaux d'intérêt général)
UN	United Nations
UNAMIR	United Nations Assistance Mission for Rwanda
UNAR	National Rwandan Union (Union nationale rwandaise)
UNDP	United Nations Development Program
UNHCR	United Nations High Commission for Refugees, also known as the UN Refugee Agency
UNHRFOR	United Nations Human Rights Mission for Rwanda
UNICEF	United Nations Fund for Children
UNOHCHR	United Nations Office of the High Commissioner for Human Rights
UPC	Uganda People's Congress
USAID	United States Agency for International Development
ZAMBATT	UN peacekeeping battalion from Zambia

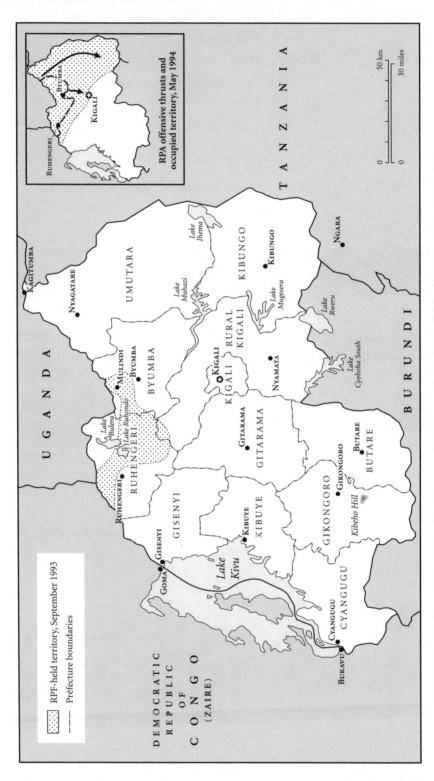

U G A N D A

KAGITUMBA

NYAGATARE

UMUTARA

Lake
Ihema

MULINDI
BYUMBA
BYUMBA

Lake
Muhazi

KIBUNGO

KIBUNGO

Lake
Mugesera

NGARA

Lake
Bulera
Lake Ruhondo
RUHENGERI
RUHENGERI

KIGALI
KIGALI RURAL KIGALI

GITARAMA
GITARAMA

NYAMATA

Lake
Rweru

Lake
Cyohoha South

GISENYI
GISENYI

KIBUYE
KIBUYE

GIKONGORO
GIKONGORO

BUTARE
BUTARE

GOMA

Lake
Kivu

Kibeho Hill

CYANGUGU
CYANGUGU

BUKAVU

T A N Z A N I A

B U R U N D I

DEMOCRATIC
REPUBLIC
OF
C O N G O
(ZAIRE)

1. Administrative boundaries during the civil war and 1994 genocide, including RPF offensive positions, 1993–94

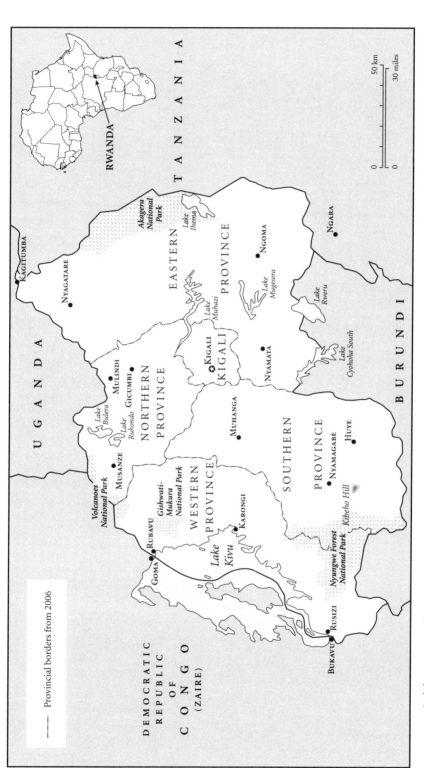

2. Administrative boundaries from 2006, with revised town names

INTRODUCTION
The "New" Rwanda

Visitors find Rwanda an alluring place, peaceful after genocide and civil war. Some in the West feel sympathy, even responsibility, for the horrors of the genocidal regime of ethnic Hutu hardliners. As a result, Rwanda benefits from an inordinate amount of goodwill as visitors—tourists, students, aid workers, journalists and diplomats alike—fall in love with Kigali's clean streets, renovated restaurants, new hotels, wireless hotspots and espresso bars serving the finest Rwandan brews. New skyscrapers, storefronts, hotels, banks, convention and shopping centers have transformed the capital. Hospitals and schools as well as roads and bridges have been rebuilt, with new ones added. In the middle of Kigali sits the main traffic circle of the revamped central business district. Pedestrians and motorists share the circle, with its six connecting roads leading to different parts of the city and eventually all corners of the country—Rwanda's road network is among the best in Africa.

Kigali is home to thirty-four private and public universities and technical schools tasked with training the next generation of leaders.[1] Operating all year round, they also provide night classes for Kigali's

1

ambitious educated elite: idleness and lack of drive are social faux pas since the 1994 genocide. Discipline and focus define contemporary Rwanda, where good citizens work tirelessly to promote national development. The official line is that thanks to government-led initiatives to promote national unity, Rwandans now live in harmony. Ethnic labels— of being Hutu, Tutsi or Twa—are a thing of the past, a relic of previous regimes who manipulated ethnicity for their own selfish political goals. Rwanda is a country on the move and Kigali its epicenter.

Or at least that is how President Paul Kagame of the ruling Rwandan Patriotic Front (RPF) would have us see it.

But the image of Rwanda he promotes internationally, the image of a country of peace and prosperity, where opportunities are there for the taking, is in fact an image that is a reality only for the privileged few. The RPF's focus on Kigali as Rwanda's economic engine is unsurprising. Like elsewhere in the world, the country's economic growth is tied to urbanization. This policy choice makes sense in a modern and globalizing world. But in a country where some 10 to 20 percent of the country are city dwellers, the benefits of such economic growth are not reaching the majority of rural Rwandans. Instead, the spoils of RPF rule, financed by economic growth averaging 8 percent per annum, are accruing to a relatively wealthy, educated and English-speaking urban elite who came to live in Rwanda only since 1994. They are both the drivers and the beneficiaries of postgenocide policies. All that Kigali has to offer is for their benefit in exchange for unbridled loyalty to the president and *his* RPF.

This pact ignores how most Rwandans actually live. Some 80 percent of the population live in the rolling hills of the countryside. Most are poor, living on less than $2 per day, and earning their keep as subsistence farmers, surviving on what they can grow. Poverty makes them risk-averse, putting how they live at odds with RPF policies to quickly upgrade their lives in the name of ethnic unity and development. Those who question or challenge RPF policy directives soon find themselves in trouble, as either agitators or people who are not committed to ethnic unity. The RPF's headstrong and top-down approach overlooks the struggles faced by the rural majority to eke out a living on small, nutrient-depleted plots of land as they work to feed large nuclear and extended families. While Kigali gives the appearance of prosperity, the average rural household of nine people struggles with food insecurity and malnutrition rooted in land disputes.[2]

The RPF is unapologetic about such realities. In its view, following President Kagame's austere and disciplined example, such daily challenges can be overcome with a mixture of proper mindset and hard work. Rwandans in all corners of the country are told to pull themselves up by their bootstraps to get unified and build the economy.

The irony of the RPF's commitment to self-reliance is Rwanda's dependence on foreign aid. Aid dependency exists when a country is unable to perform basic government functions and services without foreign funding or expertise. In 2013 alone, Rwanda received over $1 billion in net development assistance, of which more than half was dedicated to infrastructure projects.[3] While this number is not as high as the 70 percent infrastructure support that the Habyarimana regime received in the 1980s, it does highlight Rwanda's historical and contemporary dependency on aid to finance development.[4] Rwanda's aid dependency ratio has averaged 21 percent since the genocide, a number that corresponds to rates before 1994.[5] And the tiny, landlocked country is still resource-poor and population-dense. What differs today is that international aid is given freely, often without preconditions, to alleviate the collective guilt that many foreign donors feel for their failure to intervene to stop the killings in 1994.[6]

Rwanda's seemingly miraculous recovery from civil war and genocide is founded on a "deft authoritarianism"[7] that limits political rights and freedoms in exchange for national security via a mix of overt repression and subtle cooptation. The RPF's ambitious unity and development policies are designed to transform Rwanda's political and economic structures while altering individual ethnic identities. No longer will Rwandans think of themselves as Hutu, Tutsi or Twa. Instead, they will be patriotic Rwandans, ethnically unified to focus their collective energies on economic development. Under the watchful eye of President Kagame, the RPF has aggressively pursued its policy dreams at breakneck speed. Pace is important: the urgency and necessity of social, political and cultural change are used to justify an often heavy hand in remaking the country on its own terms and conditions. Foreign observers and domestic critics who comment that the political system is entrenching RPF rule instead of building a democratic system of checks and balances are denounced as traitors. Armed with the strength of conviction and the urgency of the task at hand, the RPF's position is plain: its vision for Rwanda is the only viable one to assure a genocide-free future. The fear of a return to genocidal violence informs all aspects of RPF rule, a legitimate concern given the magnitude of the violence of the 1994 genocide and the damage left in its wake. Assessing whether RPF rule could result in future episodes of mass political violence is the subject of this book.

Genocide

Some twenty years ago, Rwanda was home to the most efficient genocide of the twentieth century. By the time the civil war and genocide ended in July 1994, at least half a million ethnic Tutsi were dead in the fastest episode of mass political violence since the Holocaust. The violence was genocide as legally defined in the United Nations Genocide Convention.[8] It was a deliberate choice by a power-hungry Hutu elite who feared that political reforms would diminish their ability to enrich themselves at the expense of the general population. They used the machinery and authority of the state to systematically kill Tutsi. Returning from peace talks with the RPF in neighboring Tanzania, the aircraft of then President Juvénal Habyarimana was shot out of the sky by still unknown forces. Upon his death, a group of Hutu hardliners proceeded to eliminate their main political opponents—politically connected Hutu and Tutsi alike. They went on to form an interim Hutu Power government that declared war on a common Tutsi enemy. The hardliners then deployed loyal foot soldiers and militias to urge their Hutu brethren to exterminate Tutsi. The killing was low-tech: ordinary Hutu used machetes, hoes and other basic farm tools to kill their Tutsi neighbors. It was also intimate. Small groups did the face-to-face work of killing, usually in broad daylight and in public settings such as churches, hospitals, schools, stadiums and other everyday locales.

A handful of the killers were women; the majority were ordinary Hutu men. They killed for various reasons beyond the widely held belief that they hated Tutsi. Instead, the reasons why ordinary Hutu men killed varied by individual. Most had no prior history of sadistic violence. These husbands, fathers and farmers killed for "routine and ordinary reasons."[9] Some with vigor and a sense of duty, others to settle grudges and personal scores, and some in fear that Hutu Power militants would kill them for their lack of commitment to the cause of exterminating Tutsi. Whatever the reason, killing Tutsi was a state-sanctioned event that brought the authority of key institutions—the military, church and media—to bear.

One hundred days later, the hardliners had lost the war and fled to the refugee camps in neighboring Zaire. They urged Hutu civilians to flee with them. Millions of fearful and exhausted Rwandans did, leaving the victorious RPF in a seemingly impossible situation. People and places bore the scars of war: skeletal remains littered streets, gardens and parks; bloated corpses bobbed in waterways across the country; traffic circles and the main roads connecting them loomed large with bodies, as did churches and soccer stadiums. In addition to this, buildings, bridges and homes were damaged, sometimes beyond repair; windows, doors and roofing were looted; electricity and water were in short supply.

Just a stone's throw southeast of Kigali's main traffic circle is the Sainte-Famille parish where some two thousand Tutsi sought refuge in the first days of the genocide in April 1994. Instead of solace, they found church leaders colluding with Hutu militias. Those in charge would feed groups of Tutsi to waiting extremists, known collectively as Interahamwe (meaning "those who work together").[10] Hutu militants attacked with machetes and studded clubs. Few victims survived.

The participation of Christian churches in the genocide should come as no surprise—a historic link between church and state meant that religious leaders had long tolerated or promoted ethnic discrimination. By April 2014, as part of the commemorations to mark the twentieth anniversary of the genocide, Sainte-Famille had become a symbol of postgenocide reconciliation and reconstruction—a place full of life and hope where parishioners knelt to pray for continued peace, security and economic development on the same hard wooden benches where Tutsi had once cowered, fearing for body and soul.[11]

Surviving Genocide, Becoming Rwandan

Marie survived the genocide because of her Hutu ethnicity and her role as a young mother.[12] She stayed at home, aware of the murders at her doorstep, but not wanting to leave her young son Prosper home alone. Her Tutsi husband Bosco survived through strategic action. He joined the killing squads to demonstrate his loyalty to the cause of exterminating Tutsi. Prosper was killed at a roadblock outside of Butare on the road to Gikongoro town in May 1994. Bosco had taken him to "work" with him while Marie was out trying to plant seeds in time for the next harvest. Rwanda's long rainy season lasts from mid-March to mid-May, making it an important time to assure food security for rural households.

Bosco's job was to check ethnic identity cards, detain Tutsi and group them for murder. As family lineage passes through the father, Prosper would have been recognized as an ethnic Tutsi despite a shared Hutu ancestry from his mother. When Marie returned home on the day their infant Prosper died, her husband said that the killers chose not to spare the child because of Bosco's Tutsi identity and to remind him that he was one of them. Bosco never forgave himself for the loss of their only child, turning to drink and prostitutes while living in a UN-managed refugee camp in Zaire along Rwanda's western border, in Bukavu town. It was during this immediate postgenocide period (1994–97) that Marie believes her husband contracted AIDS. With the support of anti-retroviral drugs provided to the Rwandan government by the American organization Partners in Health, Bosco lived in relatively good health for a dozen years, having first received treatment on his return to Rwanda in 1996. Marie's children with him born since the genocide are HIV-free thanks to the donor-assisted prenatal care she received during each pregnancy.[13]

When Bosco died, Marie and her children lost most of their government-provided social services. The village health provider took the family off the rolls upon his death. As an ethnic Tutsi, Bosco was the sole true survivor of the genocide in the family. Marie, being a former Hutu, is reluctant to identify openly as a survivor given that the RPF has outlawed public discussion of, or even reference to, one's ethnicity. By the time Bosco died in 2010, a moral discourse had taken root in Rwanda, one that relies on a simple dichotomy: Tutsi are the sole survivors of the 1994 genocide, Hutu its only perpetrators.

This framing does not allow any frank or open discussion of how ethnic categories shaped the violence of the genocide. Notably, it prevents public dialogue that complicates or controverts the acceptable pseudo-ethnic groupings of (Tutsi) survivors and (Hutu) perpetrators, seeking in this way to control who can say what and when about their lived experiences of violence before, during and after the genocide. Individuals like Marie are often unable to express grievances to the government because they lack the language to do so. The

survivor–perpetrator binary also excludes other experience categories—
such as Tutsi and Twa perpetrators, Hutu and Twa rescuers, Hutu and
Twa resisters and Hutu and Twa survivors.

According to Marie, Bosco died with the shame of having killed
some fellow Tutsi without being brought to justice. Upon his death,
Marie's status as a "former Hutu" also meant that other members of the
women's cooperative shunned her. They claimed to know whom Bosco
had killed during the genocide and used this information to exclude
Marie. Losing access to social services meant that their son Joseph was
not able to enter secondary school, as Marie needed his help to provide
for their family.

The RPF's denial of ethnic identity hits people like Marie hard
emotionally, physically and spiritually. Asked about how she felt when
government assistance provided for survivors was taken away when
Bosco died, Marie's voice gradually rises while she fidgets and shifts in
her seat. "This government has made it so hard to live together since the
genocide because they don't accept what happened. People were killing,
stealing, burning. Everyone was involved because there was no way to
escape. Am I not a survivor?"

Marie displays symptoms of post-traumatic stress, a mental condition
afflicting people who have experienced severe trauma. She is not alone. As
many as 95 percent of Rwandans living in the country during the genocide witnessed, experienced or participated in extreme acts of violence.[14]
The illness brings with it major depression, insomnia and dulled, passive
behavior punctuated with violent or aggressive outbursts when reminded
of the traumatic incident or events. It can impair social and occupational
function and is particularly pernicious among the poor as they lack the
resources to seek treatment.[15] Trauma can also pass from one generation
to the next, meaning Rwanda might not outgrow the violence of the 1994
genocide. Its legacy weighs heavily on the minds of the young as the policies and programs the government has implemented to ensure mass
violence like the genocide never again happens shape their participation

in society. In some instances, such as being an adult born of rape during the genocide or having a relative who participated in the killing, young people are ashamed of their past.

Tutsi who killed other Tutsi and Hutu before, during and after the genocide have rarely been called to account for their crimes. RPF-sponsored killing squads known as *abakada*[16] fanned out across Rwanda during the genocide to control the largely Hutu population and secure territory. Anyone who resisted or challenged the RPF strategy to win the civil war at all costs was denounced or killed, often on the spot.[17] The RPF relies "on a military mode of managing political situations and choices" that began during its rebel days in Uganda and continues today.[18]

Joseph knows that his father and others like him had to steal, lie, cheat, point fingers and even kill to survive the genocide. But he is unable to talk about it. Feeling guilt and shame about what happened during the genocide and then suppressing these feelings are necessary survival skills in the new Rwanda, especially since good citizens prioritize national development over their own private needs. The RPF's expectation is that Rwandans like Marie and her family will be willing to exchange justice for the benefits of economic growth.

The Realities of Rural Life, the Promise of Kigali

Marie lives on a rural hillside outside of Huye (formerly Butare), a secondary city located in Southern Province some 120 kilometers southwest of Kigali and just 80 kilometers north of Rwanda's border with Burundi. Her one-room home is tiny for a family of four; there are hardly any visible possessions and there is no running water, electricity or gas for cooking. The modern amenities that define Kigali are conspicuously absent for Marie and millions of rural Rwandans like her. Marie's girls attend school, thanks to the provision of universal primary education. As she prepares dinner, often the only hot meal of the week, they sit on a bench doing homework in the fading afternoon light. Thirteen-year-old Grace works through math problems while nine-year-old Hope does Kinyarwanda language exercises. If these girls conform to the average, they will leave school before completing the sixth grade to help Marie cultivate the half-hectare of land that assures their survival.

Sixteen-year-old Joseph left primary school in 2012. Despite graduating near the top of his class, he was not able to enter secondary school—Marie needed him at home to help provide for the family. Joseph now works as a day laborer cultivating the land of a wealthier neighbor, a job that earns an average daily wage of 200 Rwandan francs (roughly 30 cents in 2014). In a good month, Joseph will earn as much as 4,000 francs (or US$6), enough to supplement his mother's meager income, perhaps even enough to buy medicine or clothes. This revenue is critical to the family's survival, as their small plot of land only produces enough for consumption—there is no excess to take to market.

In the rural areas, unlike in Kigali where access to the city center is tightly controlled, population density is laid bare—across the undulating hills, you see that every inch of land is in use. Plots of various sizes cover the hills, divided into rectangular patches, each a different shade of green or yellow, depending on the crop and season.[19] Land competition means that Rwandans need to find inventive and durable ways to provide enough to eat for their families. RPF policy does not allow rural farmers to make their own choices about how to use their limited resources. In efforts to address food security, the RPF mandated in 2009 which crops can be grown and when, often without concern for local growing conditions or household nutritional needs or preferences.

The cycle of having just enough to eat without reserves or excess to sell is a common condition in rural Rwanda today, as it always has been. In precolonial times, having enough to eat was also a constant preoccupation for many rural people.[20] In the late nineteenth century, as today, land was a hot-button issue as traditional patron–client relationships meant that many rural people worked the land of more socially and economically powerful patrons who in turn provided physical safety, whether from military conquest or local conflicts. Clientship "is a form of 'instrumental friendship' between two persons of relatively unequal socioeconomic status."[21] Historically, the patron (or more powerful person) extends protection or benefits to the client, who in turn provides loyalty or services such as tilling land or grazing cattle. In rural societies such as Rwanda, mobilizing resources—labor, land and livestock—was central to the growth of the state.

The legacy of these hierarchical relationships continues to cascade through postgenocide social and political life. Land was, and remains, a factor of differentiation between rich and poor, and between urban and rural residents. Marie is among the fortunate minority who owns a plot of land. Since the genocide, some 40 percent of rural residents provide for their families through daily wage labor, not from farming their own plot of land. This means that they can only provide food and other necessities for themselves and their families when they can work the land of another.

While creating off-farm jobs is a priority of the RPF government, it has yet to yield fruit despite intensive efforts in Kigali and elsewhere throughout the country. There are simply too few employers for too many job seekers. Youth employment is a policy issue of monumental proportion, as 61 percent of Rwandans are under the age of twenty-four.[22] A critical tension is the RPF's expectation that Rwandans go out and find themselves paid employment when there are few such jobs to be found. As a result, young men are "stuck" in "waithood" as they are unable to achieve the cultural benchmarks of adulthood—owning land and a home to court a spouse to then be able to have children. The inability to mature to social adulthood through marriage also affects young women as they are unable to fulfill societal expectations of what makes a desirable Rwandan woman—motherhood—without a husband and child.[23]

Like other young men and women his age, Joseph longs to leave his rural home to move to Kigali. He aspires to work as a motorcycle taxi driver, but cannot afford to make the transition. With minimal education, the best hope for young people is a job that requires few skills, such as working in construction or perhaps as a household domestic for wealthier Rwandans or foreign nationals living in the capital. Daily wage construction jobs are more plentiful, given Kigali's building boom. But they are reserved for the chosen few who have the necessary social connections and skills to take up the work. Such positions are a recent development as Kigali was largely rebuilt using prison labor in the years immediately following the 1994 genocide. By the time the private sector and foreign investors started to fund Kigali's reconstruction in the mid-2000s, young people struggled to actually settle there. It is also government policy to prevent "undesirables"—street vendors, homeless people, sex workers and beggars—from tarnishing Kigali's pristine aesthetic.[24]

As a primary school graduate, Joseph is not quite eligible to participate in state-led programs designed to educate Rwandans on living together in ethnic harmony since the genocide. Such activities are usually reserved for those matriculating in secondary school. Civic education is the vehicle through which the RPF teaches Rwandans what is expected of them as good citizens. Reeducation graduation certificates are but one of a multitude of forms and papers needed to access even the most basic rights of citizenship, including access to higher education, having a passport and the "right" to live in Kigali.[25]

Other restrictions keep rural Rwandans from settling in Kigali, further deepening an already gaping rural–urban divide. Affordable housing for low-income earners is nearly non-existent. The RPF began clearing out informal settlements in 1997 to make way for new homes and buildings, often without compensation for the displaced.[26] The result is that Kigali is not a welcoming place for most, catering instead to the political, military and economic elite. Government critics call it

"Disneyland for tourists." Kigali's shiny exterior hides the hardships of non-elite Rwandans trying to make their way. Daily wage laborers earn on average the same 200 francs as their rural counterparts. In Kigali, 200 francs is the price of a hot meal at a simple restaurant. It is far from enough to provide for food, shelter and clothing in rural areas let alone in Kigali. The chasm between the promise of Kigali and the realities of daily life is deeply felt by millions of Rwandans like Marie and her children.

A Precarious Peace

It is the transition from the horror of genocide to the stability of ethnic unity and economic development that is the focus of this book. It explains how the RPF, under the tutelage of President Paul Kagame, has been able to quickly and efficiently rebuild a war-ravaged Rwanda. It also asks how far RPF-led reconstruction and reconciliation policies produce peace, and the human cost of such rapid progress: who are the winners and losers of sweeping change in a country where the legacy of genocide touches all aspects of daily life?

Focusing on the first twenty years of RPF rule, this analysis uncovers why the government pursued the path it did while explaining the broader historical and cultural context of these decisions. It also lays bare how Rwandans experience RPF rule.[27]

As the coming pages demonstrate, the RPF has crafted a precarious peace, one that has consolidated its power and authority at the expense of other ways of imagining Rwanda's shared future and developing its people. The RPF has deepened the reach of the state into the lives of ordinary people, building on historical ways of governing the rural majority. The relationship between the RPF and the largely rural majority is premised on a mutual understanding of "submission, active support and loyalty from the population."[28] Ordinary citizens—particularly ethnic Hutu like Marie—have learned not to challenge or question

RPF rule. This raises important concerns about the durability of the rulers' postgenocide policies and the stability of the peace they have created.

The book follows a largely chronological approach. After looking at how and why the genocide came about and the conditions that made it possible, the book will then go on to consider how the country rebuilt itself, and why the RPF leadership made the policy choices it did, and the extent of their success in these efforts. Finally, we shall see why this success falls severely short—and why the peace it has built is precarious in the long term.

PART I

Genocide, and its Causes and Consequences

1

GENOCIDE
Power Politics, not Ethnic Hatred

�'t money = power

When speaking of the genocide, many Rwandans who survived the violence recount the fear they felt upon approaching roadblocks in Kigali and other towns across the country. Stomachs churned as militiamen checked national identity cards to confirm the bearer as Tutsi. Holding such an ID card, failing to produce one, or being on a list of individuals targeted for killing usually meant an immediate death sentence. Wealthier people could negotiate for their lives with on-the-spot cash payments, giving up their vehicle or making promises of land, houses and durable household goods like televisions and refrigerators. Roadblocks on main roads and barriers of cinder blocks, tree trunks and other large objects on secondary roads made passage or escape from the primary barriers nearly impossible. These bases allowed militiamen to fan out and confront anyone trying to bypass roadblocks or hide in churches, stadiums or offices while also rooting out Tutsi who sought refuge in private homes. The main roundabout in Kigali quickly became ground zero in the series of systematic murders of Tutsi that the United States and other members of the

private?

international community initially refused to call by its rightful name—genocide.[1]

On the night of April 6, 1994, ethnic Hutu hardliners within Rwanda's ruling political party sought to take control of Kigali in order to consolidate state control and eliminate political opponents. Extremist militias set up roadblocks within hours of the presidential plane being blown out of the sky. Then-President Habyarimana was returning to Kigali from peace talks held in Arusha, Tanzania, where African and Western diplomats had tried to jumpstart the stalled Arusha Peace Accords. Rwanda returned to civil war when still-unknown forces shot down Habyarimana's Dassault Falcon, a gift of the French government, on its approach to Kigali International Airport at approximately 8.30 p.m. All on board perished, including the president of Burundi, senior Rwandan government and military officials and three French crew-members. In the hours immediately following the crash, members of the Presidential Guard continued to man the roadblocks that were set up in advance of Habyarimana's arrival at the airport.

Such roadblocks were standard operating procedure throughout the civil war. Rwandans from all walks of life were subject to security searches and periodic mandatory curfews in the tense years and heady days after the civil war first started in October 1990. Kigali had been under strict nightly curfew since February 1994, following the assassination of the Minister of Public Works. Since the Arusha Peace Accords had been signed in August 1993, city residents, Rwandans and foreigners alike, lived in a permanent state of anxiety.

The accords set out a power-sharing arrangement that generally favored the now ruling RPF. The United Nations Assistance Mission for Rwanda (UNAMIR), led by Canadian General Roméo Dallaire, was to monitor the ceasefire and help secure Rwanda during the transitional period from civil war to democracy. Genocide became the culminating event as the terms and conditions of the Arusha Accords put an already embattled Hutu elite on the defensive. They were hardly going to give up their lucrative positions of political and military power without a fight. Hutu hardliners within the ruling party, the National Republican Movement for Democracy (MRND), moved quickly to shore up their control of key military and political institutions following Habyarimana's assassination.[2] Under the command of Colonel Théoneste Bagosora, the extremists formed an interim government, naming Théodore Sindikubwabo of the MRND the interim president while Republican Democratic Movement (MDR) politician Jean Kambanda was appointed interim prime minister.[3] A Hutu-dominated party with roots in south-central Rwanda, the MDR was the most powerful opposition party in the country at the time the genocide began.

By 11 pm on April 6, the killing of political moderates had begun, led by members of Habyarimana's Presidential Guard at the behest of Hutu hardliners bent on maintaining their grip on power. At the outset, the homes of Hutu politicians, journalists and civil society activists were raided systematically. Such individuals were targeted for their support of the power-sharing process or their perceived willingness to negotiate with the RPE. Hutu elites sympathetic to continued negotiations were the first targeted for death, most within twelve to twenty-four hours of the presidential plane crash. Among the dead was Prime Minister Agathe Uwilingiyimana of the MDR, a Hutu opponent of Habyarimana's MRND, along with ten Belgian peacekeepers charged with protecting her. Uwilingiyimana was the first woman to be killed in the genocide, not on the basis of her Hutu ethnicity, but rather because of her position of power and strong voice against the massacres of Rwandan Tutsi during the civil war.

The 1994 genocide marked the first episode of mass violence in which women and children were specifically targeted. Historically, and with rare exceptions, men had been the primary targets of state-sponsored violence. Throughout the civil war and genocide, all Tutsi women were at risk, even those married to Hutu men, as were Hutu women married to Tutsi men, Hutu women who tried to protect Tutsi, and Hutu women associated with groups who opposed the Habyarimana regime.[4]

The murder of the Belgian peacekeepers marked the moment when the international community definitively abandoned Rwanda. The Belgians withdrew from UNAMIR, effectively neutralizing the force while also signaling to Hutu hardliners that the unfolding violence was not a European problem. Evacuation of foreign nationals began quickly thereafter, with France going so far as to fly members of Habyarimana's family to Paris on April 9. However, there would be no international intervention force, either to stop the violence or to evacuate Rwandan civilians.[5]

Significantly, the Tutsi RPF did not support a stronger UN presence in the country, informing Dallaire on April 12 that it would not cooperate in facilitating the arrival of a more robust force.[6] Paul Kagame, in his role as commander of the Rwandan Patriotic Army (RPA-Inkotanyi)[7]—the military wing of the rebel RPF—rejected the deployment of United Nations peacekeepers lest they stand in the way of his military plans to seize political power. RPF opposition to UN peacekeepers on the ground to protect Tutsi civilians explains in small part American reluctance to support such a force.[8] Following the loss of American lives in Somalia in October 1993, tolerance for putting US boots on the ground was at an all-time low.

With sympathizers out of the way and in the face of a docile United Nations peacekeeping force, Hutu hardliners under the authority of Colonel Bagosora and a handful of senior MRND politicians, determined to hold on to positions of power, mobilized their Hutu co-ethnics to begin the work of eliminating Tutsi men, women and children. As the University of Paris sociologist André Guichaoua makes astonishingly clear in his research on the causes of the genocide, there was no sophisticated preplan to methodically kill Tutsi.[9] Instead, he persuasively documents the gradual emergence of a genocidal policy instituted by Bagosora and other Hutu hardliners somewhere around April 12, 1994. By this time, just one week after Habyarimana's death, it was clear that Hutu hardliners would be unable to end the civil war and stake their claim to State House.[10] MRND supporters were on the defensive and in disarray following the death of their president and many of his senior military advisors.[11] The rebel RPF, under Paul Kagame's military leadership, was simply too strong to be quickly and easily overthrown.

Understanding the broader political context is crucial to explaining the initial lack of a genocidal plan. The plan emerged out of a tussle between Hutu political elites who wanted to hold on to power and the RPF, who in turn sought power by military aggression. Guichaoua sums up the logic of the struggle between the warring sides with a Rwandan proverb: "Power that does not kill, that does not seek vengeance, is, like a gourd, a fragile power."[12] In other words, a zero-sum political game does not allow for power sharing—there can only be one winner. — *no power sharing*

Moreover, the militarization of Rwandan society throughout the war meant that ordinary people were predisposed to tolerate a final solution of exterminating all Tutsi to solve the political problem of power sharing with the RPF. The force and authority of the military backed the transfer of authority from the president to local leaders, even when local officials or military officers opposed or questioned the targeting of Tutsi. There was no civilian oversight of military policy or practice. And in turn, from the ensuing volatile environment that put Hutu political elites on the armed defensive, willing and able to use the apparatus and authority of the state to hold on to political power by any means possible, the plan for genocide evolved.

Army and militia units led the killing, while civilian leaders facilitated the death squads, urging every able adult Hutu man to join in.[13] Interahamwe militia and killing units led by the Presidential Guard fanned out across the country, in efforts to make sure that Hutu men did their civic duty of killing Tutsi. The squads were necessary to finish the work, as many Hutu resisted or subverted the call to arms. Those

→ what if they didnt?
21 *would they Else killed?*

who participated in the killing did so for many reasons not directly related to ethnic hatred.

Whether killers were reluctant or enthusiastic about their task, the result was the same. Within days, in addition to roadblocks and private homes, central meeting points such as schools, government buildings and hilltops marked where Tutsi died in the greatest number, often with military or paramilitary groups using modern firearms and grenades to do the deed.[14] Christian churches also served as killing fields, with more Rwandans dying in churches and parishes than anywhere else in the country—a shocking statistic in a country where almost 90 percent of the population were once members of Christian churches.

According to Scott Straus, an acclaimed scholar of the 1994 genocide, Hutu killed Tutsi for a variety of reasons, using different methods of killing.[15] In interviews with *génocidaires* (the term Rwandans use to describe those accused of acts of genocide), Straus finds that ethnic hatred was not the primary motivation. As a result, the killing took multiple forms: (1) killing, torture, rape and mutilation perpetrated against civilians—mainly Tutsi but also politically moderate Hutu—by militias, Rwandan Armed Forces (FAR) soldiers of the former Habyarimana regime and willing ordinary people; (2) killing, torture, rape and mutilation perpetrated against Tutsi by ordinary Hutu, typically under duress from local leaders; (3) intended killing of soldiers and collateral killing of civilians of all ethnicities in the course of the civil war between the RPF and the FAR; (4) killings carried out by the RPF against civilians; and (5) murder motivated by theft and looting as well as the settling of scores between ordinary people.[16]

Ordinary Rwandans understand that all of these forms of killing took place during the genocide and they use the Kinyarwanda and French phrases "*amarorerwa yo muri 94/les événements de 1994*" (the events of 1994) and "*muri 94/en 1994*" (in 1994) to describe everything that happened in 1994, not just the genocide (*itsembabwoko/le géno-cide*).[17] Some also use the language of war to describe the civil war and genocide period (*intambara/la guerre*). It was an event that defies easy explanation. Yet, as we will consider more fully in the next chapter, the RPF describes the genocide in a singular way that functions outside of the experience of many Rwandans who survived the genocide. The official line is clear: Hutu killed Tutsi because of deep-seated hatred that was introduced by Belgian colonizers and cultivated by Hutu-led postcolonial governments.

The RPF's Strategic Choices

In the thirteen weeks of the genocide, from April 6 to July 4, the RPF disrupted the killers, often by happenstance, in the act or while preparing to slaughter Tutsi. Human Rights Watch estimates that the RPF saved tens of thousands of Tutsi lives. It also sacrificed Tutsi lives in its own drive to capture political power. The RPF leadership, under General Kagame's careful tutelage, knew that its military challenge to Hutu power could provoke a dramatic loss of Tutsi life, but felt that such losses were the human cost of attaining political power in Rwanda.[18]

RPF operations were not overtly intended to save Tutsi, although some did. RPF military action aimed to secure control of territory, then political and military institutions, and finally the population. In the process, RPF soldiers—on orders from or with the knowledge of their commanders—committed reprisal killings of Hutu civilians, pillaged property and damaged hospitals and displaced persons camps before, during and after the genocide.[19] In the context of war, civilian deaths are, RPF leaders explained after the fact, an unfortunate but necessary consequence.[20] Tutsi civilian *abakada* also worked alongside the RPF to manage local populations, secure territory, and assure military victory through all necessary means. This included the disappearance and murder of Hutu and Tutsi civilians who stood in the way of the RPF's strategy to ensure its military victory on the road to political power in July 1994.

23

Academic and popular criticism of the failure of the UN to stop the killing tends to focus blame on the Security Council or the inefficiencies of its top-heavy peacekeeping bureaucracy, with the Department of Peacekeeping Operations and the Office of the Secretary-General taking most of the heat. Lost in the debris of such criticism is Kagame's military goal to install his RPF in political power. There can be no denying that the UN force in Rwanda was bungling and ineffectual in fulfilling its mandate. Nonetheless, for Kagame, the United Nations made for a convenient external scapegoat, providing cover to the RPF's military drive to both control Rwanda, and later declare itself the hero of the Rwandan tragedy for its role in stopping the killing. This does not absolve the UN for its failures. It is only to remind us that the RPF leadership, like MRND extremists, took targeted actions in seeking specific outcomes—it was hardly an innocent victim of UN inaction.

The RPF ended the genocide when it defeated the military and civilian forces responsible for organizing and implementing the genocide. Its troops encountered little in the way of opposition as they swept out from Kigali, to the south along the eastern side of the country toward the border with Tanzania, then west toward the border with Zaire.

A Country of Killers?

In a nation of an estimated seven million people, at least half a million Tutsi were killed in a hundred days. Approximately one in eight Rwandans, and nearly three in four ethnic Tutsi, perished between April and July 1994. Thousands of Hutu also lost their lives, chiefly those who opposed the genocidal campaign or refused to join in the killing. A third of Rwanda's ethnic Twa population—some ten thousand people— also met their end. As members of a marginal minority group making up around 1 percent of the population, the Twa played no visible political role in society. They were still affected, as they too live with the [politicization of ethnicity.] *

↳ no escaping
the situation

aimable

Born in 1941 and raised in western Rwanda, on a bucolic hill over-looking the shores of Lake Kivu, Aimable is an ethnic Tutsi who presents with stereotypical Twa features—physically distinguishable by his smaller height and weight. His identity card labeled him as Tutsi, but officials rarely asked to see his ID before or during the genocide. Poverty* stunted his physical growth and emotional development as a child, while a lifetime of tilling and hoeing left his face, feet and hands weathered, giving him the appearance of someone much older than his actual age. When speaking of the violence of the Social Revolution (1957–62), Aimable furrows his brow as his eyes darken: "The violence at that time was bad, but we didn't directly experience. it because it was mostly located in Kigali. The influential people [political and military elites] were fighting over power and I only heard about the struggles when our local official called a meeting at his office to tell us peasants what needed to be done to ensure security." He continues:

power = knowledge ; regular citizens kept in the dark

Even in those days, I wasn't allowed to join night patrols to look for Tutsi enemies. We [Twa-looking] are people who cannot be trusted so I was forbidden to help. The official also didn't realize I was Tutsi myself—he once insulted me as a Twa and, at that time, that was a good thing because it meant I could protect my family from the violence.

Aimable casts his eyes downward, his voice cracking as he chokes back tears:

In 1994, there was no escaping the violence, even though many people [in the western region] thought the killing wouldn't affect us. Killing squads roamed from house to house, looking to kill Tutsi. Or Tutsi were rounded up and killed at churches and government buildings. Having the appearance of a Twa saved my life. I tried to join the killing squads as a way to protect my people, but I was rejected as a member because of my small size and old age. I passed the genocide in my house, with my [Tutsi] wife. We would stay in during daylight hours, and go to try to tend [crops] during the nights.

Aimable's experience affirms that the 1994 genocide was a Hutu and Tutsi affair. A sizable witness literature attests to this, with Tutsi survivors writing about how they survived.[21] The Hutu side of the story has produced a few volumes, much of it written by foreign journalists who wanted to know why Hutu killed Tutsi.[22] This material is typically written in the third person. Few sources allow readers to learn what motivated individual Hutu to kill, why they did it and how it made them feel, in their own words.[23]

Tutsi who survived did so with pluck and wits; they often defended themselves with sticks and stones. Those living in border regions or with sufficient financial means tried to flee the country. Many failed and were found dead with bundles of their personal belongings nearby— clothes, family photos, pots and utensils. Others hid in ceilings of offices and homes, some in pit latrines or holes they themselves dug, others in rivers, swamps or forests. Some survived from the succor of Hutu or Twa, many of whom risked their own lives to provide food or a place to hide. Some of the killers readily attacked one person but not another, usually a result of bonds of family, friendship or commerce, or some mixture of all three.[24]

Michel was an established Tutsi businessman with young children when the genocide started in late April in his hometown of Butare in southern Rwanda. His father, a university professor, was killed at the end of April 1994 alongside his mother and sisters in the family home where Michel had been raised. Intellectuals were among the first targeted for killing during the genocide, and Michel's father, Joseph, was no exception. In the 1970s and 1980s, Joseph and his family lived a relatively peaceful existence as the targeting of Tutsi had diminished under President Habyarimana. By the early 1990s, ethnic tensions were on the rise again, and Joseph did his best to cultivate relationships with all Rwandans, particularly Hutu political, business and church leaders. Didier, a prominent Hutu businessman, was an acquaintance of Michel's family, who visited the family home on occasion to discuss university business. When Michel started his business of selling used cars, Didier helped him get established. Over the years, he had come to think of Didier as an uncle.

Michel heard the news that his father, mother and sisters were killed on Didier's order in the leafy main courtyard of the university, where he had gone to collect some papers from his father's office. When he arrived, he found Didier, his eyes bloodshot and stinking of a sour mixture of sweat, banana beer and cooking kerosene. Didier instantly confessed to the murders, rendering Michel numb. A bone-deep chill washing over him, Michel collapsed to his knees, head in his hands and immediately began to shake and sob. Didier knelt to comfort him. Starting to weep, Didier asked Michel for compassion: "It's war! We Hutu must do our duty!" Michel was quiet for what seemed like an eternity, processing what Didier had just confessed. Didier eventually broke the silence. "Come! Come! We can't sit here. It's not safe. The killers know your father and you are on the list of those to be killed. Come! I will take you to my home. There you can hide there until a better solution arises. Come! Come!"

Michel survived the genocide because he hid at Didier's home. Michel continues to struggle to understand how Didier, a known and perhaps even enthusiastic killer, could kill some Tutsi like his parents while saving others like him. One thing is clear—the genocide struck all Rwandans, many of whom showed incredible compassion and care for their country's people.

Somewhere between 175,000 and three million Rwandans like Didier participated in the killing, some with great zeal, others under duress. Depending on the source, there is considerable divergence in the number of alleged perpetrators. For example, human rights investigators and scholars tend to settle on the lower number of between 175,000 and 250,000 killers while the RPF-led government asserts a much higher figure of some three million perpetrators.[25] The numbers game is critically important to determine whether or not the RPF-led government is indeed administering a criminal population of Hutu perpetrators, as it began to quickly and definitely assert in late 1994.

Some perpetrators needed tangible incentive to kill while others chose to kill out of fear for their own lives. Some killed only Tutsi they did not personally know or killed Tutsi selectively, as in the case of Didier. The Hutu extremist leadership played on popular fears and greed, allowing some Hutu men to readily pick up machetes, studded clubs or garden hoes to kill friends, neighbors, colleagues and even family members. Others had to be coaxed with food, drink, cash payments and promises of land, vehicles and other property left behind by fleeing or dead Tutsi. Despite the targeted efforts of military and administrative personnel to engage Hutu in the killing of Tutsi, hundreds of thousands killed no one at all. Social bonds of family, friendship and community disrupted the Hutu extremist plan for genocide. The speed and intensity of the killing across the country varied from place to place, shaped by individual choice among a narrow set of kill-or-be-killed options and informed by local social, economic and political networks.[26] At the local level, the violence was improvised as the instructions of national political and military elites to kill Tutsi were opportunistically implemented or resisted.[27]

Some individuals killed of their own accord but they are a minority of the overall number of genocide perpetrators. Much killing during the genocide was committed in groups of ten to fifteen people, known as *igitero* (mobs), usually under the watchful eye of Interahamwe leaders.[28] These groups methodically killed crowds of people at schools, churches and stadiums once Hutu officials had found a way to arrange them in such locations. Sometimes, Tutsi were surrounded where they lived or worked by groups of killers. The group dynamic is significant as many

[left margin, handwritten] Hutu Extremist: manipulative.

[right margin, handwritten] emotions /feelings

Hutu, as well as some Tutsi and Twa, joined *igitero* for reasons beyond killing. Non-Hutu would use these groups as a form of cover, to give the impression that they were ethnic Hutu or supported the plan to exterminate Tutsi. Women also sometimes joined in the death squads, although their numbers are thought to be fewer than 3 percent of killers.[29] Social ties, particularly ties to political power at the local level, as well as friend, family and business groups, shaped how mobs were formed and who led the killing. Group dynamics meant that one or two individuals would do the deed while the others cheered or supported the murders. Communities where local leaders had close ties to the ruling MRND or the remnants of the interim government established following President Habyarimana's death were especially effective leaders of the killing.

Olivier was an influential local leader in a community in north-central Rwanda.[30] Shortly after the genocide began in early April, Olivier was appointed the *conseiller*, making him the most powerful person in his community. His political party connections facilitated this rise to power. Olivier's authority was layered on to his already established high standing in his community. When the genocide started, people looked to him to provide guidance and leadership. This power provided Olivier with *carte blanche* to follow, resist or subvert the order for genocide that came from the central authorities in Kigali. He did not blindly follow the orders to kill. Rather, Olivier's actions were strategic. As the primary powerholder in his community, Olivier was in a position to negotiate with anyone who needed a favor. In exchange for money or property, Olivier would issue new ethnic identity cards to Tutsi. In allowing them to hold documents affirming their Hutu identity, Olivier may have helped save their lives. He also allowed men he knew to be Tutsi to join the killing squads in exchange for cash, something those who could pay regularly did to save themselves. At the same time, Olivier used his authority to lure Tutsi out of hiding to certain death. The power to call meetings to order killings of Tutsi was a formidable form of local power. Olivier's ability to decide who lived and who died highlights the authority of local powerholders to determine individual fates. It also refutes the simplistic idea that Hutu killed Tutsi because of deep-seated ethnic animosity. Instead, we see that [multiple and varied factors determined who lived, who died, and how and why.] ✱ !

A Country in Ruin

By August 1994, some two million Rwandan refugees were living in neighboring countries, another million citizens were internally displaced, and a million were dead. Approximately three million people, or 40 percent of the population, remained in Rwanda at the end of August 1994. This included some 250,000 women who had been raped, almost 100,000 orphans, and an estimated 50,000 widows.[31] The stigma of rape added an extra layer of hardship and hurt, as many women lacked the personal and social resources to recover from the shame or seek medical assistance for their injuries. Interahamwe militants often sexually abused women in public, often before their own children, after their husbands had been killed. Some women were forced to become sex slaves to powerful Hutu men. The RPF also targeted Hutu women, particularly wives and daughters of powerful Hutu men, in acts of sexual revenge.[32] The goal on both sides was to sexually dominate and then socially humiliate women and girls. They succeeded, as raped women rarely reveal that they have been raped, fearing ostracism by family and community members. Moreover, some 70 percent of women who were raped during the genocide contracted HIV.[33] ↳ stigma

Overcrowded and squalid prison conditions were now the norm. By November 1994, in the main prison in the center of Kigali known as 1930, there were 4,000 inmates occupying a space designed for 1,500. Nearly all were ethnic Hutu, swept up by the military, police or *abakada* civilian patrols on the presumption of guilt regardless of available evidence. Crafting dossiers was difficult, as Rwanda boasted only thirty-one investigators and five judges at the end of the genocide.[34] In 1996, the prison population comprised around 83,000 inmates in a national prison system designed for 19,000.[35] By the late 1990s, almost every Rwandan had at least one relative, friend or neighbor in jail. Human Rights Watch researcher Carina Tertsakian concluded that awful prison conditions combined with a sense of intergenerational persecution could undermine the RPF's efforts at ethnic reconciliation:

> What Rwanda's prisoners and former prisoners think and do is not a peripheral matter. It affects a significant proportion of the Rwandan population: not only these individuals themselves, but the next generation. Children who have seen their parents imprisoned for years without justice have grown up harboring feelings of ethnic victimization. Unless these problems are addressed, they will continue to undermine Rwanda's social and ethnic cohesion, and threaten the country's future unity.[36]

The overburdened judicial system was unable to process the dossiers of the accused and inmates languished for years without being charged with particular crimes. Indeed, as the French political scientist Gérard Prunier argues, *gatunga agatoki* (finger-pointing) was the primary reason why so many Hutu found themselves in jail: neighbors and relatives would readily accuse to appropriate land or homes, or address personal grudges that preceded the genocide. Many inmates died in detention since sanitation and hygiene conditions in prisons across the country made them insalubrious.[37] Cholera, malaria and gangrene continued to claim the lives of prisoners until at least 2001.[38] Since 1996, the RPF-led government has worked closely with the International Committee of the Red Cross to manage the health and improve the welfare of the prison population. They rarely succeeded as prison conditions remained harsh and life-threatening for many, particularly women and youth. In 2014, the Rwandan Correctional Services (RCS) reported some 53,000 inmates jailed for genocide-related crimes. RCS estimates that these numbers will drop dramatically by 2020, as most inmates sentenced to twenty-five years for their genocidal crimes will be freed by then.

Emotional and Physical Scars

To have lived through the genocide was to subsist in a haze. Hollow eyes and haunted souls revealed the depth of the agony Rwandans felt in the days following the end of the genocide. The killing had touched everyone who lived in the country as "it was a hill-by-hill, home-by-home thing" carried out with machetes, hoes and other everyday implements.[39] Rwandans had killed, raped, pillaged and plundered other Rwandans, leaving an indelible mark on people and places. The genocide became part of daily life, a permanent imprint on all who were in the country at the time.

Across the country, in common gathering spots such as schools, stadiums and churches, heaps of bone-filled clothing and mummifying bodies paid testament to the magnitude of what had happened, laying bare Rwanda's collective psyche. Soccer fields, banana groves and cassava fields also bore witness. The start of the genocide coincided with one of two annual rainy seasons, when fat, low-hanging clouds discharge heavy, persistent rain. The wet added insult to injury as gaunt, glassy-eyed and often possessionless survivors tried to make sense of how and why they had survived the violence. It is nearly impossible to find a Tutsi family that survived the genocide intact. Many lost all immediate and extended family members, forever silencing their place in Rwanda's violent history.

Survivors found helping hands hard to find. Communities were fractured—suspicion reigned among lifelong friends, schoolmates, colleagues and peers. Churches, the usual center of social life in Rwanda, lost all credibility. Places of worship were the site of many massacres, with local officials and church leaders colluding to usher cowering Tutsi to "safety." For some members of the clergy, safety meant simply informing waiting Interahamwe militants or FAR soldiers of the gathered Tutsi "vermin." In the days and weeks after the genocide, churches no longer represented a place of refuge for many Rwandans. Mosques had provided cover for some Tutsi, with Muslim leaders staunchly refusing to participate in the genocide, saving hundreds of lives in the process. Most government officials, notably the locally powerful mayors such as Olivier, who might have been able to provide support, had fled or were dead.

Terrified by their past, fearful of their present, paralyzed by the loss of their loved ones, or blaming themselves for having survived, people experienced the genocide as a crime in perpetuity "against survivors, their families, and the communities who endure the repercussions indefinitely."[40] This was especially true for women who had been raped. Some who had become pregnant sought abortions, a matter rarely discussed in Rwandan culture. Women who sought an abortion did so with traditional medicines to induce the termination of the pregnancy, or with the help of female nurses they personally knew.[41] Given Rwandan cultural codes of secrecy and silence, procuring abortions for pregnancies resulting from rape during the genocide was a public secret—people knew, but few discussed it.[42]

Many members of ethnically mixed families also felt the shame of having survived. Ethnically mixed individuals and families experienced dual losses at the hands of genocidal killers and RPF soldiers. Some 95 percent of Rwandans in the country during those fateful hundred days experienced or witnessed acts of violence.[43] Some 1.2 million refugees escaped via the western border towns of Cyangugu in the south and Gisenyi in the north. Some 900,000 Rwandans also ran east to Tanzania or south to Burundi (see Map 1). The international humanitarian community estimated it to be largest exodus of people in flight since World War II.[44] Of the more than two million Rwandans who sought refuge in neighboring countries, some were former Interahamwe who oversaw the killing.

war as an experience

Survivors of all ethnicities fled on the order of local government authorities who warned the fleeing population of the possibility of gruesome RPF reprisals. Such warnings became reality when, in September 1994, UN human rights monitors found at least three hundred bodies stuffed into rusted shipping containers in the RPF-controlled northeast of the country. Mass fear of the now ruling RPF was justified, as its troops left no stone unturned in swiftly securing the country by any means necessary, both during and after the genocide.

Marked by buzzards flying overhead, the hum of swarms of flies, and the tangy smell of rotting human flesh, mass graves were commonplace throughout the country. So too was the sound of feet pounding soil as countless people fled the impending retributional assault of the RPF. Flight from western Rwanda began in earnest in June 1994, facilitated by the French military commandos who arrived in the southwest to create the Turquoise safe zone for beleaguered Tutsi civilians. The French military further facilitated the exodus of some 300,000 Rwandans into Zaire through the southern border town of Bukavu, and around 850,000 through Goma in the northwest.

Table 1. Rwandan Refugees in Neighboring Countries, August 1994*

Location	
Northern Burundi	270,000
Western Tanzania	577,000
Southwestern Uganda	10,000
Zaire (Goma)	850,000
Zaire (Bukavu)	332,000
Zaire (Uvira)	62,000
Total	**2,101,000**

* UNHCR, "The Rwandan Genocide and Its Aftermath," in *State of the World's Refugees, 2000* (Geneva: UNCHR), p. 251.

Among the huddled masses were an estimated 30,000 to 50,000 members of the army and militias of the genocide, including former officers of Habyarimana's army, as well as members of the Interahamwe and other killing squads. Perpetrators exited Rwanda hidden among the throngs of men, women and children who had sought to escape their militias. As this became known, a standard RPF practice to pull Interahamwe and other suspected killers out of the mass of refugees moving to and living in Zaire "was to lure the refugees out of their hiding places by the prospects of food distribution and then mow them down by a hail of bullets," a tactic which killed Rwandans of all ethnicities and some Congolese living in the area.[45]

While millions of Rwandans fled west into eastern Zaire, hundreds of thousands remained in the Zone Turquoise (which covered Gikongoro, Kibuye and Cyangugu provinces) under the protection of French troops.[46] Human rights defenders rightly criticized the French mission, known as Opération Turquoise, for its failure to arrest genocidal leaders of the defeated government as they fled into Zaire either through the Zone Turquoise or via the northern withdrawal route though Gisenyi into Goma, Zaire (see Map 1).[47] The camps in Zaire soon became home to the rump political and military leadership of Hutu hardliners, as well as Interahamwe militiamen, facilitated by the infrastructure and financial support of international humanitarian agencies.[48] The regional refugee crisis paled in comparison to the mind-boggling scale of what was needed at home. Embittered survivors tried to make sense of their new lives without family and their social networks as the new RPF government asked them to identify, from among their remaining friends, family and neighbors, the killers of their loved ones. Those who lost someone at the hands of the RPF and its *abakada* cadres kept mum.

The founding ideology of the RPF is one of national unity, which asks Rwandans to forget who is Hutu and who is Tutsi to advance an aim of peace and security. This "chosen amnesia" is a tall order in a country where people were killed or participated in the killing on the basis of their ethnic identity.[49] As the RPF swore in its transitional government, vowing to seek justice, truth and reconciliation for all Rwandans, only ethnic Tutsi could use the label of survivor.

Rewriting History

The genocide was the prism through which the policy choices of the new government were made, and understandably so. International donors used the same framework. Burdened by their own feelings of guilt for failing to stop the genocide, donors accepted the RPF's view that security concerns should trump respect for human rights and political openness. What many outsiders did not realize was that the RPF's mastery of information management covered up the extent to which the government sought to control Rwanda on its own terms. In a few short months, the RPF would rewrite Rwanda's complex history into a few pithy sound-bites about precolonial political harmony and ethnic unity. It also rewrote the immediate past in making the genocide about Tutsi victims, Hutu perpetrators and Western failures to intervene to save Rwandan lives. *information manipulation*

Working with expatriate journalists, aid workers and diplomats—all of whom were rightly shocked at the human suffering—RPF media handlers moved quickly to gain their commitment to a particular "intellectual image about the place and its heritage."[50] History was started afresh, as a political project that elevated the RPF while obscuring its human rights abuses at home and abroad, particularly in neighboring Zaire. This rewriting also made Hutu, particularly Hutu men, guilty of acts of genocide regardless of what they may have done or not done. Western reports soon told a single story of RPF heroism in the face of rabid Hutu extremists bent on exterminating hapless Tutsi.

The RPF's version of history is a story that was easy to swallow given the magnitude and complexity of the genocide. Friends of the new government soon came to parrot this revised history, mostly out of

36

not: war as an experience

admiration for the RPF's impressive efforts to restore security as quickly as possible. Unfortunately, the effect was that the genocide was reduced to a singular event rather than the brutal outcome of a series of complex historical, structural, political, economic and cultural processes. It would also pave the way for the RPF's partisan response to the genocide—uncritical support for Tutsi victims and no questioning of its right to rule Rwanda as it sees fit. Understanding the RPF's politicization of history is critical, as millions of innocent people have died in Rwanda over the years, their deaths the product of "intense struggles over power carried out by leaders."[51]

A one-sided take on Rwandan society, history and politics would soon inform popular writing on the country. This single story, crafted by RPF media representatives, would come to shape not just what was written, but also by whom. Just as RPA soldiers were deployed across the country, so too were media handlers who doubled as informants. They are party loyalists, employed by the Department of Military Intelligence (DMI). Rwandans who lived through the genocide understand them as a new and improved form of the *abakada* Tutsi civilian units that operated to control people, places and things under RPF command. To outsiders, they are taxi drivers, tour guides, hotel clerks and interpreters, guiding foreign journalists, aid workers and other visitors around the country to visit mass grave sites, including those in churches as well as hospitals and prisons, in the immediate postgenocide period.

By 1997, the list of approved and must-see destinations for foreigners included visiting female genocide survivors to hear their stories at government-run memorial sites across the country where mangled bodies, covered in lime, are on display. (The official sites are found at Bisesero, Gisozi, Murambi, Ntarama, Nyamata and Nyarubuye.) Visiting informal memorial sites and grave markers that were more personally meaningful to Tutsi survivors was not on the agenda, for memorializing the genocide had already become an RPF-led project

37

does this worsen the affects?

profiting off of peoples experiences w/ genocide

designed to shock foreign visitors, tourists and journalists alike.[52] Most media handlers were Uganda-born men with foreign university degrees, speaking impeccable English and having a firm grip on the RPF's singular version of Rwandan society. It did not take much prodding to have these handlers as interpreters of Rwandan culture, politics and history as they themselves had grown up learning Rwandan history as their elders recalled it.

Neatly packaged stories of Hutu hatred for Tutsi found sympathetic ears as many journalists and others writing about the genocide felt the need to atone for their failures in reporting it. The sympathy of foreign friends had a moral dimension for Paul Kagame. His people had been the victims of genocide, and shoring up the RPF as blameless leaders made sense to many outsiders at the time. Kagame would soon exploit these feelings of international shame to explain his policy choices while also laying the groundwork to justify human rights abuses in the name of national security and, later, economic development.

2

THE ROOTS OF THE GENOCIDAL STATE

The political and military choices of the RPF before, during and since the 1994 genocide cannot be understood in a vacuum. Understanding the RPF's rise and its choice to take up arms to liberate Rwandans from the Habyarimana regime helps us also understand the policy choices that the RPF, as a political party with military origins, has pursued since the genocide. This framing allows us to assess the claims of the RPF leadership, notably those of President Kagame (in charge since 2000), of occupying a moral high ground on which the RPF is the sole arbiter of Rwanda's postgenocide development. The RPF draws on deep historical wells in ways that assure its political primacy while ignoring the historical antecedents to contemporary Rwanda. As such, a historical detour is required before delving into life since the genocide. As subsequent chapters illustrate, a firmly held belief that the RPF, under the unflinching leadership of Paul Kagame, is Rwanda's rightful ruler shapes its sense of what is right and wrong for the country and its people.

All the same, the Rwanda for which the RPF fought and won was a place few of them knew first-hand. Most members of the RPF, including its leaders, grew up outside Rwanda across East and Central Africa, or in sizable diaspora communities in Europe and North America. By the mid-1980s, some one million Rwandan Tutsi lived outside of their homeland.[1] Rwanda's neighbor to the north, Uganda, became home to the majority of exiles, including young Paul Kagame.[2] He arrived in the Mbarara district of southern Uganda with his parents and siblings in 1961.

Kagame was just three years old when his family left their natal hill of Tambwe, near Gitarama town in central Rwanda. This region of the country is the historical home of the Nyiginya kingdom, one of several that emerged during the seventeenth century, and which many contemporary Tutsi elites consider to be the precursor to the modern Rwandan state. By the eighteenth century, the Nyiginya kingdom had developed a superior military, which recruited from lineages living all over the territory now known as Rwanda.[3] This militarized royal heritage matters as it informs Kagame's approach to governance, as well as the RPF's founding ideology, and its postgenocide reconstruction and reconciliation policies.[4] The centrality of royal lineages reveals an inherent contradiction in the RPF's approach to ethnicity, which relies at once on a forward-looking reconciliation narrative that eschews being Tutsi or Hutu, along with a backward-looking narrative that highlights precolonial ethnic harmony among the Tutsi and Hutu under a magnanimous *mwami* (king) in the precolonial period. Essential to this construct of ethnicity is the RPF's reductive conclusion that a key cause of the genocide was a deep-seated ethnic hatred of all Hutu for all Tutsi.

Tutsi who grew up in exile have an understandably romanticized belief in ethnic unity and the role of the precolonial royal court in fostering it. The oral histories that exiles with close family ties to royalty—like Paul Kagame—heard as children from their parents and other older relatives were rooted in a glorified past that emphasized the harmony of the royal court. Kagame was raised on a steady diet of oral histories that separated Tutsi from Hutu and glossed over the great hardships and stratified hierarchy of the precolonial period. As the American journalist Stephen Kinzer writes: "With almost mystic focus, they [young Tutsi exiles in Uganda] came to believe fate and history had assigned them a transcendent task: to find their way back to a homeland many of them barely remembered, but all had idealized."[5]

These oral narratives shared across exiled generations are rooted in a politicized version of precolonial history, which over time came to represent a central pillar in the RPF's postgenocide reconstruction and reconciliation platform, including in the secondary school history curriculum,[6] *ingando* reeducation camps[7] and national genocide museums.[8] This idealized history was and remains primarily one of Tutsi elites, first narrated by historians appointed by the king, then retold by early European explorers in their "scientific" writings, full of racist ideas about the superiority of white Europeans over black Africans. For centuries, Europeans ranked races according to each group's innate intelligence and skills, as they saw them. Their perceptions cast the Tutsi as black-skinned Europeans most able to govern Rwanda, given their sophisticated governance structures.[9]

Tutsi Rule as Natural

The Belgian anthropologist Jacques Maquet reinforced such thinking. In his 1954 book *The Premise of Inequality in Ruanda*, Maquet painted a portrait of Rwanda as a timeless feudal society, rigidly stratified by a caste-like ethnic hierarchy with royal Tutsi at the top.[10] This minority of royals within the overall Tutsi minority held all political power and controlled land, labor and crops while exploiting the majority Hutu and non-royal Tutsi.

Maquet's analysis relied on a value consensus that "all Rwandans are by birth fundamentally unequal," in which Tutsi are born to rule and Hutu are born to serve.[11] The premise of inequality was structurally enforced though an elaborate bureaucratic arrangement, the precursor to Rwanda's current state structure (discussed further in Chapter 11). Its distinguishing feature was a system of many officials with overlapping mandates, named to execute the orders of the king by any means possible. According to Maquet, this administrative ordering provided a built-in grievance mechanism, as Hutu had multiple channels of appeal in the event of injustice. Maquet failed to consider that this dense organizational structure could result in undue hardship for those subject to multiple sources of authority. At the heart of the personal histories that RPF political and military elites learned as children in exile, this reading of inequality as the natural order of things is key.

Maquet's hierarchical read of relationships in early Rwandan society is retold in the RPF's version of precolonial history and is often reproduced in the writing of authors new to Rwanda. One such mechanism is the *ubuhake* contract, which allowed cattle owners (usually Tutsi) to give cattle to their clients (usually Hutu) in usufruct, as well as protection from the more powerful, in exchange for labor, land and crops.[12] The inequalities and resultant indignities inherent in these relationships were absent from Maquet's analysis, as were the fear-based relationships they created as clients supplicated to more powerful patrons. Although some relationships were rooted in reciprocal alliances founded on respect, love and even admiration, for the majority, clientship was a divisive practice that reinforced Tutsi domination atop a political system they also controlled. It meant that Hutu land chiefs earned and lost power rapidly, usually at the whim of their superior Tutsi cattle or army chief.[13]

Maquet's interpretation of Rwandan society not only failed to capture the social, political and cultural complexity of the day; it also mirrored and rationalized the worldview of his interlocutors—Tutsi aristocrats of the Nyiginya kingdom speaking during the height of the colonial period in the late 1940s and early 1950s. Maquet refused to work with Hutu attached to the royal court, believing Tutsi to be the only competent sources on Rwanda's political organization, an idea developed in consultation with Abbé Alexis Kagame (1912–81, no relation to Paul Kagame). A member of the Nyiginya court and the great-nephew of an important Tutsi commander to King Rwabugiri (*c.* 1860–95), Alexis Kagame saw no need to assess the opinions and knowledge of Rwandans; the goal of his research with Maquet was to understand the country's political organization. Their finding—that precolonial ethnic relations between Hutu and Tutsi were mutually beneficial—is at the heart of the RPF's approach to postgenocide reconciliation, which seeks to restore the presumed natural ethnic unity of Rwandans as the basis of the country's peace and security.

The defining life event for many of the RPF's founding members was the difficult and dangerous decision to flee Rwanda, cast out by ethnic violence and invective that began in the dying days of Belgian colonial rule in the late 1950s. Subsequent personal experiences of flight, exile and return to Rwanda as armed rebels, seeking to restore democratic governance and ethnic unity to a society they believe was torn asunder by capricious colonizers and unprincipled postcolonial Hutu political elites, inform their ideology. The RPF's telling of its mythical history is reinforced by what the Smith College historian David Newbury calls the myth of elitist agency. Rooted in the "assumption that the words of political leaders [. . .] represent the thoughts and worldview of those outside elite status," this fiction informs the thinking of many, including numerous current government officials, as well as some foreign observers.[14]

The Social Revolution (1957–62)

By the middle of the twentieth century, colonizers across the African continent were facing increased domestic demands for more power and autonomy. Rwanda was no exception in the call for independent statehood. It was mostly Tutsi political elites who wanted to send their Belgian administrators packing. By the late colonial period (1957–62), the Belgian authorities faced increasing demands from an educated and aspirant Hutu counterelite who sought to right the power imbalance between Hutu and Tutsi.[15] Many of these men (they were all men) found themselves excluded from upward social and economic mobility simply because of their status as Hutu. This, in turn, bred a sense of resentment and feeling of persecution.[16] Using "organizational networks and politics ties forged through the Catholic Church," these Hutu elites began to challenge both Belgian and Tutsi elites.[17] For them, the Belgians were not moving quickly enough to institute political and social reform. Simultaneously, the Tutsi old guard aimed to preserve the existing system of power and privilege, and rejected Hutu demands for inclusion. For Tutsi powerholders, the main issues at hand were economic and social disparity, not ethnic discrimination.

In early 1957, Tutsi rulers issued a "Statement of Views," calling for an accelerated move to self-government, with emphasis on extending educational opportunities to all Rwandans, opening up political competition and instituting social and economic reforms. The statement recognized one kind of discrimination in Rwanda—that between the Belgians as Europeans and Rwandans as Africans. There was no mention of the racial discrimination that the Hutu as a group had experienced.

In March of the same year, nine Hutu intellectuals issued the "Bahutu Manifesto." Released as a response to the "Statement of Views," the manifesto asserted that the most important political problem facing Rwanda was the Tutsi–Hutu divide. Twa, in their peripheral position in Rwandan society, were not included in the debates of the day. The manifesto was directed at the Belgians, calling on them to recognize the "Hutu–Tutsi problem"—defined as the Tutsi monopoly on political, socio-economic and cultural life. The Hutu intellectuals wanted Belgian-introduced identity cards to remain, claiming that without ethnic categories it would be impossible to know whether more equitable political institutions, social structures and economic opportunities were being created for Hutu. Ultimately, the manifesto called for a change in attitude, away from the idea that only Tutsi could act as elites, and demanding a double liberation for Hutu, from Belgian colonizers and the Tutsi old guard.[18]

Swayed by these arguments and the feverish climate of the day, the Belgians threw their weight behind the Hutu authors of the "Bahutu Manifesto," striking fear into Tutsi, who made up only 16 percent of the population.[19] The response of Tutsi powerholders, as a minority within a minority, "was to downplay the importance of domestic ethnic difference."[20] The aspirant Hutu elite continued to insist on the importance of racial categories, using the language of democracy, freedom and justice as the birthright of the Hutu majority (comprising some 80 percent of Rwandans). In so doing, the manifesto "recognizes race as the marker of oppression and therefore of [Hutu] liberation."[21] For the majority Hutu, ethnic categories became the sole avenue to democratic emancipation.

By mid-1957, seminary-educated Grégoire Kayibanda had formed the Hutu Social Movement, with the intention of pursuing the objectives set out in the manifesto. It later became the Hutu Emancipation Movement Party (PARMEHUTU). Two other political parties also operated at the time—the mainly Hutu APROMOSA (Association for the Social Promotion of the Masses) and UNAR (National Rwandan Union), which represented the interests of elite Tutsi.[22] In November 1959, social revolution came to Rwanda, sending the Tutsi elite and many of their clients into exile. It ended twenty-two months later, following elections and a September 1961 referendum that rejected the Tutsi monarchy. In recognition of the results of the referendum, the Belgians shifted their support to Hutu elites. Ethnically motivated violence punctuated this transition period. By 1962, the Belgians had left and in July Rwanda gained formal independence, with Kayibanda becoming Rwanda's first postcolonial president.

President Kayibanda conflated the Hutu ethnic majority with a democratic one. PARMEHUTU's ideology focused on creating ethnic unity among Hutu. Having successfully freed his Hutu co-ethnics of their Tutsi overlords, Kayibanda presented his victory as a democratic one for the rural masses. In throwing off the shackles of Tutsi feudalists, the state would now serve the interests of the Hutu majority. Ethnic Tutsi were expected to accept Hutu majority rule and to make no claims on power.[23] As the Kayibanda regime moved to shore up the security and safety of the formerly downtrodden majority Hutu, it practiced capricious violence against Tutsi who challenged the new political order. The new president promised to respect the political rights of minority Tutsi while at the same time reminding them not to challenge his authority. Kayibanda's rhetoric was unequivocal: Tutsi who challenged the notion of Hutu leaders provoked violence against themselves. The result was the absence of a political middle ground—space for political tolerance and cooperation among Hutu and Tutsi elites all but evaporated, foreshadowing the Hutu nationalist rhetoric that called for the destruction of Tutsi in the early 1990s.

Waves of Persecution (1959–73)

Rather than a social revolution in which elite Hutu tried to secure their piece of the political pie, to this day the RPF leadership conceives the events of 1957–62 as a practice genocide—a warm-up for what was to come in 1994. This framing glosses over the socio-economic issues of the day, while neglecting the ways in which political elites—Hutu and Tutsi alike—employ ethnicity to rationalize their attempts to seek power. In the minds of the current RPF leadership, a fear of sharing power with Hutu is legitimate. Not only have Hutu political elites targeted Tutsi when under political pressure, they are more interested in maintaining their power than assuring the security of all Rwandans. As we will see in coming chapters, the political choices of the RPF are security-seeking, intended to contain a restive Hutu population while assuring the safety of politically loyal Tutsi as an ethnic minority.

The hasty transfer of power at the dusk of the colonial period had lasting repercussions on Rwandan political life, shaping a power dynamic that would later facilitate Rwanda's civil war (1990–94) and the 1994 genocide. Thanks to Kayibanda's framing of his victory as the freeing of the Hutu majority from the grips of Tutsi domination, violence against ethnic Tutsi became commonplace. As a result, Tutsi fled the country in multiple waves: 1959–61, 1963–64 and again in 1973.

The first wave of Tutsi departed before Kayibanda acceded to power as violence targeted Tutsi members of the aristocracy and others in positions of power during the late colonial period (1957–62). Hutu aspirations for greater power sharing frightened Tutsi powerholders. In November 1959, a small group of Hutu leaders, future President Kayibanda among them, used the rumor that a Hutu hill chief, one of only ten in the country, had been killed (he had not) to attack numerous Tutsi, who then launched retaliatory raids on Hutu. For the Hutu leadership, that Tutsi youth would dare attack a Hutu chief was read as a provocation, in turn justifying their violent response. The uprising clearly "demonstrated the depth of rural discontent with Tutsi domination and the ability of Hutu to destabilize the authority of the state."[24] The violence soon included attacks by Tutsi youth against Hutu political leaders, which led to counterattacks by Hutu crowds against Tutsi elites that resulted in Tutsi families—Paul Kagame's among them—being targeted and attacked. The final exodus of many powerful Tutsi came in July 1960 when the sitting Tutsi king Kigeli Ndahindurwa fled, followed by thousands of his mostly Tutsi followers and their clients.[25]

Most Tutsi expected to be away from Rwanda for a short time, and foresaw returning to their positions of authority and power once the political situation had settled down. Few expected that it would take almost thirty years and an armed struggle to return.

The Second and Third Waves

In 1963, a second wave of ethnic violence targeted ordinary rural people—they were attacked simply for being Tutsi as their Tutsi "brothers" in neighboring countries had attacked Rwanda. The targeting of ordinary people marked a shift in the pattern of crises impacting Rwandan governance. Historically, violence was limited "to a relatively small group of key participants in the competition, often members of the same ethnic group. The losers—usually high placed political actors—often faced death or exile."[26] Now, ordinary Rwandans were the victims of political violence. A strictly ethnic reading of political struggle emerged—it was now Hutu versus Tutsi, not elite versus elite.

Tutsi refugee leaders living in Uganda instigated this second wave of flight into exile. Between 1963 and 1967, in hopes of expediting their return home, they directed a series of raids into Rwanda from their base in Uganda. The reaction of the Kayibanda government to the raids became the precedent for eliminating opponents. Organizing citizens into a mandatory system of civilian defense, Kayibanda's PARMEHUTU placed Rwandans on alert for possible Tutsi infiltrators entering the country under cover of night from Burundi, Zaire and Uganda.[27] The Tutsi refugee attacks triggered reprisals on Tutsi still living in Rwanda, particularly in border areas, as the Kayibanda regime redoubled its efforts to eliminate dissent, among both ordinary people and political elites.[28] Government tactics involved guarding roadblocks and barriers to verify the ethnic identity of passersby and carrying out foot patrols to root out perceived or real infiltrators.

In some areas—notably along Rwanda's northern border with Uganda—local officials encouraged Hutu attacks on Tutsi living in their communities, blaming them for having helped or planning to help the Tutsi leading the raids from outside. In places where ordinary people were hesitant to scapegoat their Tutsi neighbors, senior government officials returned to their hills of origin to incite attacks on Tutsi. When the Tutsi fled, these same Hutu officials confiscated their land and other property to give to their Hutu followers, or gave them the jobs that the Tutsi had once held.

In 1962, PARMEHUTU became the only party allowed to operate.[29] By 1965, Kayibanda had dismantled opposition politics. Like Kagame today, Kayibanda claimed political opposition distracted Rwandans from the work of development. Instead, "disciplined freedom" became the hallmark of his regime, as Kayibanda regularly reminded the masses "that actions that destabilized and divided the country undermined democratic development and social tranquility."[30]

The Rwandan political crisis of 1972–73 saw a final wave of Tutsi refugees flee the country, when Major General Juvénal Habyarimana seized power from Kayibanda and PARMEHUTU. The coup was relatively peaceful. Compared to the dramatic upheaval of the previous two rounds of violence that sent Tutsi into exile, bloodshed was minimal.[31] During his tenure, Kayibanda had openly favored those Hutu closest to him, meaning other Hutu men educated in colonial seminaries in central Rwanda. His rule also served to sharpen internal regional divisions and favoritism. Many key powerholders in government came from Kayibanda's home area of Gitarama. The University of Wisconsin political scientist Scott Straus notes that personalized rivalries and divisions marked the Kayibanda regime, making for a regionalist and fractious authoritarian system of personal rule.[32]

Following his coup in July 1973, Habyarimana pitted Kayibanda loyalists against one another on a regional basis as a means to break their grip on power. Even so, many officials who served under Kayibanda joined the second postcolonial republic (1973–94). Some elite Tutsi, skittish after years of repression and hardship under Kayibanda, fled the country before Habyarimana's coup. All the same, educated urban elites met Habyarimana with open arms—Hutu and Tutsi alike. Politically moderate Hutu who sought consensus across ethnic lines had high hopes. Habyarimana's promises of national security, peace and development resonated with urbanites, and ushered in a period of ethnic optimism as he sought to unify Rwandans following the divisive politics of the Kayibanda regime. For rural Rwandans, being able to feed themselves and their families remained the most pressing issue of the day.

Like kings and Kayibanda before him, Habyarimana oversaw the election or appointment of government officials, from the lowest administrative posts to senior government and military officials. Within little time, northerners felt they were getting their rightful share of the political and economic pie, which in turn increased the resentment felt by politicians from central and southern Rwanda. Born of ethnic and regional grievance, containing these injustices was the primary task of Habyarimana's Second Republic. This was the rationale that Rwanda's new president used to explain his focus on building strong state structures, using the language of economic development and ethnic balance to promote harmonious relations among Hutu, Tutsi and Twa.[33]

Habyarimana Promises Peace and Development for All

In the early days of his rule, soon after the third wave of Tutsi refugees departed, attacks on local Tutsi ceased and Habyarimana began to cooperate with some Tutsi economic and political elites. The politics of ethnic discrimination receded into the background. Elite Tutsi, notably wealthy businesspeople who had remained in Rwanda, were generally left to get on with their lives. Throughout the 1970s and early 1980s, urban and elite Tutsi successfully worked almost exclusively in the private sector. The unspoken agreement of the day was straightforward: politics was the preserve of elite Hutu. The rural masses, who had little to do with Kigali political games, met Habyarimana's presidency with a collective shrug—their lives remained one of daily economic hardship and toil.

For all the indications of progress, Habyarimana did not abolish ethnic identity cards. Instead, he added the category of place of residence to each card, effectively fixing one's place of origin, thus cementing the regional divides Kayibanda's rule had formalized. Even so, the first decade and a half of Habyarimana's rule was a time of reprieve for

Rwanda's remaining Tutsi. Scapegoating of Tutsi as an ethnic "other" would not begin in earnest until the late 1980s, when multiple economic and political factors converged to put Hutu elites on the defensive.[34]

By 1975, civic optimism yielded to resignation as Habyarimana declared Rwanda a single-party state. Eager to extend his control throughout the country, Habyarimana founded a new party, the National Republican Movement for Democracy (MRND). He quickly and easily constructed a cohesive political monolith, building on the solid foundation of hierarchy and oppression that defined the precolonial state.

Just as Paul Kagame does today, Habyarimana had a coterie of military leaders advising him on political and social affairs, including how to deal with the press and civil society. Military commanders held key political and economic positions, including in the education, transport and infrastructure ministries. Habyarimana justified the need for a single party and controlled political space to "unify Rwanda and work more efficiently for its development."[35] State structures and party personnel amalgamated—all Rwandans were automatically members of the MRND. This in turn reinforced preexisting socio-economic hierarchy as party practice encouraged rural people not to question the directives of those in positions of authority, particularly those in government and the Catholic Church.[36] As Hutu political leaders told ordinary people to accept their lot in life, Maquet's functional interpretation of inequality in Rwanda came full circle.

Over the years, a culture of quiescence became entrenched as Habyarimana pushed his party's administrative control downward to the most local level, an informal political unit of ten households (*nyumbakumi*) that was supervised by an unpaid MRND representative of the same name. This is not to suggest that rural people did not push back against authority in lively and forceful ways. They did, as the Belgian anthropologist Johan Pottier found in his research within cooperatives in southern Rwanda.[37] Rather, it is to highlight the increasing density of the structures of the state, which in turn made conformity a political good to be bartered by even the lowliest of Rwanda's poor, rural non-elite.

Under Habyarimana, the primary building blocks of the regime were communes. The smallest formal administrative unit was the *cellule* (cell) whose jurisdiction averaged fifty households per unit. The next largest unit, the *secteur* (sector), varied in size, with an estimated five hundred to a thousand homes per unit. Communes subsumed both cells and sectors, with each one having on average eleven sectors, each sector in turn having ten to twenty cells. The head of the commune was the *bourgmestre* (mayor), the position occupied by Olivier, whom we met in Chapter 1. The mayor was the most powerful local official, controlling the security apparatus and wielding the most authority in his bailiwick. These men (they were almost exclusively men) exercised direct and persuasive power over the ordinary people in their jurisdiction, as well as those living in smaller administrative units (sectors, cells and *nyumbakumi*).[38] Such bureaucratic density meant that Rwandans were subject to multiple and overlapping administrative requirements. This would later facilitate the speed and intensity of murder during the 1994 genocide.

Table 2. Hierarchy of the Rwandan State under Habyarimana (1975–94)

Entity	Number	Responsible Official
National Government	1	President
Préfecture (Province)	12	*Préfet* (Governor)
Sous-Préfecture (District)	22	*Sous-Préfet* (Sub-Governor)
Commune	154	*Bourgmestre* (Mayor)
Secteur (Sector)	1,531	*Conseiller* (Councilor)
Cellule (Cell)	8,987	*Responsable* (Responsible)
Nyumbakumi	+/-150,000	*Nyumbakumi* (head of ten houses)

Habyarimana handpicked and maintained close connections with his mayors. With a singular focus on economic development, the MRND established weekly *umuganda* (work for the public good)— repairing roads, digging anti-erosion ditches, or clearing brush. *Umuganda* was implemented as an activity of the state, sold to Rwandans as part of their civic duty. The *nyumbakumi* official took attendance and fined those who failed to appear. MRND loyalists also mobilized Rwandans to glorify the party and its heads in regular "animation" propaganda meetings where teams of singers and dancers competed in praising Habyarimana. Rwandans could also express their loyalty by wearing a presidential portrait pin, posting Habyarimana's picture in their home and business, or swearing allegiance to him personally (rather than the office) when they assumed public office or a position paid by the state.

The media also served the one-party state. Habyarimana established the Rwandan Information Office (ORINFOR) to oversee two approved newspapers (one in Kinyarwanda and one in French), and the national radio (Radio Rwanda). Radio was particularly influential, acting as a mouthpiece for both the president and his government, helping to build loyalty to Habyarimana and the party. Radio broadcasts called officials to meetings, announced appointments to or removal from government posts, and released the results of admission examinations to secondary schools. The music mostly comprised MRND songs, praising Habyarimana and the party.

By 1990, radio had become the primary vector through which party propaganda was communicated to all corners of the country and beyond.[39] Starting in the late 1980s, party officials began to use the radio to define Tutsi as a common enemy. Regime rhetoric divided Tutsi into two broad categories. The first were Tutsi, inside or outside the country, nostalgic for any kind of political power. The second were those who supported the hegemonic goals of elite Tutsi living in exile, seeking to return to Rwanda to recapture power from the Hutu. The effect was a singular definition of Tutsi as a common enemy. Hutu who questioned this portrayal were denounced as unpatriotic. Hutu solidarity—lining up behind the common goal of eliminating Tutsi—became an important part of regime rhetoric.

Tutsi refugees in countries bordering Rwanda also listened to Radio Rwanda. The unmitigated praise for Habyarimana incensed many Tutsi refugees, as his presidency was the main hurdle between them and home. In Uganda, the specter of single-party rule under Habyarimana further politicized the children of Tutsi refugees, including young Paul Kagame and other founding members of the RPF. Many Tutsi who fled in the late 1950s and early 1960s died in exile, far from home. Refugee children born abroad were filled with collective shame because they had been unable to help return their parents to their rightful homes.

Throughout their long exile, social and cultural clubs kept Tutsi in contact with one another and provided an avenue for political discussion. These groups and their publications perpetuated a romanticized view of their native land; a return to Rwanda was the only way to ensure the dignity and restore the humanity of Tutsi refugees. The social and political realities under Habyarimana were largely ignored by ambitious young exiles determined to return whatever the cost. Refugees in southern Uganda, closest to Rwanda and with access to the news of the day through multiple channels, dismissed regime declarations that overpopulation and land shortage prevented Tutsi refugees from returning home. Tutsi exiles living in Uganda also underestimated the racism of the Habyarimana regime, built as it was on Hutu supremacy. They did not register how widespread was the image of Tutsi as arrogant, wily and oppressive leaders, bent on returning to Rwanda to once again enslave Hutu. As Rwanda inched closer to civil war (1990–94) and genocide (1994), these issues served to shape the choices and actions of both the MRND government and the rebel RPF.

3

REFUGEE REBELS
Preparing for Civil War

The calming of ethnic tensions in the early years of Habyarimana's rule, along with his policy of allowing Tutsi to operate freely in the private sector, raised hopes of a peaceful return among refugees residing in Uganda. The refugees' terrifying flight and the harsh realities of exile gave young Rwandans like Paul Kagame a driving sense of purpose. Kagame's parents, like other elders, considered education as the path to end their exile, and to give their children a sense of hope for the future—a future in Rwanda. Studying was more than a way to please one's parents; it also politicized many young exiles, as they came to understand how much they had lost in fleeing Rwanda. Kagame speaks of how, as a young teenager, he and other young Rwandan exiles developed political consciousness about their human rights and their right to return to their homeland to liberate Rwandans from the oppression of the Habyarimana regime: "Even as a kid, we would discuss the future of Rwanda. We were refugees in a refugee camp in a grass-thatched house for all this period. So it was eating up our minds, even as kids. The political consciousness was there. We had ideas of our rights."[1]

after reach of local politics?

To add insult to injury, many Tutsi refugees faced derision and abuse on a daily basis, driven in large part by local politics in southwestern Uganda, where most Rwandan Tutsi had settled in camps. Rwandan refugees found it difficult to secure coveted school places, further fueling their sense of persecution. When they did, teachers complained that the Rwandans were disruptive. Ugandan students' taunts and insults of their Rwandan counterparts provoked angry reactions.

Many Rwandan exiles hailed from a group of hereditary nobles, meaning that many were unfit or unwilling to engage in "low" farm labor—hoeing and harvesting—to provide food for their families. Lore of the time highlights the bravery and resilience of those Rwandan refugees who could put aside their traditional royal status to work the fields and do other menial tasks. Paul Kagame experienced this at first hand—his mother dismissed her privilege to work, while his father languished. A hereditary Tutsi noble, Kagame's father withered in exile, and died when young Paul was just fifteen years old.[2]

Losing a parent to the hardships of exile was a common experience for young Rwandan refugees. For Kagame, it shaped his resolve to return to Rwanda on his own terms, and informed the longing he and many other refugees like him felt for home. It is possible that the trauma of his parents, including the resilience of his mother and needless death of his father, shaped Kagame's politics, leadership style and sense of duty to liberate his fellow Tutsi from the grips of Hutu oppression. As early as 1978, young Kagame claims he realized armed struggle would be the only way to address Rwanda's problems: "Deep in our hearts and minds we knew we belonged in Rwanda. And if they [the government] did not want to resolve the problem [of return] politically then armed struggle would be the alternative."[3]

Common adversity along with local military and political dynamics in Uganda shaped the rise of the RPF as a rebel army.[4] When the first Rwandan refugees arrived, Milton Obote of the Uganda People's Congress (UPC) was Uganda's president, serving from 1962 to 1971 and then again from 1980 to 1985 after Idi Amin's overthrow. Initially, Obote supported legal protection for Rwandans, but his benevolence was short-lived, as he soon identified Tutsi refugees as a "public enemy against whom to unite his party."[5] Domestic woes meant the foreigners' presence became increasingly politicized, and in 1970, Rwandans were banned from paid employment. Obote's policy was about to take effect when Idi Amin overthrew the UPC in 1971. Within a year, Amin was himself persecuting Rwandan refugees due to Kigali's support of Obote's rebel force, "even though the Tutsi refugees shared Amin's hatred of the Rwandan regime."[6]

Following Habyarimana's 1973 coup, Amin changed course, and attempted to recruit Rwandans into his infamously brutal security apparatus. Several years later, in a last-ditch effort to save his regime, Amin yet again blamed Tutsi in Uganda for the country's ills. When Obote's troops finally overthrew Amin in late 1979, Tutsi again became the target of a government desperate to hold on to political power.

Ethnic persecution at home and abroad spurred many young Tutsi refugees to action. The precursor to the RPF was the Rwanda Refugee Welfare Foundation, established to provide assistance to refugees who were suffering in Uganda. By late 1979, the group's primary goal had evolved to force an eventual return to Rwanda for exiled Tutsi and it was renamed the Rwandese Alliance for National Unity (RANU). Espousing unanimity among exiles in Uganda, RANU stressed ethnic unity as the basis of good governance and economic development. Between 1981 and 1986, Obote was back in power and, for all its brave intentions, RANU was rendered toothless. Its leaders had fled to Nairobi, where the organization existed in name only.

In December 1980, Obote branded Rwandan refugees as alien foreigners and forced them into heavily guarded camps. Not long after, Uganda's defense minister at the time, Yoweri Museveni, took to the bush with the aim of overthrowing Obote. Sensing dissension in his government, Obote moved to label Rwandan Tutsi as the "natural allies of his political foe Yoweri Museveni of the National Resistance *power = ability to negotiate*

Movement (NRM)."[7] Museveni promised to award Ugandan citizenship to Rwandans who sent their sons to fight his cause. Tutsi exiles welcomed the promise of political integration, as this would allow them to leave the refugee camps most called home. Many young Rwandan men flocked to join Museveni's National Resistance Army (NRA) to overthrow the capricious Obote.

Museveni framed his rebellion as a struggle for freedom and democracy in Uganda, themes which resonated deeply with some young Tutsi refugees.[8] The Ugandan scholar Mahmood Mamdani estimates that approximately a quarter of the NRA membership of sixteen thousand were Rwandan refugees.[9] When Museveni finally seized political power in 1986, he rewarded them for their critical roles in overthrowing Obote with plum posts in government, business and the military. Ugandans again scapegoated Tutsi refugees, complaining bitterly to Museveni that foreigners were receiving the most powerful and prestigious posts in the NRM. In addition, many members of the global Tutsi diaspora descended on Uganda, declaring it the next best thing to being back in Rwanda.[10] The new arrivals increased tensions among Museveni's friends and foes alike; no one could abide the president's willingness to tolerate the presence of increasing numbers of Tutsi "foreigners."

By 1988, anti-refugee sentiment in Uganda had reached a tipping point. Tutsi who had either participated in the anti-Obote struggle, or who had instructed their children to join the fight, could no longer tolerate their situation. Many felt Ugandans were ungrateful for their efforts to overthrow Obote and install Museveni in State House in Kampala. The Tutsi community also perceived that Museveni himself was insufficiently grateful for its many sacrifices. The Rwandans surmised that if Museveni condoned anti-Tutsi feeling, then returning to Rwanda via armed struggle might be their best option.

The large number of Rwandans in senior NRA positions forced Museveni to respond to public criticism that they were coopting Uganda's political leadership. In late 1989, Museveni dismissed two high-ranking

Rwandan officers—Paul Kagame (deputy chief of military intelligence) and Fred Rwigyema (deputy minister of defense).[11] Their departure provided the RPF with the impetus to organize its invasion. As Rwandans recognized integration in Uganda to be an empty promise, RANU's membership jumped dramatically. At its annual meeting in December 1987, RANU renamed itself the Rwandan Patriotic Front. Planning for the armed struggle ahead began in earnest. Its task was facilitated by the floundering joint Rwanda–Uganda ministerial commission. Set up in February 1988, the commission was charged with finding a way to peacefully and quickly send Tutsi refugees residing in Uganda home to Rwanda. President Habyarimana refused to accept the mass repatriation of Tutsi refugees from Uganda, allowing only for the return of those who would make no land claims on arrival.

Preparing for a Liberation War (1988–90)

Paul Kagame and Fred Rwigyema were the driving forces of the newly formed RPF. Much of the popular literature views the two men as childhood friends.[12] Rwandans, particularly Hutu political opponents and those who have recently defected from the ranks of the RPF, contend that Kagame and Rwigyema were far from friendly. They were adversaries with differing personalities as well as differing visions of how best to retake, and eventually remake, Rwanda.

Kagame is serious, studious and quick-tempered. Among RPF cadres, he quickly earned a reputation as cold and careful, preferring to spend his time reading or writing rather than building camaraderie with the rank-and-file. Kagame was every bit the caricature of a military intelligence officer—politically astute, emotionally distant and whip smart. He also had a reputation as a fighter, someone who could explode if he felt misunderstood or pressured. Rwandans in Uganda saw Kagame as both emotionally cold and a hot-blooded man of anger. Such was his "air of seriousness that even older people curbed their rowdiness and

Kagame's personality

rough language" in Kagame's presence.[13] For the young professional soldier, work was always a priority. This austerity continues to inform his professional and personal life to this day. Even his June 1989 marriage to Jeannette Nyiramongi, a fellow Rwandan Tutsi who had grown up in exile in Burundi, was a simple affair with only the couple's closest family and friends in attendance. Kagame, always a tactician, can be forgiven for his singular focus, as he had Rwanda's liberation from the tyranny of the Habyarimana regime on his mind. Just fifteen months after his wedding, the RPF would enter Rwanda from Uganda, launching the civil war that concluded only with the 1994 genocide.

Rwigyema, on the other hand, was effusive and friendly. His charismatic and warm personality made him popular with the troops during his time as a leader in Museveni's NRM and later, when recruiting Tutsi refugees to the RPF. Kagame and Rwigyema met as children in a makeshift refugee camp in southwestern Uganda sometime in the mid-1970s. Like Kagame, Rwigyema had also been born in Gitarama in 1957 and fled to safety in Uganda with his parents in 1960. However, their paths diverged as teenagers as Rwigyema sought full integration into Ugandan society as a citizen while Kagame longed to return home. After years fighting in the bush with Museveni, Rwigyema felt entirely Ugandan. He was also confident that his now close personal friend Museveni would reward Tutsi refugees for their service with full Ugandan citizenship. When this did not happen, Rwigyema became disillusioned and "his shabby treatment at the hands of the president after years of faithful service embittered him."[14] To add insult to injury, Museveni publicly pronounced on numerous occasions that he had no interest in being the keeper of Tutsi refugees. Once Museveni had relieved Kagame and Rwigyema of their leadership posts in his army, both men turned to zealously work toward Rwanda's liberation from the grip of the dictatorial Habyarimana.

Kagame was not always destined to lead the RPF or to eventually become Rwanda's president.[15] Many founding and now exiled members

Kagame = opposite → Rwigyema = all work

Rwigyema = opposite

of the RPF claim that it was Rwigyema who orchestrated the military plan to return to Rwanda by way of civil war. They contend that Kagame was marginal to Rwigyema's plan of attack; it was no accident that Kagame was away when the civil war started. When the RPA entered Rwanda from Uganda on October 1, 1990, Kagame was in the United States, in training at the Army Command and General Staff College at Fort Leavenworth in Kansas. As several now exiled RPF members recall, Kagame was reportedly incensed at being excluded from the final planning. Rwigyema and a handful of his closest lieutenants were killed in the first days of battle, and, feeling his exclusion keenly, Kagame immediately returned to Kampala to assume leadership of the RPF and continue the struggle.[16]

At the time, Rwigyema's battlefield death was attributed to friendly fire. However, many of Kagame's postgenocide political foes, including former founding members of the RPF, believe Rwigyema was murdered on the battlefield on Kagame's order. Two commanding officers, Chris Bunyenyezi and Peter Bayingana, allegedly killed Rwigyema, his death the product of internal struggles over military strategy and the overall plan to take Kigali.[17] Rwigyema sought to conduct a thunder run on the capital to oust Habyarimana, while Kagame wanted to maintain the liberation roots of the RPF. Bunyenyezi and Bayingana were soon arrested and charged with treason, put on trial and executed, also allegedly on Kagame's order. Their execution paved the way for Kagame to take full command of the RPF. Rwigyema's murder raises many still unanswered questions, and the available evidence is hearsay. A key unanswered question is: how did Paul Kagame manage to obtain total control of the RPF between October 1990 and January 1991?

In death, Rwigyema became a martyr and hero to many young Tutsi exiles. Soon after, the social and cultural clubs that linked the otherwise scattered Tutsi diaspora intensified their efforts to fund the fledgling RPF. Within months, by the end of 1990, a global network of Tutsi funders was pouring in an estimated $1 million annually into RPF coffers. Despite this broad funding base, the RPF itself was "dominated by refugees from Rwanda who had roots in RANU, the National Resistance Army, or both."[18]

At the start of Rwanda's civil war, the RPF's military objectives were: 1) the negotiation of the return of Tutsi refugees to Rwanda, and 2) the creation of a government of national ethnic unity. By this point, RPF leadership had also crafted its own nationalist ideology that would later form the core of its postgenocide reconstruction and reconciliation policies: the notion that ethnic categories are a colonial construct that served only to divide Rwandans.[19] Meanwhile, Museveni provided tacit support to the RPF by allowing southern Uganda to be used as the rebels' operational base. Rwandan exiles living in foreign capitals, notably Washington, Brussels, Paris and London, lobbied foreign governments to support the RPF's struggle to overthrow Habyarimana.[20]

For all its intent, the RPF lacked military and political intelligence from within Rwanda. In 1990, the country's political climate was highly volatile; as tensions within the Habyarimana regime rose, political infighting began among key actors. The single-party state that had become the norm in the post-independence period was now under threat as dissident groups in Rwanda clamored for democratic rule. In an ironic twist, the RPF also did not "support the democratization process since it undermined an essential reason for invasion, that is to overthrow an oppressive government."[21]

Encouraged by key foreign donors—notably France—civil society leaders and other critics of the Habyarimana regime pressed to loosen Rwanda's constrictive political system. Even as the World Bank introduced strict financial austerity measures, Habyarimana continued to rely on his rhetoric of development and prosperity to demonstrate to domestic and international critics that his government could still deliver economic growth. The regime's message focused on urging all Rwandans to continue to work hard to ensure ethnic unity—which in turn needed a strong single party.[22]

Habyarimana's regime could not whitewash Rwanda's economic woes. Only foreign aid provided an illusion of prosperity: the country was in financial freefall. The Belgian development scholar Peter Uvin argues that prior to the genocide Rwanda's international donor community saw the country as a model of African development. Its praise was rooted in impressive development outcomes, such as high GNP growth and growing industrial production. Rwanda also had strong human development indicators, such as high vaccination rates, low maternal mortality and a robust civil society.[23] Rwanda's donors lent credence to the official portrayal of Rwanda as a peaceable, poor but hardworking Christian country. However compelling the statistics, these could not resolve the issue of how a country where more than 80 percent of the population depended on farming, but where there was too little land to feed and house them all, could possibly sustain itself.[24]

By the end of the 1980s, regime critics, including journalists, human rights defenders and even some members of the usually tacit clergy, began to report on increasing corruption and favoritism for Hutu from Habyarimana's northern region. The circle of regime insiders deepened the effects of the economic crisis. Simultaneously, when the price of coffee—Rwanda's chief export—took a plunge on the world market, Rwanda fell into economic crisis. Coffee harvests were already threatened by widespread drought, and famine loomed large in significant portions of the country. The crisis was apparent as rural smallholders sold their plots in distress to pay for basics such as food and medicine. Local conflicts over land usage and rights also erupted. In 1988, in a fit of defiance, rural producers began to pull up coffee trees they had planted on government orders to instead grow bananas, beans and other crops they could use to feed their hungry families. Bananas could also be turned into banana beer, a product with a sizable local market. However they tried, the situation did not improve. By the early 1990s, rural farmers were simply unable to make ends meet.

Seeking to offset Rwanda's economic misfortune, Habyarimana called on his network of personal relationships and explained away the crisis as a product of foreign efforts to introduce multi-party politics. Habyarimana expertly exploited Rwanda's top-down administrative structure through an elaborate network of cronies and loyalists. The heads of state corporations that controlled public services like gas, electricity, water and transportation, as well as those that oversaw the production of cash crops such as coffee and tea, backed the president. Appearing to support Habyarimana and his economic policies was critical to the personal survival of many of these leaders. Openly criticizing the president, or choosing not to act on his instructions, were risky propositions that few dared to attempt. Even the intellectual elite, including professors, journalists, lawyers and doctors, dared not criticize Habyarimana. Business leaders in the private sector also remained mum on the nature of the economic crisis facing Rwanda in the late 1980s, as they needed Habyarimana's approval for the state concessions that made their businesses profitable.

Rwanda's business, social and political elites owed their professional status and income to Habyarimana. As the economy plummeted, the president called on these elites to return to their hills of origin and spread the word that there was no economic crisis; rural farmers were to be reminded of their role in economic development. Having a high-status person come home to the rural hill where they grew up to share important news from Kigali was a symbolic form of power. Making elites the messengers served a dual function: it reminded the bearer that he owed his position to Habyarimana, and let the rural peasantry know that the message was critical, as an important person from Kigali had come all the way to the countryside to communicate it. The concept of performed deference was not new to Rwanda. It had its roots in the precolonial state and is captured in a proverb, "orders from above spread quickly, in the form of rules."[25] But when an important person came home to communicate something from the president himself, rural Rwandans recognized this as a sign of crisis.

For all the government's failings in driving economic policy, it was efficient in getting its message out quickly. Habyarimana's commitment to economic development resulted in an impressive road network and telephone infrastructure, both of which enabled political and military leaders to communicate with their counterparts and the population. Then as today, roads served an important function, moving both people and goods in a landlocked country with no rail system.

allow for media filtration and censorship? manipulation?

The RPF Invades from Uganda (1990)

Despite his best efforts to maintain control and loyalty, Habyarimana was forced to yield to pressure from international donors and open Rwanda's political system to multi-partyism. Much-needed donor aid, particularly from France and Belgium, was tied to multi-party politics. Rather than risk losing everything, Habyarimana reluctantly accepted the end of the single-party state in early 1991, permitting other political parties to form.

another ex: of power giving the ability to negotiate

In addition to external pressure, Rwandan politics were impacted by the start of the civil war. The RPF attack from the Ugandan border town of Kagitumba surprised Habyarimana's Rwandan Armed Forces (FAR). Following their first offensive, the RPF marched to Gabiro town, 60 kilometers north of Kigali, without encountering significant military resistance. The RPF expected to find a welcoming population, jubilant for their efforts to liberate the country. Instead, they found masses of frightened and hungry rural residents, cowering from two concurrent invaders: foreign rebels whom they did not know and government officials who cared little for them. Kagame would later say that the lack of welcome was an insult to the RPF's liberation mission.[26] This lack of gratitude came to shape the RPF government's post-1994 attempts to reeducate the rural masses on the importance of a unified

this time it is Rwanda as a country without the power

national ethnic identity, as well as the importance of discipline, sacrifice and loyalty. What RPF leaders, including Kagame, did not fully absorb was that rural Rwandans had learned to adapt to, and largely ignore, the moral musings of political leaders. Instead, they hunkered down for another period of political uncertainty, spoken of as *igihirahiro*.

Habyarimana wasted no time in asking for assistance from France, Belgium and neighboring Zaire, without which analysts believe that the RPF would have easily continued its advance to Kigali. To highlight the need for external assistance, Habyarimana ordered his FAR to stage a mock attack on Kigali on October 4, 1990. French paratroopers supported the FAR and pushed the RPF back to Uganda. The rebels suffered heavy casualties in the withdrawal, including the death of Fred Rwigyema on the second day of fighting.

Despite this initial setback, the RPF was able to occupy much of Rwanda's northern border region (see Map 1). Here, the rebels corralled the local population into camps it viciously controlled. Many rural residents fled the military advance, too scared to wait and discover what life might be like under the RPF. At the end of 1990, the RPF's dream of indoctrinating civilians to their noble vision of national ethnic unity had few takers. The ordinary men and women who remained in RPF-held territory in the north were forced into internally displaced persons camps (IDPs), ostensibly established to provide safety to the largely Hutu civilian population, while ensuring their indoctrination into the goals of the RPF's liberation struggle. The RPF saw holding civilians in camps as straightforwardly logical; a captive population could not aid and abet Habyarimana's FAR.

Conditions in the camps were difficult, with few amenities. Food and water were scarce. Shelter was makeshift; residents built what they could cobble together from scraps of young trees, dried banana leaves and mud they found on site. With the rural population detained in camps, villages were deserted. Abandoned *shambas* (personal gardens) became overgrown, while crops of cassava, beans and bananas went unharvested. The tea estates of Mulindi some 80 kilometers outside of Kigali, where the RPF would come to set up camp, sat untended as once-manicured bushes became unruly trees.

The civil war provided the Habyarimana regime with the necessary pretext to pursue any and all measures needed to protect itself from an enemy that was both external (the RPF and the exiled refugees who supported it) and internal (all Tutsi and Hutu political opponents). The minister of justice soon declared all Tutsi in Rwanda as *ibyitso* (accomplices). Habyarimana started to persecute all Tutsi, regardless of their station in life, or their real or perceived alliance with the rebels. In time, many senior government and military officials deployed the term *ibyitso* to justify mass arrests. Tutsi were perceived as the natural allies and spies of the RPF "invaders," and became victims of arbitrary arrests, political assassinations and organized massacres in urban centers across the country. By the beginning of 1991, more than eleven thousand mostly Tutsi detainees were being held without charge, in deplorable conditions. Many were tortured and died.

Hutu began to murder their Tutsi neighbors in sporadic bursts soon after the RPF arrived. Local officials directed the murders, targeting Tutsi and Tutsi-related people, including Hutu spouses and children. Fear blanketed Rwanda, as killings which targeted Tutsi increased indiscriminately. At all times, persons of authority incited and directed the killing. The leaders were local officials, central government authorities and, at times, military officials. Typically, attacks took place when MRND leaders and their loyalists felt threatened, sometimes by events related to the civil war, sometimes by pressure from rival political parties. The targeting of ethnic Tutsi, along with perceived or real opponents of the Habyarimana government, "contributed to the fragmentation of the political landscape and to the introduction of weapons and warriors difficult to control. Increasingly, a culture of violence took hold in which political solutions became increasingly difficult."[27] It was in this climate that peace negotiations began in Arusha, Tanzania.

The Arusha Peace Accords (1990–93)[28]

Emerging opposition political parties in Rwanda forced the reluctant Habyarimana regime to negotiate with the RPF. The leadership of the Hutu-dominated Republican Democratic Movement (MDR), the Social Democratic Party (PSD) and the pro-Tutsi Liberal Party (PL) were weary at the lack of progress in peace talks, noting the absence of good faith on both sides, and hoped negotiations would make space for their parties to actively participate in politics. The PSD tried to distinguish itself as free of ethnic politics, seeking instead to advance the regional interests of Butare prefecture in the south.

In the first two years of the war (1990–92), the MDR, the PL and the PSD were bit players in the peace process. Habyarimana viewed the opposition parties as potential or actual allies of the RPF, which heightened his distrust. Occasional talks resulted in no significant progress toward peace. Ceasefires were broken as quickly as they were signed, usually before the ink was dry. Then, in April 1992, representatives from each opposition party openly and formally met with the RPF for the first time. Habyarimana and the MRND were pushed to the negotiating table at Arusha, Tanzania, where the Organisation of African Unity (OAU) and the American government facilitated talks. In July 1992, the MRND agreed to a ceasefire, and in August it signed a new peace agreement.

The Arusha Accords included protocols on uniting the FAR and RPF armies, the repatriation of Tutsi refugees, and the resettlement of persons displaced by the civil war. It also included provisions for power sharing among the signatories, including the creation of a national unity and reconciliation commission and a national summit on unity and reconciliation. It further laid out a timetable for installing a broad-based transitional government, which was to be made up of representatives from all of Rwanda's political parties.

Chief among the peace protocols was an armed international mission to Rwanda. The United Nations Security Council authorized the United

Nations Assistance Mission in Rwanda (UNAMIR) on October 5, 1993. Under this agreement, the United Nations was to provide a peace-keeping force to oversee the implementation of the ceasefire protocol. To save money, the UN limited the force to 2800 troops, far below the 5000 requested by the preliminary assessment team. It took another two months before peacekeepers arrived in Rwanda, underfunded, poorly trained and ill-equipped. The best-prepared and largest number of troops hailed from Belgium. Meanwhile, UN officials in New York further hamstrung the force. Both before and during the genocide, UNAMIR officers tried to avert and minimize violence targeting Tutsi and other civilians, but New York restricted all such efforts.[29]

On the surface, Habyarimana appeared to relinquish some state control as a show of good faith. Behind the scenes, members of the MRND's inner circle broke away to form their own Hutu extremist party, the Coalition for the Defense of the Republic (CDR). The CDR not only opposed peace talks with the RPF; it favored a Hutu-only Rwanda. The RPF leadership refused to negotiate with the CDR, arguing it was not a political party at all, but an extremist splinter group of the MRND. International mediators encouraged the RPF to compromise and allow the CDR to join the power-sharing agreement. The RPF held firm, rejecting the argument that bringing hardliners into government where they could be managed was preferable to leaving them out of the agreement where they could wreak havoc.

Further undermining peace talks was a widespread lack of support among many of the FAR's rank-and-file. Some opposed the accords because they believed they could attain total victory on the battlefield, while others resisted eventual forced demobilization, which would cost them their professional status and livelihood. This was especially true of senior officers who feared forced retirement. In a chilling letter dated end July 1992, the head of military intelligence warned Habyarimana that if he continued to compromise at the negotiating table, disgruntled military officers could overthrow him.[30] Having himself orchestrated a

coup that took power from Kayibanda in 1973, Habyarimana understood the threat. The letter contained an eerie prediction: if Habyarimana
continued to allow the RPF to gain ground, the military would target
and kill politicians, and the population would rise up and kill Tutsi—
exactly what happened when the killing started in April 1994.

Feeling squeezed by his armed forces, opposition politicians, and
Hutu chauvinists within his own party, Habyarimana also faced
increasing international pressure. In a bid to kowtow to all sides,
Habyarimana pursued a twisting path along which he first signed then
disavowed the accords. The RPF's recurring use of force during negotiations made observers question its commitment to peace talks. Members
of the opposition coalition believed the RPF wanted to seize power by
any means necessary, and not share it with lowly Hutu. Inasmuch as the
RPF's engagement with the peace process appeared questionable, its
February 1993 attack on FAR units at Byumba near the Ugandan border
gave the rebels the advantage on the battlefield, further forcing
Habyarimana's already-weakened hand. The international community
continued to pressure the virtually bankrupt MRND to end the war,
threatening to cut all foreign aid. The French also withdrew much of
their military assistance in recognition of the RPF's strength on the
battlefield, thereby further bolstering its strategic position.

On August 4, 1993, the MRND at last signed the final protocol of
the Arusha Accords. The agreement provided for a transitional government with political power to be shared among three blocks: Habyarimana
and his loyalists; domestic parties opposed to him (MDR, PL and
PSD); and the RPF. Habyarimana would remain president in name, but
in essence would become a figurehead, as most of his powers would be
exercised by a council of ministers, a body on which the MRND had
only five of nineteen seats. The RPF was also assigned five seats on the
council of ministers, and received the new position of vice prime
minister. The internal opposition parties were allocated nine ministries,
plus the post of prime minister. The CDR rejected the accords and was

shut out of government. Its leaders, along with disgruntled MRND members, went so far as to proclaim that the international diplomats who were brokering the accords were in fact RPF accomplices who had willingly given it too much power. In truth, the terms of the agreement recognized the RPF's superior negotiating skills and military position. Diplomatic priorities mirrored those of the RPF—democratization and multi-party politics—which gave the appearance of international support for the rebels.

According to the terms of the agreement, the RPF negotiated a plum deal. The new Rwandan Army was to draw 60 percent of its troops from the FAR and 40 percent from the RPF. Command posts were to be shared equally between FAR and RPF officers down to the level of battalion. The new force was not to exceed nineteen thousand, including six thousand national police, meaning that both the FAR and the RPF would have to demobilize about half of their troops (thirty thousand government troops and twenty thousand RPF forces).[31]

Although the peace agreement reduced the number of RPF troops on the ground, those remaining in uniform continued to see action, as regional shocks shaped the actions of Rwandan Hutu hardliners. In Burundi, which shares the same ethnic make-up as Rwanda, ethnic Tutsi had held power after independence. In June 1993, Burundian voters elected Melichor Ndadaye, the country's first Hutu president. A peaceful transition to majority rule followed and Burundi was hailed a democratic success story. However, Burundian Tutsi military officers in Burundi assassinated Ndadaye in October 1993, causing the CDR and ethnic extremists within the MRND, along with a few hardline members of the MDR who defected from the opposition, to paint his murder as undeniable proof that Tutsi anywhere would do anything to gain power. The RPF added insult to injury by issuing a bland statement of regret at the passing of the Burundian president, while welcoming Ndadaye's assassination among those Rwandan refugees still in Uganda. The RPF's two-faced response tipped the balance of power toward Hutu extremists.

The impact of events in Burundi reached into the lives of all Rwandans as Ndadaye's assassination and the ethnic killings that followed instantly and dramatically worsened the political situation.[32] By the end of 1993, some 300,000 mostly Hutu Burundian refugees took up residence in southern Rwanda, where they joined other Burundians living there following previous episodes of violence. These Burundian refugees lived in misery in refugee camps in the southern prefectures of Butare and Gikongoro. For Rwandans living in the south, their bare-bones existence was evidence of the damage a Tutsi-run army could do. The increased numbers of Hutu refugees provided leverage to Habyarimana's supporters. For nearly two years, from the end of 1991, in clear violation of international convention, Burundian Hutu living in refugee camps had been receiving military training from the Habyarimana government. As the number of new arrivals increased from mid-1993, so too did military training.[33]

The international community, in demonstrating its willingness to tolerate ethnic "slaughter in the pursuit of political ends," also affected the Rwandan situation.[34] International pressure to restore normalcy in Burundi only extended to restoring civilian control of the government. Donor governments did little to bring the Tutsi architects of the violence in Burundi to justice, signaling that ethnic violence was tolerable. Neither the Tutsi officers who assassinated Ndadaye and other Burundian political leaders nor the Hutu administrators and ordinary people who killed Tutsi were held accountable. Following Ndadaye's assassination, Rwandan Hutu attacked Tutsi in many parts of Rwanda, killing almost a hundred people and driving thousands more from their homes. Hutu who tried to protect Tutsi also suffered. For example, hardliners attacked Alphonse-Marie Nkubito, a senior judicial official and Hutu human rights defender who regularly defended Tutsi. He survived.

As Burundian Hutu developed combat skills, Rwandan radio allocated considerable attention to Ndadaye's assassination. Commentators claimed he was castrated at the time of his murder and his body had been violated. Although later proved untrue, these assertions were already public, and radio announcers reminded listeners that Tutsi kings would castrate defeated enemies, using their genitals to decorate the royal drum (the drum being a symbol of royal power). Disinformation about Ndadaye's mistreatment reinforced popular fear and hatred of the Tutsi, and their intentions to again dominate the Hutu majority. A proverb sums up the deep roots of Hutu skepticism about Tutsi powerholders: "When you lodge a Tutsi in your house, he chases you out of your bed."

Ndadaye's assassination galvanized popular sentiment. Within weeks, Hutu Power made its first appearance as a political entity at a November 1993 rally in Gitarama, not far from Paul Kagame's childhood home. A second rally in Kigali was broadcast on radio, and featured Froduald Karamira, second vice president of the MDR, as guest speaker. Karamira addressed a mixed audience of MDR, MRND, CDR and PL supporters, alleging in ethnically charged language that RPF leader Kagame had helped plan Ndadaye's assassination, depriving Burundian Hutu of democracy, while asserting that Kagame would surely do the same in Rwanda. Karamira also mocked and denigrated those MDR politicians who still trusted the RPF, calling them puppets of the Tutsi. He then baptized the radical wing of his MDR *"Pawa"* (a variation on the English word "power"), marking a clear ideological shift in Hutu extremist politics. Hutu Pawa nationalists publicly and definitively labeled Tutsi the common enemy. The rally resulted in the full polarization of Rwandan political alliances—on one side, a new Hutu coalition in the form of Hutu Pawa, and on the other, the RPF. Political moderates were sidelined as space for the voices of tolerance and negotiation quickly evaporated.

A Military Solution? (1993–94)

Recruitment and training of militias, particularly the Interahamwe, continued through 1993, intensifying in the latter part of the year and early 1994.[35] In Kigali, at secluded military camps, as well as at remote locations in Akagera game park in the east and Gishwati forest in the northwest, Rwandan soldiers trained militias to use firearms and other weapons (see Map 2). When international diplomats and human rights observers asked about these programs, the minister of defense said that the recruits were being trained to serve as guards for the forest preserve. Meanwhile, military trainers boasted that their recruits could kill a thousand Tutsi in twenty minutes. Elsewhere, active Interahamwe units were found in communes where burgomasters were overt supporters of the MRND or CDR. The Interahamwe rarely operated in central and southern Rwandan communes, where local officials belonged to other political parties.[36]

In early 1993, military and political leaders close to Habyarimana began to organize civilian self-defense units. Male participants were recruited according to their commune of residency, the rationale being that the government could draft far more men this way than if they relied on political party membership lists. The government framed civilian self-defense units as a nationwide project committed to the security of all citizens, something other political parties could not do. In so doing, this recruitment method also served to subtly reassert the dominance of the ruling MRND.

Self-defense units had historical roots dating back to the 1960s, when civilians patrolled and guarded barriers from raids by Tutsi refugees. At the time, self-defense units were generally unarmed, as their task was surveillance, not population control. In late 1993 and early 1994, the civilian self-defense units came to the fore once again, and were central to a broader collaboration between the ministry of defense, the national police, and those political parties able to defend the idea of the republic. Participation was restricted to include only republican political parties, which meant the MRND and CDR were involved in all aspects of planning. The units' program of protection was not only limited to defense against RPF combatants in uniform, but extended to "disguised RPF" and their "acolytes," language so broad as to be interpreted to mean Tutsi civilians as well.[37]

The government's racial construct of Tutsi is evidenced in the rhetoric of its key supporters. A soldier from the north, who headed the civilian self-defense program for the Ministry of Defense, Colonel Bagosora kept records on the evolution of the units throughout this time. Bagosora was once close to Habyarimana and his wife, and owed his prominent military position to regional prejudice, not merit. Under the transition to multi-partyism, Bagosora became an ardent member of the CDR and its racist ideas. He believed that Rwanda's civil war was the latest manifestation of an age-old struggle between Hutu and Tutsi. Bagosora saw Tutsi as arrogant, cruel, dictatorial masters of deceit, in contrast to Hutu who were modest, open-hearted and loyal. According to Bagosora, Rwanda belonged to the Hutu, who had lived peacefully with the docile Twa until wily Tutsi imposed supremacy over the rightful local inhabitants. For Bagosora, the RPF was simply a Tutsi supremacist party, determined to restore "feudal-royalist servitude" with the help of Ugandan President Museveni.[38]

Colonel Bagosora's ethnically charged language has roots in the Hamitic Hypothesis, which helped fuel the propaganda created by Hutu hardliners.[39] The myth contends that Tutsi are members of a superior Caucasoid race from northeastern Africa, and, as such, are "invaders" in Rwanda. Hutu extremists drew on imagery of Tutsi superiority and foreignness to strike fear in the hearts of the rural Hutu majority, warning them that all Tutsi needed to be annihilated lest they once again seek to assert their oppressive dominance over Hutu. In conversation with Prudence Bushnell, the most senior American diplomat working on Rwanda in April 1994, Bagosora was unequivocal. He considered the genocide to be "a spontaneous reaction by the population to the RPF offensive." In lieu of the orchestrated massacres of civilians by the Hutu-led government forces that they were, Bagosora understood the violence of genocide as an uncontrollable effect of RPF attacks.[40]

The inflammatory, ethnically divisive language of regime hardliners did more than dehumanize and scapegoat all Tutsi. It also made it possible to target Tutsi for death on the basis of a physical stereotype:

tall and thin, with long faces and fine features. In reality, these characteristics can hardly be applied to all Tutsi. While some Tutsi did conform to the ideal, many others did not. This fluidity made marking Tutsi for death according to their physical appearance difficult, particularly for people born of mixed ethnic marriages. These children always took the ethnic affiliation of their father, but those born of a Tutsi father might have the stereotypical Hutu characteristics of their mother—short, with a husky build, dark skin and broad, flat facial features—which added further diversity to the categories of Tutsi and Hutu.

Lists and record keeping were part of a broader set of bureaucratic and administrative rules of Rwandan society to promote national security. Rwandan government practice requiring communal mayors and other local administrators to provide data about the populations they governed further underpinned ethnic stereotypes. This included quarterly reports on the numbers of births, deaths, arrivals and departures by age, sex and ethnic group. Such detailed information facilitated the creation of myriad lists, including records of Tutsi and dissident Hutu who had been arrested for political activity, or were thought to have left to join the RPF. Regional lists were refined into a mechanism for genocide and the killing of Tutsi. Lists did more than identify suspected RPF supporters; they were also used in the early days and weeks of the genocide to persuade reluctant Hutu to attack Tutsi. Oftentimes, local officials revealed collections of machetes and other tools used to kill Tutsi as supposed proof of Tutsi plotting against Hutu or the government.

As soon as Habyarimana's plane had been shot down, Hutu hardliners moved to shore up their own power and authority. Within seventy-two hours, they had outwitted moderates within their ranks to install a new extremist government. At the same time, the rebel RPF advanced from their positions in and around Kigali, reigniting the battle for control of the country and setting the stage for genocide.

PART II

Transitioning to Peace?

4

A SEMBLANCE OF NORMALITY

Rwandans made heroic efforts to return to some semblance of normality once the genocide had ended. Rural farmers, government officials and political elites alike busied themselves with work. Urgency and survival were the orders of the day.

Adults and orphaned children returned to the fields to salvage what they could of the June harvest. Anyone who survived had to figure out a way to recover emotionally and spiritually while mustering the physical strength to harvest ripe fields of maize and sorghum—staples of the Rwandan diet, particularly for rural people who subsist on what they grow. Women carried much of the burden, tending livestock, rebuilding roofs, fences and stockades while caring for surviving relatives and neighbors. Many women also took on primary economic responsibility for their households—the men they knew were dead, in prison or in exile. Staff at pharmacies, grocery stores and other small businesses scrambled to stock their shelves amid electricity and water rationing. Revenge killings, whether related to the genocide, personal grudges or tussles over land or property, were a daily reality.

Meanwhile, government coffers were empty—humanitarian support had yet to arrive. France, Habyarimana's primary donor, had suspended aid, and Rwanda's new bilateral donors—the US, Britain and the Netherlands—were divided over how best to support the new government.[1] They were concerned about the ethnic make-up and intentions of the new government, specifically whether the RPF would lead a revenge campaign against Hutu opponents.[2]

Foreign debt repayment was an additional stumbling block, as representatives of the World Bank and International Monetary Fund (IMF) sought to schedule repayment of Rwanda's pregenocide debt before releasing any new funds. Foreign dollars only began to flow in November 1994, when the European Union "unilaterally broke the deadlock in giving $88 million with preconditions."[3] Only then did Rwanda's bilateral and multilateral donors finally release US$1 billion in aid, representing 95 percent of the country's budget from 1994 to 1996.[4] International funding was accompanied by technical expertise as donors deployed qualified citizens to facilitate the implementation of social services in health and education, special support to survivors of the genocide, and reconstruction of infrastructure and the economy.[5] The arrival of foreign "experts" affronted the RPF leadership; the government preferred to set its own reconstruction priorities and have Rwandans it trusted undertake the work.

Donors failed to appreciate how the RPF interpreted their collective actions. Western condescension and paternalism about what the government should do to rebuild after genocide was deeply felt; donors wanted to focus on justice, while the RPF prioritized securing Rwanda's borders and restoring basic services. Foreign inability to understand the "flesh and blood, visceral worldview of a regime that had won a narrow victory against a genocidal regime that still survived" shapes Rwanda's donor relations to this day.[6] By 1996, in domestic and international speeches the RPF leadership stressed Rwandan self-reliance and survivor resilience, and rejected colonial mentalities of dependence on outsiders.[7]

Meanwhile, in late 1994, the international community remained preoccupied with the refugee crisis that the genocide had generated. It took months before humanitarians understood that the refugee camps, particularly those in Zaire, had become an extension of the genocide by other means.[8] Leaders among the rump elements of the former Habyarimana regime, the former FAR, and Interahamwe militias correctly calculated that the international community would provide food, medicine and other services to the camps.[9] Hutu camp leaders organized refugees by their hill of origin, complete with commune and sector officials, along with parallel military and church authorities.[10] Where officials of the old order could not be found (often they could not), new ones were appointed and given the task of controlling the camp population. Dirt footpaths snaked through the tent city, revealing the status of inhabitants. The most powerful could stand in their tents, while the poorest slept on the ground, wrapped in UN-issued canvas or plastic sheeting.

The real power in refugee camps lay in the hands of Hutu extremists, who threatened to kill any civilians who tried to return home to Rwanda. Anyone who questioned the rules of the camps or complained to international humanitarian workers were harassed, disappeared or were killed.[11] Others stayed willingly, fearful of returning to the RPF's Rwanda.

The extremists' unquestioned authority allowed them to provide food and medical care for their own kind, as well as soldiers and militia members who continued killing Tutsi.[12] Conditions in the camps were squalid for most, but relatively comfortable for camp elites. Those who lived among the open sewage pits and makeshift graves acknowledged their precariousness by ironically declaring their UN-issued tarp shelters as "bombproof."[13] Exhaustion resulting from chronic malnutrition, diseases like dysentery, cholera and malaria, and revenge killings took their toll; at the end of 1994, the United Nations Children's Fund (UNICEF) estimated that at least fifty-eight people a day died in UN-run health clinics. UNICEF reckoned that its own figures were too low, as some 90 percent of refugees in camps in Zaire did not have access to medical care.[14]

The militarization of the camps and their control by former members of the Habyarimana regime kept the RPF on high alert and made their troops volatile. RPA soldiers arbitrarily executed and detained civilians—Hutu or Tutsi—if they were suspected of associating with the former genocidal regime or being hostile to the new government.[15] RPF leaders distanced themselves from these killings by blaming them on undisciplined or newly recruited RPA soldiers who killed in revenge for the genocide, not as the result of senior officials' orders. The RPF's carefully phrased explanations informed the thinking of Rwanda's foreign donors who, if renewed violence broke out, did not want to explain to their domestic constituencies why they were funding an ethnic war in a tiny Central African country. This feeling was particularly acute for the US, having only recently suffered the humiliation of seeing the naked bodies of its marines dragged through the streets of Mogadishu in November 1993 as part of the United Nations Assistance Mission to Somalia.[16] By September 1995, only $245 million of the more than $1 billion pledged had been released.[17] At issue was the amount being spent on refugee camps around Rwanda. Almost half of all aid was being used to maintain refugee camps in Burundi, Tanzania and Zaire. As disbursements failed to keep up with donors' pledges, the RPF was further aggrieved by what it perceived as a foreign lack of confidence in the new Rwandan government.

Many donors, including an ashamed United Nations, continued to sit on their hands. Led by the US, donors sought reassurance that a government comprised of minority Tutsi could bring peace to troubled Rwanda. There were concerns from the first months of RPF rule as it sought ensure the safety and security of the country. It often did so with a heavy hand—disappearances, abductions and killing at the hands of RPA personnel and their civilian *abakada* counterparts were commonplace.[18]

Relations between the RPF and some donors warmed by late 1994, once funds had been fully released. Even so, early foot-dragging would be read by the RPF for years to come as a show of donor non-confidence. This early fumbling, combined with an overall sense of shame and guilt shown by the international community, was exploited tirelessly by the RPF evoking external failure to stop the genocide, and served to inform donor relations in the fragile interim period (1994–97) and throughout the transition to development (1998–2000). To this day, the RPF leadership has "a deep distrust of the UN and international non-governmental organisations."[19]

The Transitional Government of National Unity

The efforts to craft a government of ethnic unity began in July 1994, when the Arusha Accords provided for the creation of a transitional government. International and regional partners welcomed such an arrangement, especially when considering the alternative, in which the victorious RPF could have unilaterally imposed a military and political monopoly without due concern for democratic principles. This observation appeased many outsiders, but merely annoyed Paul Kagame, for whom democracy was hardly a priority. Kagame felt that his government could only assure national security by tracking down Rwanda's genocidal enemies. For Kagame and the RPF, security was job one, even if it meant sending Rwandan troops into the refugee camps in neighboring Zaire to forcibly bring refugees home to face justice. In an interview with American journalist Philip Gourevitch, Vice President Kagame highlighted the RPF's generous and conciliatory spirit in sharing political power and welcomed the integration of former FAR soldiers into the postgenocide RPA.

Noting the challenges of rebuilding Rwanda in the wake of the genocide, Kagame reinforced the hero status of the RPF as the sole entity that stopped the 1994 genocide. Acknowledging that the head of a minority Tutsi government was now responsible for governing a majority Hutu population, Kagame doubled down on his commitment to national unity, stating: "If I wanted to be a [political] problem, I would actually be a problem."[20] It was also a stern reminder of who held ultimate power in Rwanda as the RPF "faked inclusion" while working to take full military and political control of the country.[21]

In the aftermath of the genocide, the government's public relations machinery worked to reassure local and international observers of the RPF's commitment to pluralistic government, as well as the terms and spirit of the Arusha Accord.[22] Habyarimana's former party, the MRND, and the extremist Hutu party, CDR, were banned but other opposition parties took up their seats in a National Unity government. All the same, the RPF held the upper hand. Its decisive military victory meant that it could, and would, extend its political and military might over the country. As Gerald Gahima, a founding member of the RPF who defected in 2009, recalls: "The RPF interpreted its military victory over the organizers of the genocide as a mandate to reconstruct Rwanda on its own terms."[23]

At first, the Government of National Unity appeared to fulfill the ethnic power-sharing requirements of the Arusha Accords. Newly appointed President Pasteur Bizimungu was an RPF Hutu who previously worked as a civil servant during the Habyarimana regime in the 1980s. Of all appointed government ministers, just over a third were members of the RPF.

It seemed as though the RPF would establish an inclusive government that was genuinely committed to national unity and reconciliation. The optics of the new cabinet were impressive, consisting of a Hutu majority (sixteen of twenty-two posts), including the president (Pasteur Bizimungu, RPF) and the prime minister (Faustin Twagiramungu, MDR). Twagiramungu was a Hutu political moderate who had been in opposition during the Habyarimana regime. Politicians, civil servants, judges and military who served under the previous regime stayed in Kigali and "indicated their willingness to co-operate with the RPF."[24] The RPF also negotiated with the French military, which continued to occupy and control the Zone Turquoise, to honor its commitment to withdraw on August 21, 1994. All the many constituencies within Rwandan society appeared to be represented—Hutu and Tutsi, Franco- and Anglophone, survivors from within Rwanda and those who returned from abroad.

For all the window dressing of power-sharing, the RPF manifested its full control of the new arrangement by unilaterally creating the post of vice president. No such position was foreseen in the Arusha Accords, nor were the duties of the vice president defined publicly. The Rwandan parliament appointed Paul Kagame to the position. The title was far from honorific; as head of the military and chairman of the RPF, Vice President Kagame was the country's only true authority, albeit de facto the "power from behind the throne."[25] Kagame would rule from behind the scenes until March 2000, when he ascended unelected to the presidency.[26]

Human Rights Abuses

No sooner had the Government of National Unity been established than concerns about RPF military abuses began to emerge from Rwandan and international human rights communities alike. Timothy Longman, then Human Rights Watch country director for Rwanda, now at Boston University, recalls that bloodshed continued well after the RPF had allegedly stopped the genocide. "People would take me around [in 1995] and say, 'There's a mass grave right over here,' and you would ask, 'From when?' And they would say, 'Just from a few weeks ago—not from the genocide.'"[27]

Concrete evidence of RPF abuses appeared as early as September 1994 in the form of the Gersony Report,[28] which cited "convincing evidence of widespread, systematic killings by the RPF."[29] Initially, the RPF expected the results of Gersony's fact-finding to support its efforts to forcibly return refugees, and so allowed the team to travel and work without escorts, which was not the norm at the time.[30] Gersony's team visited 91 sites in 41 of 145 communes, gathering information about ten other communes and making site visits to nine refugee camps. Most of the team's work took place in the provinces of Butare, Gisenyi and Kibungo. Gersony's team conducted interviews with more than two hundred individuals and facilitated over one hundred group discussions. Completed in October 1994, the Gersony Report provided credible eyewitness accounts of numerous RPA crimes, including between fifteen and thirty thousand execution-style deaths in just four communes within its survey area. As a team member reported to the American journalist Howard French: "What we found was a well-organized military-style operation, with military command and control, and these were military-campaign-style mass murders."[31]

In a show of support for the new government, the UN and the US suppressed distribution of the Gersony Report. Both were concerned about being seen as pressuring the RPF's young government, which many believed had just ended the genocide. Ambassador Susan Rice personally felt the weight of America's perceived failures during the genocide. In 1994—at the time of the now-infamous debate around whether the US ought to describe the killings in Rwanda as "genocide," lest an international legal obligation to intervene arise—Rice was new to government officialdom.[32] In an exchange reported in *A Problem from Hell*, Samantha Power's award-winning book, Rice is portrayed as a loyal aide to then President Bill Clinton, reading the loss of Rwandan lives through the frame of domestic politics. Rice stunned her colleagues with the words: "If we use the word 'genocide' and are seen as doing nothing, what will be the effect on the November [congressional] election?"[33] Rice quickly came to regret her statement, and told Power: "I swore to myself that if I ever faced such a crisis again, I would come down on the side of dramatic action, going down in flames if that was required."[34]

Rice also blocked the printing and distribution of the Gersony Report. Soon after, then UN Secretary-General Kofi Annan directed the UN High Commissioner for Refugees to embargo the report. Gersony and his team were told never to speak of their findings. To this day, many close to or affiliated with the RPF deny the report's existence, calling it propaganda prepared by those seeking to discredit the new government. Vice President Kagame went further, issuing a warning to foreigners "who preach ethnic divisions."[35] A copy of the alleged report surfaced on the internet in 2010.[36]

Many Rwandans were aware of RPF killings and systematic massacres. Those who could used the political cover of the RPF's language of openness and ethnic unity to denounce what they considered as a climate of terror. In November 1994, Prime Minister Faustin Twagiramungu published a document in which he critiqued the government, including the creation of the vice presidential post, RPF harassment of the political opposition, the practice of mass arrests without evidence, and arbitrary killings.[37] Kagame rejected Twagiramungu's claims, and instead reaffirmed the government's commitment to political openness and ethnic unity in a televised public debate.

By January 1995, the Twagiramungu and Kagame affair revealed internal tensions in the new government. The prime minister urged the government of national unity to provide security, while the vice president defended the honor of the RPA.[38] Behind the scenes, the RPF was busy identifying its internal enemies. From January to March 1995, reports of the Intelligence and Security Departments of the National Gendarmerie or police identified numerous "subversives." These lists included opposition politicians, journalists and civil servants, as well as certain foreign diplomats and international NGO personnel based in Kigali.

The Kibeho Massacre

The murder of Rwandans who took refuge in a camp on Kibeho hill in April 1995 made clear that the RPF controlled both the Government of National Unity and Rwanda's military. By the time the camp had been cleared of civilians in late April 1995, under the pretext that Hutu militants had infiltrated it to continue their murderous work, Paul Kagame was squarely at the helm of Rwandan political life. Kagame and other senior RPF officials demonstrated the extent to which they alone made decisions with military goals in mind. The Kibeho massacres further illustrated how the RPF would rule—as securocrats, not democrats and through military might with its own security in mind.

A decrease in the number of killings, disappearances and imprisonments by late 1994 suggested that the RPF anticipated increased international scrutiny following the suppression of the Gersony Report. The UN and the US had agreed to look the other way provided the RPF curtailed its campaign to secure Rwanda by any means. The RPF was aware that rump elements of the Interahamwe and others bent on continuing the work of eliminating Tutsi remained active in the country. Ordinary Rwandans knew this too, and many feared for their lives, caught in the crossfire as they were. Adult men bore the brunt of the violence of the day. Arbitrary arrests, beatings and torture at the hands of the RPF were commonplace, all in the name of security.[39] While some rural residents returned home, a steady flow of people continued to seek shelter in IDP camps, terrified of the violence in the hills. Despite the international community's entreaties to limit its military activities, by early 1995 the RPF was no longer swayed by international condemnation or sanction.

Housing between 90,000 and 120,000 Rwandans, most of Hutu origin, Kibeho was the largest IDP camp in the country (see Map 1). For the RPF, the imperative to have Rwandans at home was paramount. The leadership did not want refugees to languish in refugee camps outside of the country. Instead, the thinking was that Rwandans should return home as soon as possible, lest they remain politicized to the extremist goals of Hutu Power. The camp was an offshoot of Opération Turquoise, the French-run humanitarian "safe zone" that provided refuge to Hutu extremist members of the former government in eastern Zaire. When the French left Rwanda in August 1994, the UN set up a special

Integrated Operations Centre (IOC) to manage the repatriation of internally displaced Rwandans. The RPF kept a close watch on the IOC camps, believing them to be sites of Hutu extremist activity, despite housing a mostly civilian population of rural subsistence farmers who likely did not participate in the genocide. There was no way to determine individual culpability. Judicial investigations to identify *génocidaires* were not yet under way, but a finger-pointing, shoot-first-ask-questions-later mentality was already entrenched.

Like other IDP and refugee camps, Kibeho provided the barest necessities to its residents. Water was in short supply; sanitation facilities absent. Many Kibeho inhabitants displayed evidence of marasmus, with swollen bellies indicative of the first stages of malnutrition. Infectious disease was rife; cholera, diarrhea, dysentery and malaria rampant. Already physically weak from long journeys on foot after attempting to escape the genocide, many Rwandans succumbed to the inhumane conditions of the camps.

Four days prior to the massacre, on April 17, 1995, the governor of Butare province ordered all IDP camps in his jurisdiction to be closed, including the ill-fated Kibeho camp in neighboring Gikongoro province. The order came as part of broader government efforts to return IDPs to their hills of origin as quickly as possible. The RPF leadership needed civilians to return home to begin the work of rebuilding their houses, planting next season's crops and restoring basic infrastructure such as wells, animal pens and government offices. RPA soldiers were deployed to oversee the exercise. Military overseers expected compliance as the population waited for instructions to once and for all return home.

A UN peacekeeping battalion from Zambia (ZAMBATT) was stationed near the camp and bore witness to subsequent events. In the small hours of Tuesday, April 18, two RPA battalions surrounded Kibeho and fired shots into the air to awaken and move people out of the camp. According to an eyewitness, the American journalist Donatella Lorch, "bodies lay crumpled, some hardly visible among the piles of burlap sacks, cooking pots and clothes. Among them: a mother whose child still was tied to her back, a boy thrown over the torso of a man, another curled up in between the ashes of cooking fires. And everywhere there was blood and flies."[40] RPA soldiers then torched the camp's makeshift shelters to ensure residents had nowhere to return. On orders from UNAMIR command, ZAMBATT did not intervene.

Kigali met the news of the violence that occurred during the clearing of the camp with dismay at a poorly executed mission that had disgusted the international community. The RPF leadership quickly moved into face-saving mode. At a press conference that evening, RPF Minister of Rehabilitation Jacques Bihozagara commended the RPA, noting "if it were the government's intention then it would have gone ahead and killed the people within the camps. After all, the camps are part of Rwandan territory."[41] The subtext was clear—the RPF held sovereignty over Rwandans, and would do whatever it wanted, to whomever it wished.

The next day, Wednesday, April 19, Interior Minister Seth Sendashonga, an ethnic Hutu member of the RPF, traveled to Kibeho to defuse the situation. The army refused Sendashonga access to the camp. Later the same day, President Bizimungu arrived. In a briefing with RPA commanders on site, he was told that only a handful of people had died in the melee. The RPA attributed any loss of life in the camp to criminal gangs of *génocidaires*, whose goal was to frustrate the RPF's efforts to resettle the amassed IDPs. Bizimungu accepted this official version of events, concluding that Hutu "criminals" inside the camp had brought about their own demise. He continued: "It is a pity that people have died. But people inside the camp had arms and were violent. The international community has been shocked because they have been told lies."[42]

Bizimungu returned to Kigali on Thursday, April 20, and immediately was summoned to a meeting organized by Sendashonga. Once the minister had assembled representatives of the UN, international NGOs and the government, he publicly stated that he felt the RPA was not in control of the situation at Kibeho. Kagame, in his dual role as vice president and minister of defense, assured Sendashonga that he would ensure the relocation would proceed peacefully.

The next day, Friday, April 21, the RPA closed all roads in and out of Kibeho, and forbade international humanitarian food and water convoys from entering. An estimated hundred thousand surviving refugees were herded together outside the camp; many chose to walk to Butare town, some 32 kilometers east. Others headed straight for Burundi, unwilling to risk resettling in Rwanda. In panic, a group of young refugee men tried to clear a path for relief vehicles to enter the camp. RPA soldiers opened fire, instantly killing them. True to their UN non-intervention mandate, ZAMBATT soldiers stood by and did nothing. Already horrifying, the events of Tuesday through Friday were but a warm-up for the main event of emptying the camp.

Exhausted residents spent Friday night standing shoulder to shoulder, wondering what the morning would bring. At noon on Saturday, April 22, 1995, when RPA soldiers fired into the air to frighten and force the crowd out of the camp, many were trampled to death. Terrified residents burst the cordoned lines of exit; in response, the RPA fired mortars directly into the crowd.[43]

By the end of the day, somewhere between one and four thousand people had died[44]—although international human rights investigators believe this number is too low.[45] The RPF acknowledged that 338 Rwandans had died, but still declared the repatriation effort a success. Before the RPA closed more roads, the NGO Australian Medical Corps had a team of thirty-two personnel on site. Its staff counted some four thousand dead before the RPA called a halt to their work. Paul Jordan, an Australian eyewitness, later wrote: "While there was little that we could have done to stop the killings, I believe that, if Australians had not been there as witnesses to the massacre, the RPA would have killed every single person in the camp."[46] Conversely, UNAMIR Vice Provost, British Major Mark Cuthbert-Brown, finds this figure "an incredible claim," stating that the Australian medics were not present overnight on April 22.[47]

A Doctors Without Borders (MSF) nurse estimated some ten to fifteen thousand men, women and children passed her truck on the Butare–Runyinya road during the day of Sunday, April 23. Many had bullet wounds and showed signs of having been beaten. Months later, in an interview with Philip Gourevitch, Vice President Kagame suggested the deaths were justified: some lives were lost while IDPs were being repatriated, but these deaths were unavoidable in the context of securing territory and capturing *génocidaires* who had used civilians as human shields.[48]

The respective responses of the RPF and the international community were telling in their own ways. For many Rwandans and some diplomats, any notion that the RPF would respect the rule of law, uphold human rights, and promote ethnic unity disappeared after the Kibeho massacre. The event continues to hold sway in the hearts and minds of many. In southwest Rwanda, it is rare to find someone who has not been touched by the Kibeho events, whether as a survivor or as the loved one of someone who died during the massacre. Judging by the many loved ones they never saw again, they know the number of casualties to be much higher than the RPF admits to, but they do not speak of their losses for fear of imprisonment, or worse, being accused of promoting ethnic division.

In the aftermath of the Kibeho massacre, promises of democratization and political openness rang hollow for many Hutu and Tutsi who had lived through the 1994 genocide. Interior Minister Sendashonga agitated for an independent commission of inquiry to assess RPA actions at Kibeho. President Bizimungu snubbed him and instead appointed an international commission of inquiry, whose terms of reference were drafted by his office. The report toed the RPF line, stating that Kibeho was a haven for criminals, while affirming the professionalism of the RPA. The report acknowledged that RPA actions were disproportionate, but as the massacre was not a planned event, it was likely that deaths resulted from equipment and communication deficiencies.

Members of Rwanda's political opposition, notably Hutu living in the diaspora, held out Kibeho as the first concrete example of the exact kind of oversight the RPF intended to mete out on majority Hutu. For them, any rhetoric of national ethnic unity was nothing but a fiction designed to mask the RPF's intention to fully control Rwanda. But in the mid-1990s, no one was listening to such warnings. The collective remorse of being bystanders to genocide made the international community willfully blind and overly accommodating to the RPF.

The muted and near non-existent response of the international community—including humanitarians, diplomats and UN staff—suited the RPF. Many in the international community, save a handful of human rights monitors and journalists, including the influential Gourevitch, swallowed the RPF's party line that the mess they had to clean up in places like Kibeho stemmed from international failures to intervene to stop the genocide. The RPF demonstrated considerable acumen in controlling the story—the number of dead, and the way they died, were reported in foreign media outlets as a product of an RPF struggle to control criminal Hutu elements of the population.

There is a broad consensus among Rwanda scholars about the ways that the RPF controlled the narrative of the Kibeho massacre. Pottier notes: "Kibeho was a half-way stage in the development of Kagame's doctrine of tight information control."[49] Scholars generally agree that the way the RPF organized the Kibeho massacre and then effectively managed information flows about what had happened, and to whom, foreshadowed its subsequent managing of news about its attack on neighboring Zaire in 1996 (discussed further in the next chapter).

A few donors vigorously opposed the Kibeho killings and disputed the RPF's narrative, but their initial ardor soon cooled. The EU froze direct aid pending the results of the commission of inquiry. Belgium suspended aid until a full independent investigation was held. Such an investigation never happened, and both donors soon restored their aid. The US and the UK not only failed to protest the massacres, they unquestioningly accepted the RPF's explanation of events, signaling to Kigali that it could proceed unfettered in its drive to secure the country as they saw fit. This early habit of turning a blind eye to the excesses of the RPF government paved the way for bigger and more brazen RPF crimes, both in Zaire and at home.

The Kibeho massacre made it impossible to deny that the RPF was carrying out systematic killings as a means to hold all Hutu accountable for genocide crimes, regardless of actual guilt or innocence.[50] For any Hutu in government, including Prime Minister Twagiramungu, the massacre signaled to opposition politicians that the RPF endorsed the very impunity it carefully denounced to foreign audiences. The RPF's control over the country's judiciary and police ensured that there would be little, if any, risk of punishment for its crimes. That political elites act in their best interest, with little regard for the daily trials and tribulations of ordinary people, is not news to Rwandans. All the same, resignation about a culture of impunity, in turn, creates a repressive environment, resulting in feelings of isolation or helplessness in some, and anger or desperation in others. Speaking up about injustices like the loss of life at Kibeho was made difficult for some and impossible for others.

Concentrating Power

Human rights abuses by the RPF led moderates within the party to question its commitment to national unity. Members of the political opposition tried—and failed—to hold the RPF accountable for its crimes. The lack of donor sanctions in the face of RPF violence, combined with the entrenchment of a culture of impunity, signaled that life after the genocide would not be so different than it was before. The country's leadership may have changed, but its style of governance was all too familiar. In the wake of the Kibeho massacre, some individuals, including RPF veterans, remarked on the contradictions between the democratic principles and political liberalization espoused as the ideological backbone of the RPF as a rebel group, and how it practiced governance. Those who dared noted in private how the RPF, under Kagame, had become extremist in its Tutsi favoritism. Such hardline positioning was not new in Rwanda; extremist positions among political and military elites distinguish Rwandan politics. The RPF soon came to embody this tension, speaking in the name of Tutsi victims of the genocide, while simultaneously denying their suffering (discussed further in Chapter 12).

Driving the perception of "politics as usual" was the increasingly superficial role of Hutu opposition members in government and the clear marginalization of political moderates who wanted to move Rwanda away from divisive ethnic politics. They had little, if any, decision-making power and held public office only as long as they did not challenge the RPF's actions and accepted its repressive practices.

In August 1995, numerous prominent Hutu politicians and long-time RPF allies resigned, partly in response to the whitewashing of the Kibeho investigation, and to make it clear to Rwanda's new donors that any talk of national unity was merely a cover for the RPF to consolidate its political control of the country by any means possible. Deserters included ministers, judges, civil servants, army officers, journalists, religious leaders and "even players in the national soccer team."[51] Interior Minister Sendashonga (RPF), Justice Minister Alphonse-Marie Nkubito (PSD) and Prime Minister Twagiramungu (MDR) resigned their seats.

This gesture marked the near-disappearance of any opposition to the new Rwandan government. Between 1995 and 1998, more than forty prominent political figures—Hutu and Tutsi—fled into exile. Several others disappeared, or were assassinated or imprisoned. It was the first purge of moderate voices by the RPF. Nkubito died under mysterious circumstances in Rwanda in 1997. RPF operatives allegedly killed Sendashonga in Nairobi, Kenya, in July 1998. Seeing the writing on the wall, Twagiramungu went into self-imposed exile in Belgium.

Nkubito's death sent a wave of defeat that rippled through Rwanda's nascent postgenocide human rights community. Top-ranking members of the RPF who had long-standing suspicions concerning the role of the RPA in downing Habyarimana's aircraft were silenced. Shortly before his death, Nkubito shared with American Embassy officials "detailed notes" of his research on RPA responsibility for the attack on Habyarimana.[52] As the former state prosecutor prior to the genocide, Nkubito was also a leading human rights activist during the Habyarimana regime. Following his resignation in 1995, Nkubito returned to human rights work. His sudden death in 1997 was deemed suspicious by family and colleagues, and they requested a post-mortem. The RPF refused.[53]

The spate of political resignations in 1995 meant that there were cabinet vacancies to be filled. The RPF appointed new Hutu to cabinet posts, while installing loyalists as deputies within Hutu-led ministries. "*Hutu de service*" (token Hutu) were selected to give the appearance of an ethnically balanced government while the real power within ministries lay with RPF appointees, almost all of whom were returnees from Uganda, Congo or Burundi.

By mid-1995, it was clear that the RPF inner circle was replete with party members who had been exiled in Uganda—these individuals held the country's real power. Proof of this came in August 1995 when, out of 145 positions, Kagame appointed 117 Uganda Tutsi returnees to the locally powerful post of mayor.[54] When questioned about these appointments, Vice President Kagame replied that ethnicity was a fictional hangover from Belgian colonial rule while boasting that Hutu were well represented in his government.[55] Kagame reminded foreign journalists that his commitment to sharing power with Hutu politicians was "sincere," since, if he wanted to, he could have "taken over everything but the fact is that we did it differently" (opting for a power-sharing government).[56]

From October to December 1995, the RPF continued its now established pattern of human rights abuses. Hutu men remained especially subject to arbitrary arrest on suspicion of committing acts of genocide; many were jailed for years without formal charge. The RPF explained these arrests as "necessary," given the incursions of Interahamwe and others intent on destabilizing Rwanda from the refugee camps in Zaire.[57] Political power was now firmly concentrated in RPF hands.

5

SECURING PEOPLE AND PLACE

As mostly Tutsi returnees returned, the most vulnerable victims of the genocide—widows and orphans—were either cast out or unable to return to their homes and fields. At first a trickle, then a raging river, returnees soon numbered some four hundred thousand by December 1994. Like Kagame and the RPF before them, many expected a warmer welcome than they received. Rather than negotiate or pay for property, many returnees appropriated homes or farms they found empty, assuming such assets belonged to Hutu perpetrators of the genocide.

The situation was compounded by a lack of available housing. Most habitable buildings had been burned or destroyed during the war and genocide. Many people lived in the open air, whether in internally displaced persons camps, or on the spot where the family home once stood. UN plastic tarp shelters, in the ubiquitous blue that marks temporary shelters in refugee crises the world over, served double duty as walls and ceilings to some of these makeshift postgenocide homes.

"Returnees" is a catchall category that includes Tutsi who lived in exile or who were born abroad to exiled parents. Those who returned to

Rwanda following flight in the 1950s and 1960s were described as "old-caseload." The majority of old-caseload returnees hailed from Uganda. Others returned from other African countries and farther afield—Burundi, Kenya, Tanzania, Nigeria, South Africa and Zaire, as well as Belgium, Canada and the United States. Having long romanticized their motherland, returnees were ill-prepared for life upon arrival. Most had never spent time in the country previously, and few could speak the national language of Kinyarwanda. Returnees often found their relatives dead or in exile. Romantic nostalgia turned to antipathy as the returnees realized there were few jobs outside of the international diplomatic and humanitarian or domestic non-governmental sectors. Scarce resources—such as shelter and paid employment, as well as access to phone lines, water and electricity—fractured the returnee community and further perpetuated fissures throughout society. Divisions within families were common as years of exile weighed on individuals.

Placide is a sixty-something-year-old Tutsi man, raised in the Nyamata area of southeast Rwanda. His mother was Hutu, his father Tutsi, meaning Placide and his siblings were identified as Tutsi in the pregenocide period, as ethnicity is patrilineal. In 1959, when political violence targeting Tutsi intensified in central Rwanda, some 200 kilometers from Placide's childhood village of Rusumo (near Rwanda's eastern border with Tanzania and southern border with Burundi), his family scattered as the fear of violence spread across the country. Placide's two younger siblings escaped on foot to Tanzania with their Hutu mother, walking for three days until they found a welcoming village. His father, Ephram, loaded Placide and his older brother into the family car, driving all night to find safety in Burundi. The family hoped to be reunited in a few short weeks.

Placide would not meet the surviving members of his family until 1996, after returning to Rwanda in 1995. As an "old-caseload" refugee, Placide was educated in the French language. He was able to continue his primary education, eventually studying at the national university in Bujumbura, the capital of Burundi, and then training as an accountant courtesy of the scholarships and bursaries the Burundian government made available to qualified Rwandan refugees. Placide's success story is hardly representative of most Rwandans who fled to Burundi in the late 1950s and early 1960s. Most lived precariously with few opportunities or rights. As a wealthy businessman, Ephram's status sheltered the family from the usual hardships of poor peasant Rwandans, the majority of whom arrived in Burundi on foot and with little more than the clothes on their back.

Ephram died in 1972, without returning to his native Rwanda. As he planned his father's funeral, Placide tried to find his mother and sisters through family and professional networks. They had taken up residence in western Tanzania, adopting local customs, habits and language in an effort to fit in. This included changing their family name, as individuals of Rwandan origin were rarely welcomed. Due to her facility with language, Placide's mother, Anysie, picked up Kiswahili quickly and was able to find work as a domestic in the homes of wealthier Tanzanians. Prior to the political upheaval that pushed the family to take flight, Anysie had regularly crossed Tanzania's open border to sell foodstuffs at local markets. She had the necessary social and economic networks that, combined with Tanzania's open-door policy of the time, allowed her to buy land to cultivate, and to send Placide's sisters to primary school. All the same, in time, she found it increasingly difficult to secure the necessary funds to pay for her daughters' schooling, meaning both girls only received the equivalent of a fourth-grade education.

Placide's sisters, Esther and Gisele, returned to Kigali in 1996 when the Tanzanian government forcibly repatriated Rwandans who fled the genocide. Anysie was dead, killed by a low-ranking Tanzanian soldier in late 1994. The influx of refugees from Rwanda following the genocide had changed local living conditions in Tanzania for long-time refugees like Anysie and her daughters. Anti-refugee sentiment surged and crime soared. To this day, the deaths of numerous Rwandans living in towns and villages along the Tanzanian border remain uninvestigated.

Placide and his siblings were finally reunited in November 1996 at a UNHCR repatriation center. Upon his arrival in Kigali in mid-1995, Placide was soon employed as a caseworker at the repatriation center. Many genocide survivors were too emotionally traumatized or physically frail to take up the task of rebuilding the country. Those willing to work often lacked the necessary qualifications or skills. Newly arrived educated Tutsi, like Placide, soon held most staff positions in government and international non-governmental organizations. Placide was tasked to reunite families that had been torn apart by the violence of the 1994 genocide. Upon their arrival at the reunification center, Esther and Gisele were assigned a caseworker. As he documented their family history, Placide and his sisters realized that they were long-lost siblings. They had not seen each other in more than thirty years.

Such delayed reunions were commonplace in the years immediately following the genocide. Educated, male, French-speaking, middle-class, urban and politically connected, Placide had a different set of options available to him than did his poorer, rural and less educated sisters. Gender norms also shaped his siblings' experience of return. Since they are historically subordinate to men in Rwandan society, women derive personhood through the men to whom they are related. Their social realm is the homestead, where they raise children and work the land to feed the family.

Having failed to marry, the sisters occupied a marginal position in postgenocide society, as they could also not own or inherit land. Having failed to fulfill cultural expectations of becoming wives and mothers, unmarried, childless women are viewed as barren and thus of little value to society. Moreover, not having lived in Rwanda during the genocide, Esther and Gisele were not eligible for already limited social welfare benefits. As sisters to Placide, Esther and Gisele had some societal status, but lacked the more coveted rank of wives and mothers.[1]

In his culturally mandated role as head of the household, Placide knew he would have to provide for his sisters and help them return to their childhood home in eastern Rwanda. In the early months, full of love and regret for all that they had missed as siblings, he did so willingly, despite numerous hurdles. Given the decades that had passed since they lived in Rusumo, the likelihood that another family had taken up residence on their homestead was near certain. Moreover, without Placide's presence to stake a claim to the family property, Esther and Gisele would not be able to claim their former home. In any case, by 1996, once local officials declared a site officially abandoned, returnees were able to formally stake claims to the property, and the opportunity to reclaim family homes diminished to near zero. Additionally, favoritism for Ugandan returnees had crept into the Rwandan political order as this group quickly asserted themselves as refugees who had suffered the most in exile, and who in turn liberated Rwanda from the tyranny of the Habyarimana regime.[2] Rwanda was now theirs.

Old-caseload returnees had limited knowledge of rural life and lacked the necessary skills to cultivate the land and grow their own food. More critically, they feared living in rural areas—with limited infrastructure and services—surrounded by Hutu who they believed perpetrated the genocide. The old-caseloads were further hampered by their disdain for those Rwandans who lived through the genocide. Many were suspicious of Tutsi who survived 1994, concluding that they must have colluded with the killers to have lived. Nearly all returnees lived in fear of their Hutu neighbors. In reality, Hutu who were in Rwanda following the genocide were most likely innocent of the crimes committed in their name. The guilty quickly fled into exile when it became clear that the RPF would win the civil war that ended the genocide.

All the same, returnee fear was not entirely baseless as many Hutu who remained in the country met the RPF with a sneer as an illegitimate occupying force. Years of propaganda and evidence of violent RPF reprisals resulted in some Hutu internalizing resentment of Tutsi. To minimize the scope and scale of Tutsi suffering, others even denied that genocide had occurred. Few Tutsi returnees chose to live in rural areas, congregating instead in Kigali and other urban centers across the country in the hope of taking up salaried jobs with international human-itarian organizations, and eventually as government officials and small business owners. By late 1994, Tutsi returnees, particularly those from Uganda, dominated local economies.

Given the impossibility of his sisters' return to Rusumo, Placide instead welcomed them into his small house in the Nyamirambo neighborhood of Kigali. The three-room home easily accommodated the adult siblings. For Esther and Gisele, Placide's house was the summit of luxury; they had never lived in a home with cement floors, electricity and indoor plumbing. While the cost of living in Kigali skyrocketed after the genocide, as a UN employee, Placide earned US$1,200 a month, just enough to cover the family's daily needs.

Affronted that she had to surrender part of their home to her husband's relatives, Placide's Burundian wife, Jolie, felt differently. She did not like having strangers in the house and made her displeasure known. Daily tensions in the household revolved around money, language and religion. Unable to speak French—the primary working language of government and the non-governmental community at the time—neither sister could find work.

Fruitless job searching prompted Gisele to move to Rusumo to repossess the family homestead despite the known challenges. Soon after, she was killed in a skirmish with the new occupants. Such violence was common throughout Rwanda. As Tutsi returnees streamed back into the country, land and property conflicts about what belonged to whom raised the stakes for squatter residents; some had lived in homes abandoned for decades, often as far back as 1959. Local government officials were either unable or unwilling to prevent violence related to property ownership, and property-related murders were common.

Deforestation and soil quality compounded land conflicts. Not all the land returnees tried to claim was arable. There were—and remain—intense local conflicts over land quality and parcel size, and frictions were exacerbated by demographic shifts following the genocide.[3] Recognizing these tensions and fearful of meeting the same end as her sister, Esther continued to look for salaried employment in the city. Eventually, she found work as a household domestic, working for one of Placide's foreign colleagues. Esther earned just over US$125 a month, an astronomical wage for someone of her social and educational status. Despite her good fortune, Esther's relations with her brother soured. Placide forced Esther out of his home in 1997, citing a lack of familial similitude. Placide and Jolie were raising their boys in the Muslim faith, making their religion a minority one in predominantly Christian Rwanda. In 2009, unable to adapt as Francophones to new government rules mandating English as the official language of education and business, Placide and his wife left Rwanda to live in the capital of Burundi, Bujumbura.[4]

The RPF ideology of national ethnic unity as the basis of peace and security, that so many returnees imbibed as exiles, was insufficient to hold Placide's family together. Theirs was not an isolated case. Infighting based on where one had lived during exile became commonplace in old-caseload returnee communities. By late 1995, returnees understood one another as Ugandans, Zaireans, Tanzanians and Burundians. Those from other countries were lumped in a single category of "other," as the numbers of returnees coming from other parts of Africa and the West were too few to register as allies or to build solidarity networks.[5] Returnees from countries bordering Rwanda all jockeyed to expand their economic opportunities and political control. Ultimately, the most powerful group to emerge were those who fought for the RPA during the civil war and genocide, and members of their immediate families. This meant that Ugandans from within the RPF and RPA and their loyalists became the most influential individuals in the country.

Forced Repatriation of Refugees

At the end of 1996, the UNHCR estimated that almost 1,200,000 refugees were living in eastern Zaire, with another 600,000 residing in western Tanzania. The UN registered some 270,000 Rwandan refugees in Burundi, along with 90,000 more living in Uganda.[6] The sheer number of refugees, the complexity of the humanitarian situation in the North and South Kivu regions of Zaire, and limited collective knowledge of a fluid political situation meant that humanitarian organizations had little ability to effectively manage the camps. By adopting an explicitly apolitical stance, international humanitarians failed to recognize that the camps had been organized by fleeing elites according to Rwandan geographic regions and administrative structures as a means to control local and refugee populations, as well as to coopt the distribution of humanitarian aid. Unlike the international community, the RPF-led government was well aware of the political dynamics at play in the camps. Throughout 1995 and into 1996, the RPF repeatedly asked the international community to separate armed members of the former government from unarmed civilians. The international community failed to act, leading the RPF to take matters into its own hands and force their mass repatriation.

The RPF took up arms with a dual purpose—to repatriate refugees it believed responsible for the 1994 genocide and to dispose of then Zairian military dictator and President Mobutu Sese Seko. Mobutu had been a close friend of Habyarimana, and—much to Kigali's chagrin—was an open and enthusiastic supporter of Rwandan Hutu rebels.

What is now known as the first Congo war began in late 1996. Hutu militants living in the refugee camps incited attacks on Congolese Tutsi living in the area, confirming RPF suspicions that elements of the genocidal former regime were intent on finishing what they had started. Hoping that the hordes of Rwandan refugees would return home of their own accord, local and regional Zairian authorities did not intervene to stop these attacks. In September 1996, the deputy governor of South Kivu announced on local radio that if the Banyamulenge (meaning all Kinyarwanda speakers living in eastern Congo) did not leave within a week they would be imprisoned in the camps and killed. This announcement provided the necessary moral cover for the RPF to attack and dismantle the refugee camps. Again, the RPF asked the international community to disarm the Hutu Power forces and their Zairian counterparts. When their request went unheeded, the RPF and local Banyamulenge took matters into their own hands, and attacked their attackers.

During August and September 1996, Banyamulenge rebels attacked Interahamwe and Zairian army forces stationed in the refugee camps. The RPF engaged with brutal precision and potency; no one was spared. According to the Rwandan Ministry of Defense, young Hutu men were believed to have been politicized to continue the work of killing Tutsi, and so were singled out as the most dangerous element in the camps. Josephat, a Hutu boy who was sixteen at the time, remembers the RPF's actions well: "Anyone who was young got harassed, beat up and even killed when questioned by the RPF. There was no authority in the camps and the RPF killed, but so did the Interahamwe. When I saw someone in uniform or with a weapon, I really feared for my life!"

By November 1996, the Banyamulenge rebellion had both a name, Alliance of Democratic Forces for the Liberation of Congo-Zaire (AFDL), and a leader. Laurent-Désiré Kabila was handpicked by the RPF to give their military exercise a Zairian face. Tens of thousands of refugees—ordinary Rwandan Hutu and Tutsi—were caught up in the crossfire and many died.[7] Assisted by Rwandan troops, the AFDL rebels quickly moved from south to north, gaining control of the 480 kilometers of Zaire's eastern border in a series of attacks between October 1996 and May 1997.[8] Plain to see was the RPA's control of the camps and the military strategy to evacuate by any means the Rwandans seeking shelter there.

In November 1996, some 600,000 refugees began the arduous trek back to Rwanda. Walking in stony silence, exhausted bodies dragged along even weaker ones under the blazing sun, the only audible noise being the occasional yelp of a young child or fragile elder, the last gasps of those who lay down by the roadside to die, and the shuffling of feet moving toward an uncertain future in the RPF's Rwanda. UN observers described this river of people as the highway to hell.

RPA soldiers, rifles at the ready, ushered this sea of people home to Rwanda, towards UNHCR transit points which would register all who had returned. Refugees who tried to veer off the RPF-patrolled path to avoid the transit camps were shot dead or jailed. Once they arrived at the transit points, individual refugees received a small care kit of rice, kerosene and soap, had their fingerprints taken and their transit documents stamped, enabling them to return to their hills of origin.

Once again, the international community stood by and watched as RPF-aided AFDL rebels repatriated most refugees to Rwanda in 1997. In the face of such passivity, the RPF was further emboldened to resettle its mostly Hutu refugee population by any means possible. Fearing for their lives, approximately four hundred thousand refugees fled deep into Zaire, as afraid of the RPF and AFDL as they were of the Interahamwe militias and other members of the former regime. Zairian civilians were also caught up in the fighting, with tens of thousands losing their lives or livelihoods in the war between the RPF, its AFDL proxy and the Interahamwe militias, who were in turn supported by Zairian troops supplied by President Mobutu.[9]

Mobutu was ousted in May 1997, and Kabila ascended to the presidency of Zaire, renaming it in 1998 the Democratic Republic of Congo (DRC). AFDL rebels, backed by the RPA, massacred thousands of civilian rebels in the process; tens of thousands of deaths were caused by inhumane camp conditions through cholera, dysentery and malaria.

In another unfortunate turn of events, shortly after the forcible camp closures in Zaire, the Tanzanian government announced that all Rwandan refugees in Tanzania must leave by the end of December 1996.[10] Ignoring their right to return home voluntarily, Tanzanian security forces began removing refugees under duress. Nearly 300,000 of the 500,000 Rwandans residing in Ngara camp fled western Tanzania to avoid being sent home (see Map 1). For many, the flight was in vain. Tanzanian army forces intercepted them and channeled them toward the Rwandan border where the UNHCR struggled to register them all. Under the direction of RPA soldiers, refugees limped back to their home communities, only to find their homes occupied or destroyed and their fields planted. Further compounding their misery, Tanzanian soldiers, at the request of the RPF, arrested thousands of these refugees on suspicion of genocide. Genocide survivors and returnees often made false accusations of participation in genocide against Hutu who returned from Tanzania to prevent them from reclaiming their homes and property.

Those who returned from postgenocide camps in neighboring countries became known as "new-caseload" returnees. With ongoing communal violence and the legacy of the Kibeho massacre hanging over them, few wished to be back in their country of origin. Once in Rwanda, many met a hostile welcome from newly appointed local officials as presumed *génocidaires*, and found themselves homeless as other returnees had appropriated the abodes they had fled in 1994.

The experience of being forced to return to Rwanda under the watch of the RPF and RPA would play into later government-led justice and reconciliation processes, which began in 2001 and continue to the present. New caseloads wanted to talk about their suffering, have their postgenocide losses addressed, and grievances acknowledged. Few would get the opportunity to speak.

The worries of new-caseload returnees were worsened by the continued ineffectiveness of the UNHCR and other international aid agencies. UNHCR staff were unable to cope with the volume of hundreds of thousands of refugees streaming back into Rwanda haphazardly. It abandoned the usual registration processes, instead leaving the administration of new-caseload returnees to inexperienced and hostile RPA soldiers. Many refugees were harassed and worse by the RPA at local transit camps.

Few were surprised to learn that the RPA used the transit camps to apprehend tens of thousands of Hutu refugees on genocide crimes. Detainees were sent directly to prison without due process. By 2000, Rwanda's prison population had ballooned to 120,000 prisoners in a system designed for 55,000.[11] Many languished without dossiers or investigators. Unfortunately, for many, there was no way to prove their guilt or innocence. By mid-2000, only 1,292 genocide suspects had been tried for their alleged crimes. Tens of thousands more still awaited trial. Despite the efforts of international donors to link their dollars to justice and reconciliation, the government had yet to dedicate itself to such initiatives.[12] The RPF's focus remained on securing Rwanda's borders and rebuilding basic infrastructure so that the work of developing the country could begin in earnest.

Settling In

With all the new-caseload returnees, it was abundantly clear that there was not enough land to go around. Land conflicts resulted in food shortages. The perennial October to December rainy season, during which subsistence farmers plant and tend to their maize and other staples, had passed. Widows, and other women without male relatives, were those most likely to have lost or forfeited ownership of the land they had abandoned during the genocide. Customary legal practice in Rwanda holds that women cannot inherit land from their fathers. It is the cultural duty of a husband to provide land for his wife. When the husband dies, the woman holds the property in usufruct to meet the needs of her male relatives, particularly her sons. If she has no heirs to inherit assets, a widow's ability to stay on her land depends on the good-will and courtesy of her late husband's kin.[13]

The economic security that land provides makes it a commodity unlike any other for some 80 percent of the Rwandan population. Subsistence farmers rely on their land to provide for their families. Land ownership and usage is also an emotional good, especially for those who wish to remain on the land where they were raised or married, or to connect the living to the dead through inheritance.[14] Most importantly, land provides a sense of belonging, something all Rwandans who had lived through the 1994 genocide yearned for.

The RPF recognized the need to revise the inheritance law to avoid male exploitation of land, and did so with a sweeping piece of legisla-tion.[15] In 1999, a new succession law was passed allowing women and girls to legally reclaim their land. Such a law was desperately needed as the number of woman-headed and child-headed households in Rwanda was now substantial. Suddenly, male kin no longer controlled land hold-ings; women and girls were able to inherit land and decide on its usage independent of male family members. The law also gave women rights to enter into contracts, seek paid employment, own property in their own names (not their husbands'), and open bank accounts without the permission of male relatives. One shortcoming of the 1999 law was that it only applied to married women, a significant oversight as most women who had lost their land were widows. These women remained unable to challenge male relatives, or male squatters who simply annexed unused plots.[16] However well intentioned, the legislation did not immediately change things on the ground, but it laid the groundwork for women's increased role in Rwandan public life.

Uprooting the Rural Poor[17]

In the shadow of the mass returnee resettlement, the government began to uproot the rural poor, often without consulting them, and rarely compensating them. In December 1996, the government adopted a National Habitat Policy that required all Rwandans living in scattered homesteads on hills across the country to live instead in government-mandated "villages" called *imidugudu*, which were designed to upgrade the traditional way of living. The rationale was to end the land and housing crisis provoked by the mass population displacement caused by the genocide. Hundreds of thousands of homeless Rwandans, most of them Tutsi survivors and new-caseload returnees, moved willingly into *imidugudu* in the hope of recovering hearth and home as quickly as possible. Simultaneously, despite their opposition to the villages policy, hundreds of thousands were forced to move. Local officials gave land to old-caseload returnees who had none. Those who failed to cede their land were imprisoned; some who criticized the policy disappeared. Some of those forced to move already had a home. Local government officials regularly used force to relocate people. The RPF punished those who failed to cooperate with government directives or spoke out about the *imidugudu* policy with fines or arrest.

International donors poured tens of millions of dollars into the *imidugudu* initiative. The first groups of rural Rwandans to move received move-in-ready homes, or the necessary materials to build their own. However, three years later, by 1999, more recently displaced individuals received little, if any support. These people lived for as long as two years in temporary shelters of grass, leaves or UNHCR-issued tarps. Female- and child-headed households were disproportionally affected by the policy. They lacked the economic and social networks to be able to build homes in accordance with government regulations. Additional hardship came in the form of government favoritism for old-caseload Tutsi returnees. Local authorities regularly appropriated land for RPF political and military officials and their associates, including businesspeople, who then confiscated large tracts of land for themselves. The RPF justified this reallocation by promising to develop large-scale farms that would provide local jobs while benefiting the national economy.

Local reaction to life in villages was muted. The policy was not the product of public consultation and it is difficult to know what people felt about policy decisions taken in their name. What is clear is that a policy implemented with the stated goal of improving rural lives has in the twenty years since the genocide failed to do so, with many Rwandans saying that they felt more impoverished and more fearful of their neighbors since moving. A key factor behind these emotions is the policy's lack of concern for how rural subsistence farmers actually provide for themselves and their families. Noting that similar villagization schemes elsewhere in Africa, including neighboring Tanzania, had failed miserably in reaching the desired policy outcomes, Rwanda's international donors expressed skepticism but did not withdraw their aid.[18]

By the end of 2000, most villages still lacked the services and amenities they had been promised. Homesteads were built close together or alongside main roads, which meant that daily efforts to cultivate one's crops became a challenge. The structure of *imidugudu* meant that rural subsistence farmers had to walk much farther to tend their fields, and to gather everyday basics like water or firewood—tasks which fall primarily on women and girls. Distance from one's fields also made people more susceptible to theft, and made caring for cows, goats and other livestock difficult as there was insufficient space for pasturage in many *imidugudu*.

The practical and cultural role of banana groves in rural life was also not considered. Bananas are a staple of the Rwandan subsistence diet. With shallow root systems, the trees do best when they are protected from wind and rain. They also provide shade to homes, while helping to compost household waste. The *imidugudu* design did not provide toilets for each home, affecting crop yields as human waste is quickly neutralized as it fertilizes the banana trees. Beer brewed from bananas became harder to produce and more expensive, given chronic shortages in some areas. Known as *urwagwa*, banana beer is shared on special feasting occasions such as weddings or funerals, as well as to mark social bonds

111

between families and neighbors. Guests share *urwagwa* from a single straw in calabash jugs, as a sign of solidarity and alliance but also of respect and courtesy.[19] Generally speaking, the relocation process improved citizens' physical security, but in moving as many rural people as they could into villages, the government overlooked key cultural elements of daily life, which served to increase local animosity towards the *imidugudu* process.

Quelling the Insurgency

From the end of 1997 and throughout 1998, many Rwandans lived first hand with a Hutu insurgency in the northwest, and feared the war would come to their doorsteps.[20] Many grew weary of life under a cloud of disquietude and mistrust. Innocent, a twenty-something ethnic Hutu living in Gisenyi town, summed up local sentiment well when he said: "I don't want to stay here anymore. I just want to make something of a life. The dying, the death—how can this government say the genocide has ended?"

Most northern Rwandans are ethnic Hutu, which explains why many residents in the natal region of former President Habyarimana perceived the new Tutsi-centric RPF government as an alien force. Many in the region feared a return to traditional power structures, in which Tutsi aristocrats ruled over Hutu peasants. Such was the rhetoric that many imbibed during the propaganda campaign that helped fuel the civil war and genocide. Habyarimana's MRND strategically broadcast its anti-Tutsi message over the radio, reminding rural Hutu farmers of the oppressive nature of Tutsi rule, and urging them not to let Tutsi once again dominate Hutu. Only a short time after the war, this language still resonated with many Hutu, particularly those old enough to remember the profound sense of Hutu marginalization that informed the social revolution of 1957–1962. Jean-Pierre, a retired Hutu government official now in his seventies, relates what he learned as a boy from his elders about the extractive qualities of Tutsi King Rwabugiri's oppressive rule, linking them to the RPF's counterinsurgency. In the darkness of his windowless single-room home, Jean-Pierre says:

My father, my uncles, even my mother's brothers and father had to pledge allegiance to chiefs. In their day, the chiefs were mostly Hutu. Rwabugiri was a Tutsi and was known for his cruel power. He was so vicious—he even killed people close to him! Advisors could die at any time! Low people like my ancestors survived because we belonged to a powerful lineage. It was a time of pride. We were powerful because our chief was powerful. He protected us against royal warriors. We worked together to cultivate and make sure we harvested well, to please our patron. This was the dynamic—the powerful protected and the weaker sought protection. By the time the Belgians arrived, we had no one to protect us because hill chiefs became Tutsi. I was about thirty years old when the [1959] revolution took place. I hoped for a better future because I knew by then that Tutsi only wanted power for Tutsi. Hutu like me had been excluded. I was a good student but didn't go to university because school seats were reserved for Tutsi! Imagine the pain I felt when the RPF entered our region [in 1990]. They killed us [Hutu] then and they are killing us now. We need to push to overthrow this government. These people [RPF Tutsi] want to restore dictatorship!

Jean-Pierre's words reveal the messiness of history. The ways in which past events have been taught to successive generations of Rwandan students have been shaped by whichever ethnic group holds power.[21] As the American historian Alison Des Forges notes, ethnic elites have skillfully exploited distortions of history to suit their political goals.[22] In the case of Hutu, individuals like Jean-Pierre have, over the years, learned of wily Tutsi from the stories of elders and in their secondary school and university classrooms. In fact, historically, Rwanda's northern region had enjoyed significant autonomy from the Tutsi royal kingdom that ruled from present-day central Rwanda when the German Count von Götzen first arrived in 1894. Strong and centralized structures were already the hallmark of the Rwandan state at that time. And contrary to the RPF's official history, there was no singular Rwandan response, first to the arrival of Germans, or later, to the Belgians, who set up camp in the Kinyaga region in the west. Not only did Rwanda's renowned military fail to repulse the foreign occupiers, the royal courts largely collaborated with the Germans, who had established colonial rule by 1898.[23] Although some members of the court continued to resist their European counterparts while others collaborated, "many maneuvered to create opportunities" for themselves and their clients.[24]

Many Tutsi chiefs acted as intermediaries for the colonial administration, gaining new and more reliable forms of political and social power in the process. The result was the creation of two complementary systems of power that fed the interests of the colonizers and the ruling royal Tutsi. The royal court, under Rwabugiri and with the help of German colonizers, led a series of factional struggles in peripheral regions of the territory that would eventually become the borders of contemporary Rwanda. Rwabugiri focused particular attention on the Hutu-led lineages in the north that resisted royal efforts to control them. Rwabugiri used all available means to bring lineage heads under his control and conflicts were often violent with loss of life and livelihood common. History helps explain why men like Jean-Pierre see Vice President Kagame as the Rwabugiri of his day. The aforementioned quote reflects a feeling shared by many northerners, that they do not feel liberated by RPF rule. Instead, people like Jean-Pierre hope for liberation from the RPF, a sentiment the RPF wishes to extinguish.

Just as the Habyarimana regime managed RPF incursions in the northwest through the 1990–94 civil war, the RPF framed its military operations to the international media and local people as necessarily countering threats from Hutu extremists and *abacengezi* (infiltrators). Both adopted a "deliberate strategy of confusion so as to be able to blame attacks on each other."[25] Northwesterners became targets of arbitrary violence by one side or the other. The RPF saw Hutu and Tutsi who lived in the region during and before the 1994 genocide as sympathizers to the *abacengezi*, while many locals viewed the RPF as infiltrators who had imposed themselves on Hutu of the north. The RPA's viciousness toward the general population and widespread support for the region's extremists made it difficult for the Rwandan military to garner much local support for their efforts.[26]

The northwest region was always populated by a Hutu majority, and policies instituted by then President Habyarimana before 1994 meant most Tutsi lived in southern portions of Rwanda. But some Tutsi called the northwest region home through to the end of the twentieth century. The few that remained were wiped out during the genocide.[27] By 1997, there were very few Tutsi-identified Rwandans living in the northwest. They had either died or fled.

From the 1970s onward, Habyarimana had established a system of ethnic quotas, ostensibly to assure equitable distribution of government resources and opportunities to all Rwandans. In practice, government officials used the quotas to restrict Tutsi access to jobs and school placements, and to discriminate against Hutu from other parts of Rwanda besides the north.[28] By the time it came to power, the RPF leadership was already familiar with this pattern of regional bias, and believed it was dealing with a recalcitrant population bred on Habyarimana's brand of Hutu supremacy, which excluded non-northerners as well as Tutsi: "By the mid-1980s, Habyarimana's home prefecture of Gisenyi, one of ten in the country at the time, had provided the office holders for one-third of the most important jobs in government as well as virtually all the leaders of the army and security service."[29]

Hutu insurgents only numbered several thousand but they were highly mobile and well embedded in local communities. During 1998,

RPF-appointed local officials fled their posts in Gisenyi province because they feared for their own safety. Again, history helps explain why some locals in the northwest willingly provided food and shelter to Hutu insurgents. Many did so out of fear for their lives, lest they be killed for failing to support the military goals of their Hutu brethren. Either way, the RPF was unable to quickly bring the northwest under its command.

Searching individual homes to identify those who were hiding or feeding the infiltrators was a key tactic used by the RPF to flush out the insurgents. This was the same ploy Habyarimana's FAR used to identify those who hid RPF rebels during the early 1990s. Those who did not aid their efforts saw their homes and crops burned and their livestock slaughtered. Many were killed.

Fighting raged between the two sides throughout 1998 and into 1999. Widespread insecurity meant crops went unplanted, and famine affected hundreds of thousands of people in eastern Zaire and northern Rwanda—a cruel irony as the region is one of Rwanda's most fertile.[30] Regional instability was such that the RPF regularly banned travel by road, and transporting food brought in from other parts of the country became impossible. Travel restrictions applied equally to the UN, international reconstruction projects and human rights monitoring teams. The region's usually lush verdant hills bore visible signs of insurgency. Fields burned to a crisp, crops were uprooted. Homes stood empty, unlocked doors rattling in the wind. Whole villages were deserted.

Determining the number of insurgency casualties was difficult. The brutality of the incursion and RPA reprisals precluded human rights investigations. Moreover, the collapse of health care, social and economic systems meant that many wounded may have died prematurely.[31] Regardless, the RPF government saw no reason to invest scarce government resources to investigate alleged human rights abuses in the region. Not even the UN Human Rights Mission for Rwanda (UNHRFOR) was able to send in its teams to document crimes allegedly committed by both sides.[32] With teams operating in every corner of Rwanda,

UNHRFOR was often the only international organization with boots on the ground to document atrocities.[33] As the RPF turned up the heat on the *abacengezi*, it became increasingly difficult for human rights monitors to work, meaning knowledge of who killed whom and how was nearly impossible to obtain.

The RPF media machine also did its part in suppressing the numbers of lives lost during the insurgency. As with the 1995 Kibeho massacre, media handlers working within the military and the president's advisory team did not deny that civilians had been killed; rather, they minimized the number of dead. New casualties were pinned on those already dead for their presumed links to the Hutu rebels. Presidential advisor Claude Dusaidi pronounced: "if civilians were killed, they were accomplices, persons who sympathized with these armed men."[34] In a 1998 report, Amnesty International alleged that throughout the northwestern insurgency, the RPF attempted to blame the majority of deaths on the insurgents.[35] Meanwhile, according to the report, the RPA was the primary source of what human rights monitors call "excess mortality"; Rwandan soldiers committed thousands of murders or more, while the *abacengezi* were responsible for several hundred deaths at least. The dry, legal language of the report fails to capture the extent to which both sides deliberately and indiscriminately targeted innocent men, women and children.

By the end of 1997, the human rights situation had become so grave, the security situation so severe, and fears about reporting on RPF and RPA abuses so acute, that domestic and international organizations stopped issuing public statements on rights violations in Rwanda. By mid-1998, disappearances engineered by RPF security forces were so commonplace that affected families stopped reporting the absence of their loved ones to local and international agencies alike. Fear was the common denominator among all regional residents—fear that they too would disappear in the reporting process, or fear that nothing could be done. Young men and boys of fighting age were especially vulnerable to disappearance; the RPF would apprehend them in forced recruitment drives to serve in the army.[36] According to Amnesty International, heavy casualties by the RPA meant active recruitment of new military personnel was ongoing.[37] The few who were released from military round-ups spoke of being held in detention centers or military camps, subject to abuse and forced into weapons training to battle the *abacengezi*.[38] In time, these tactics allowed the RPA to gain the upper hand in the northwest. The population had lost almost everything, and was unable to sustain either side. In addition, the RPF had made some progress in convincing locals to side with the government through newly installed local authorities. War-weary civilians welcomed the end of open conflict.

By the end of 1999, the RPA finally had the full military control of the country it had been seeking since the civil war began. While the insurgency had ended, its effects continued to ripple across the country. There were no commissions of inquiry or other government-led efforts to uncover who did what to whom during the insurgency. The human rights community was frustrated at every turn as it sought to document abuses to hold the offending parties accountable. The bitter pill of impunity left a sour taste for all who survived it. That the RPF's policy of ethnic unity did not include Hutu, particularly northerners, was the one thing made abundantly clear by the insurgency.

The end of the insurgency offered an unstable peace—the absence of open conflict did not include truth or justice. The government made sure that foreign and local journalists reported on attacks it attributed to the *abacengezi*, without reference to RPA killings of civilians. Rwandans who lived through the insurgency knew this to be untrue, but had no way to protest against such injustices, and lacked the ability to question the RPF's version of events; doing so could result in their arbitrary arrest, detention or death.

6

CONTROL AT HOME AND ABROAD

A legitimate fear of a return to genocidal violence shaped the RPF's efforts to assure physical security throughout the country. This in turn resulted in widespread feelings of fear and uncertainty for the majority of rural Rwandans as the ethnic killings that shaped life before and during the genocide continued in many parts of the country. The primary difference was that ethnic Hutu were now the main targets, although Rwandans of all ethnicities were caught in the crossfire as both sides of the insurgency in the northwest region killed with impunity.[1] The RPA, as well as Rwandan-organized and trained troops of its Zairian proxy, the AFDL, were partially responsible for continued violence as they also organized cross-border killings in both Rwanda and Zaire (also known from 1998 as the Democratic Republic of Congo or DRC).

Security became a perverse concept for many Rwandans and Congolese civilians when, in August 1998, Vice President Kagame ordered a new military invasion into the DRC, just as President Kabila of the DRC ordered all foreign soldiers out of *his* Congo. Kabila's heavy-handedness incensed Kagame, making the return to war simple. As Kagame told American Ambassador Robert Gribben, the RPF was "honor bound to support the [Banyamulenge] mutiny on grounds of ethnic solidarity, but also to rectify the error of putting Kabila in power."[2] Senior RPF officials sold foreign donors the idea of renewed war on humanitarian grounds, as they believed Kabila was targeting Congolese Tutsi by arming Rwandan Hutu militias. There was truth to this claim. Like Mobutu before him, Kabila scapegoated the Congolese Tutsi community, which made it easy for Kagame to mount a Rwanda-sponsored, anti-Kabila rebellion. The Congolese Rally for Democracy (Rassemblement congolais pour la démocratie, RCD), a Rwandan proxy militia funded by Kigali, led this second Congolese war with RPF materiel and intelligence.

The targets of RCD militants were a mixed group linked to the Habyarimana regime—ex-FAR soldiers, Interahamwe, and others opposed to the new Rwandan government. They came together as the Army for the Liberation of Rwanda (ALiR), linked by the sole purpose of overthrowing the Tutsi-led government in Kigali. In 2000–1, some eight to sixteen thousand Hutu rebels fighting as the ALiR regrouped under the banner of the Democratic Forces for the Liberation of Rwanda (FDLR).[3] Eliminating the FDLR to assure Rwandan territorial and national security soon become the RPF's sole rationale for maintaining a military presence in eastern DRC. RPF officials consistently cited the FDLR as a destabilizing force for Rwandan security. By 2003, when the second Congo war ended, it was clear that the FDLR lacked the personnel and munitions to successfully over-throw the RPF; independent human rights and military analysts deemed the FDLR too weak to be of real threat to Rwanda's national security.[4]

When the war officially ended in July 2003, millions of civilians had been displaced over a period of five years. At least three million died. Although the RPF-led government was an official signatory to the peace agreement that ended the war, Rwanda continued to send its troops across the border to Congo, claiming the Kivus region to be a base for Hutu extremists determined to continue the genocide. To many observers, the government's claims rang hollow; numerous founding and senior members of the RPF were greatly enriched by military access to Congo's natural resources, including gold, coltan and timber. Donor dollars were allocated to infrastructure and other development projects, but, while ordinary Rwandans continued to live at subsistence levels, they saw that senior members of the RPF were enjoying their share of Congo's ill-gotten mineral wealth.

While its troops maintained security along Rwanda's western border, the government engaged in broad-based consultations to guide reconstruction and reconciliation. The main consultations, held at the presidential compound from May 1998 to March 1999, were known as the Urugwiro Village talks.[5] True to form, RPF-style consultations were not broad-based participative affairs, with key stakeholders and individuals weighing in on policy decisions. Rather, the government used the consultations as a forum from which to communicate its policy preferences in an information-sharing and instructional format.[6] Government priorities remained managing access to land, poverty alleviation and the provision of essential services, such as water, access roads, schools and health care.[7] Much to the dismay of genocide survivors, justice and reconciliation did not yet feature on the list.

The government's indifference to survivors' suffering produced a widespread sense of betrayal, which informed relationships between ordinary Rwandans and RPF officials. Tutsi genocide survivors generally felt free to speak about what had happened to them or their loved ones during and after the genocide, while most Hutu felt constrained from speaking, fearing they would be accused of participating in the genocide or of promoting ethnic divisionism.[8] Members of both groups felt they lacked the ability to critique a government dominated by former refugees from Uganda.

Although mental health and trauma initiatives were not a government priority, numerous survivor groups provided counseling on an ad hoc basis.[9] Survivors learned to nuance existing language to capture the unexplainable—surviving genocide, being a member of the living dead (*gupfa uhagaze*). For survivors, the indescribable effects of having one's world turned upside down by virtue of being Tutsi are captured in the sensation of not being able to breathe, accompanied by intense feelings of helplessness, vulnerability and loss of hope.[10] The language of trauma had yet to take hold in Rwanda, but such western concepts were widely used by international aid workers to explain the inner emotional worlds of the survivors.

Sparking Development

In 2000, the government launched its Vision 2020 policy to international fanfare. Designed to transform the country into a middle-income, service-based economy in two decades, this was a most ambitious plan, especially given Rwanda's historical reliance on subsistence farming and foreign aid. The announcement came as a great relief to donors, who had long wanted the RPF to prioritize economic development as the basis of peace and security. The RPF leadership understood their sense of urgency as they too delighted in the shift from security and reconstruction to economic development.

Vision 2020 was the RPF's most ambitious project to date, but it was not its first lofty initiative. A few months earlier, the government inaugurated the National Unity and Reconciliation Commission (NURC), whose primary task was (and remains) educating Rwandans on the importance of ethnic unity, as well as denouncing and fighting any kind of ethnic discrimination or intolerance. The NURC's mission is to ensure that genocide "never again" happens.

That same year, the RPF arbitrarily extended the mandate of the Government of National Unity, which was set to expire in July 1999 after its initial five-year term. The government claimed its primary justification for the move was to manage ethnic identities to prevent future genocides. In practice, the mantra "never again" became the standard response to all RPF policy choices, and the actions it took to implement those policies. When the RPF unilaterally decreed an extension of its national unity mandate into 2003, it also claimed it needed more time to assure national security before rolling out any justice and reconciliation initiatives, and stated its intent to continue nationwide consultations on the constitution to include the opinions of as many Rwandans as possible. Meanwhile, government critics deemed the extension to be a power play aimed at giving the RPF more time to consolidate its control of local populations and communities before the pivotal 2003 presidential and parliamentary vote—Rwanda's first national elections since the genocide.

Much public skepticism of RPF decrees, however muted, directly resulted from the RPF's chronic allergy to real or perceived criticism. The government was especially sensitive to accusations of human rights abuses, including killing, torture, disappearances and arbitrary detentions across the country.[11] Senior government representatives, including President Bizimungu and Vice President Kagame, sternly rebuked criticism of any sort on three grounds: first, as a product of genocide denial; second, as a lack of foreign commitment to the "truth" of what "really" happened in Rwanda; and lastly, as a sign of Western arrogance, when prescribing peacebuilding to the RPF for a country they had abandoned. There was at least some truth in the RPF's rejection of such criticism: military violence was perhaps arbitrary, but it was not one-sided. Hutu extremist insurgents also committed abuses in their efforts to infiltrate Rwanda. As always, ordinary people were caught in the crossfire.

Justice or Revenge?

Politically dominant and in full military control of the country, the RPF unilaterally decided how the government would prosecute genocide crimes. From 1998 to 2000, it laid the groundwork of its justice policy: maximal prosecution for crimes of genocide and crimes of humanity committed during the civil war and genocide, limited to the period from October 1, 1990 to December 31, 1994. The government's rationale for this harsh course was to end the culture of impunity that the RPF believed gave rise to the genocide in the first place, and to institute a system of justice that included all Rwandans.

The RPF's no-stone-left-unturned approach to postgenocide justice cut across levels of the judicial system before it became official policy with the 2001 introduction of the neo-traditional, *gacaca* courts. The courts are a system of grassroots justice inspired by the Rwandan tradition that disputes are best settled at the community level. In addition to the *gacaca* courts, some genocide crimes were pursued in military and domestic trials, under the principle of universal jurisdiction. Universal jurisdiction allows domestic courts to try perpetrators of crimes so heinous that they amount to crimes against the whole of humanity. The ghastly nature of crimes against humanity means that any competent court can hear genocide cases, regardless of where they occurred, or the nationality of the victims or perpetrators.[12] According to universal jurisdiction, alleged Rwandan perpetrators of the 1994 genocide were tried in the countries where they sought refuge or took up residence, typically in Belgium, Canada, Finland, France, the Netherlands, Switzerland and the United States.

The Rwandan genocide had its own international court as well. Established in December 1994, the International Criminal Tribunal for Rwanda (ICTR) was domiciled in Arusha, Tanzania. The court closed its doors in 2015 without finding legal evidence of a Hutu Power conspiracy to commit genocide. This is not to say that the court itself was a failure. Acts of genocide did take place in Rwanda, as defined by the Geneva Conventions. The conventions establish a legal minimum standard of practice in international law in times of war. However, the ICTR finding suggests the absence of a preexisting plan for genocide prior to April 1994. In its twenty-one years of operation, the court found more than sixty senior political leaders and military officers of the former regime guilty of acts of genocide.[13]

Meanwhile, the Office of the Prosecutor (OtP) at the ICTR took few steps to prosecute RPF crimes in violation of a fundamental principle of international humanitarian law—that individuals from all sides of an armed conflict should be prosecuted.[14] The first chief prosecutor, Richard Goldstone, serving from 1994 to 1996, accepted the RPF's claim that it only perpetrated revenge killings. Goldstone felt that securing Kigali's cooperation to support the work of the court was more important than investigating alleged crimes of the RPF and the RPA. This milquetoast response would shape the relationship between the Rwandan government and ICTR officials, as successive prosecutors— Louise Arbour of Canada (1996–99), Carla Del Ponte of Switzerland (1999–2003) and Hassan Jallow of Gambia (2003–15)—worked to try RPF crimes before the international tribunal, with greatly varying degrees of success.

Real and imagined shortcomings hampered the prosecution's ability to secure indictments against the RPF for its alleged crimes. From the start, the government impeded ICTR officials from investigating RPF crimes, and led a smear campaign disputing the court's sincerity in seeking justice for Rwandans. By this time, when the government spoke of justice for Rwandans, it meant only Tutsi survivors of the genocide. Repeatedly, the RPF made it clear to chief prosecutors Arbour and Del Ponte that it would cooperate with the court on its terms: there would be no investigations into alleged crimes of the RPF and the RPA, including the critical matter of who shot President Habyarimana's plane out of the sky on April 6, 1994.

When Del Ponte announced "a full-fledged investigation into RPF crimes" in December 2000, the government, supported by Washington and London, sought to shame and pressure the ICTR to drop the case.[15] It succeeded. The United Nations Security Council removed Del Ponte from her post in August 2003, and appointed Hassan Jallow in her stead. Unlike Del Ponte, Jallow showed no stomach for the politicking required to secure RPF indictments. Under his tenure, Rwanda's impunity gap widened as RPF crimes were not even investigated, let alone prosecuted.[16] Jallow pursued a policy of conciliation and compromise. From 2003 to the end of 2015, the court failed to investigate a single alleged RPF crime from before, during or after the 1994 genocide. Conversely, from 1998 to 2000, the ICTR had started to prosecute some of the so-called "big fish" of the genocide, meaning those who played a key role in its implementation.

Under the watch of chief prosecutor Louise Arbour, the ICTR issued its first judgments in 1998. Jean-Paul Akayesu, mayor of Taba commune in Gitarama province, and Jean Kambanda, interim prime minister during the genocide, both received life sentences, the tribunal's maximum penalty.[17] Both cases were groundbreaking in international law. The Akayesu ruling marked the first case of its kind to rule that rape is a crime of genocide, while Kambanda publicly pleaded guilty during his trial. Kambanda's acknowledgment of the genocide and his role in organizing it was significant as it directly challenged those who sought to deny genocide had occurred.[18] As part of the RPF's overall control of the media, the results of both cases were not well publicized within Rwanda, muting their potential contribution to national reconciliation.

The ICTR prosecutors carried out their work at once helped and hindered by government cooperation and interference. RPF leaders repeatedly besieged the OtP to render a legal determination of genocide with two aims in mind. First, the RPF sought to clarify that it did not order the downing of the presidential plane, which would absolve President Kagame and other senior officials of any role in that fateful event. And second, the RPF aspired to the court's recognition of its official version of the genocide's origin, and its heroic role in stopping it.

Back in Rwanda, the national courts began work in December 1996, with the trials of several hundred people in twelve specialized chambers, established with the sole purpose of dealing with cases of genocide.[19] The work of domestic courts was overshadowed by the RPF's continued pattern of arbitrary arrest and detention.[20] By 2001, the number of persons in custody was down from 120,000 to 110,000, as the government released several thousand people for lack of evidence, or because they were minors, elderly or ill. Even so, to this day, tens of thousands of accused remain crammed into detention centers and prisons across the country, with little prospect of being tried in their lifetimes.[21] Of the approximately 1,300 people who were tried domestically, some were sentenced to death, others received various terms of incarceration, while a handful were acquitted.

In April 1998, the government staged public executions by firing squad at five locations across the country: Kigali, Gikongoro, Nyamata, Murambi and Kibungo.[22] Those on the docket were the first Rwandans to be found guilty of participating in the genocide. The condemned included Froduald Karamira, a ranking member and ideologue of the now-banned Hutu Power wing of the otherwise moderate MDR party, as well as other local government officials, and two Catholic priests who ordered or directed the killing at churches in their communes. At each location, large crowds gathered to witness these state-sanctioned displays of violence, with a mixture of fright and bitter delight at the first public acts of retribution for the genocide.

Some Hutu saw the executions as a gruesome display of Tutsi power. Etienne, a young Hutu who survived the genocide, said mournfully: "The Tutsis will kill us all now in revenge and so that they can always rule Rwanda." For some ethnic Tutsi who lost loved ones in the genocide, the executions marked more than a moment of justice; they were an opportunity to revel in revenge. Liberata, a middle-aged Tutsi woman who lost most of the members of her family, said with a twinkle in her eye, "This is what justice looks like. It is better to see your enemies dead than to worry they will rise up to kill again."

Domestic and international human rights organizations, including UNHRFOR, raised questions about the trials that had resulted in executions. In some cases, guilt had not been established beyond a reasonable doubt, and in others, concerns about unfair trials leading to conviction were expressed.[23] Violations included having no lawyer present, not being able to call defense witnesses, and judicial expediency. Cases leading to execution lasted on average four hours. The RPF brushed aside such criticism, claiming it needed to send a clear message to Hutu extremists that they could not escape justice.

According to the Foreign Affairs Minister Anastase Gasana, the executions served an educational function, although he did not clarify the lesson. It may be that the executions stemmed from Rwandan cultural codes about collective revenge. The Belgian anthropologist Danielle de Lame notes that, historically, Rwandan society had a long-standing culture of violence, focused on avenging the losses of one's lineage.[24] This right of revenge results in the "omnipresence of fear" shaped by a near-constant threat, including loss of life in periods of both peace and war. Perhaps the RPF wanted to send a message—as ruler of the new Rwanda, it now possessed the authority to regulate fear, as a form of both power and punishment. This public display of power and dominance was informed by precolonial royal authority, as the authority and legitimacy of precolonial Tutsi kings was built on "the right to kill and to enrich."[25]

The cycles of revenge that characterize the historical resolution of political conflict in Rwanda mean that those elites who employed violence to hold power feared later being targeted for death in response to the violence they ordered. Elite power struggles—shaped by winner-takes-all conflicts and the historical exclusion of the losers in politics and the economy—also have important implications for the security of ordinary people like Etienne and Liberata. Both Hutu and Tutsi tie their emotional and physical security to a righting of past wrongs. History is cyclical, meaning Hutu elites are to revenge the hurts and losses of all Hutu, while Tutsi elites are to do the same for all Tutsi. This cultural response was reflected in the reactions of some domestic human rights groups to the executions. Pro-Tutsi and pro-RPF groups saw the executions as therapeutic to survivors of the genocide, while pro-Hutu ones chose not to comment publicly. A handful of independent local human rights organizations, in which Hutu and Tutsi worked together to promote and protect all Rwanda regardless of ethnicity, issued statements of concern that the government then denounced as a form of genocide denial.[26] Only the Rwandan journalist and priest André Sibomana was prepared to say publicly what some discussed privately—that the executions represented a grave violation of human rights and were a threat to heart-felt reconciliation.[27]

Tight control of judicial proceedings and messages about the role of executions in promoting justice was coupled with government efforts to monitor and muzzle the work of human rights defenders, the press, religious leaders, political opponents and other real or suspected critics. By 1999, domestic human rights organizations had begun to self-censor, which in turn narrowed space for democratic dialogue on the reconstruction and reconciliation vision of the RPF. Rather than publish reports that could be perceived as critical of the RPF or the RPA, or sympathetic to the *abacengezi*, Rwandan human rights activists began focusing on areas where there was controlled government endorsement, including human rights education, conditions in overcrowded prisons, and government efforts to restore the justice sector.[28] Rwanda's international donors, particularly Belgium and the United States, were key supporters of the latter.

The RPF's strong-arm tactics and intimidation caused the demise of the international human rights community in Rwanda. Soon after the UNHRFOR criticized the government's use of executions as justice, the Ministry of Justice began a review of its mandate, with the intent to stop its investigative and monitoring functions. High-level negotiations between the UN and the government failed, and in July 1998 the UNHRFOR mission was permanently shuttered, and its staff expelled. In private, members of the domestic human rights community noted that UNHRFOR's departure marked the moment of consolidation between Rwanda's culture of impunity and a tightening of control over information provided to foreign audiences.

Among independent journalists, civil society activists and members of the political opposition, the forced exit of UNHRFOR made for defeat and despair. The season of hope that the RPF planted when it successfully stopped the genocide was over by the end of 1999. By this time, the government had suppressed or coopted its critics, and information about the actual human rights and governance situation on the ground was muted, if it was available at all. Most international media based outside Rwanda relied on information provided by government-controlled media, or on briefings provided by government officials. When foreign journalists tried to access or investigate independent information, their efforts were often met with frustration; RPF loyalists had infiltrated "UN agencies, local and foreign NGOs and key businesses to monitor attitudes towards the government and general activities."[29] Government control of information painted an overall rosy picture of daily life, which was dutifully reported to the outside world. Within this climate the RPF was able to turn its attention to crafting a uniquely Rwandan style of democracy.

7

MILITARIZED DEMOCRACY

As the counterinsurgency in the northwest abated, the RPF shifted its focus toward creating accountable and responsive political institutions. Increasingly, the government sought to free itself from the ties of foreign aid by developing the economy, while demonstrating its commitment to ethnic unity through the implementation of social and cultural policies. Members of the international community, including diplomats, aid workers and journalists living in Kigali, were buoyed by this commitment to democracy, while failing to consider for whom Rwanda's new institutions would work. They also neglected to see history repeating itself; the RPF's portrayal of itself as the "best able and willing to guide Rwanda along the 'right' path to peace, security, ethnic unity and development," mirrored the rhetoric and practice of the Habyarimana regime.[1]

For Rwandans who lived in the country before the genocide, the RPF's style of governance was all too familiar; for many, the RPF-led government was as intrusive, controlling and violent as previous regimes had been before. A singular difference was that the government was now Tutsi-led. Although the RPF claimed to espouse democracy, its approach to public participation was informed by its distrust and dislike of ethnic Hutu. This common antipathy to all Hutu was firmly rooted in the belief that the RPF had inherited a "mostly hostile, mostly Hutu" underclass of potential enemies.[2] A senior member of the RPF recounted an oft-cited proverb to justify the government's mistrust: "If you teach a Hutu to shoot a bow, he'll shoot an arrow into your stomach." The RPF's ingrained enmity toward Hutu meant that its real and perceived political opponents were intensely coerced to conform through the use of tactics far subtler—and more effective by far—than those practiced by the Habyarimana and Kayibanda regimes.

The donor community provided little oversight of the early excesses of RPF rule. Most were unfamiliar with cultural intricacies, and the local, national, regional and international dynamics that drove the security and governance choices of the RPF. In particular, donors failed to appreciate Rwanda's longstanding culture of "an excessively centralized state," which uses its muscle to monitor the daily activities, mundane and otherwise, of Rwandans (a theme discussed further in Chapter 11).[3] Diplomats saw the counterinsurgency in the northwest as necessary for securing the country, certain that it was but a short-term military deployment to contain the threat of Hutu extremists returning to continue killing Tutsi.[4] This viewpoint was in part shaped by the RPF's control of who could access the theatre of war in the northwest to report on casualties. All the same, the international community was both pleased and placated by the seriousness with which the government approached the complex task of rebuilding Rwanda.

With spoilers like Sendashonga, Twagiramungu and other political opponents now forced out of government, the work of bringing democracy to the masses could proceed. Like foreign donors, old-caseload returnees, many of whom had supported the RPF since its early days in Uganda, shared in the optimism of the moment. They were, after all, its main beneficiaries, as government jobs and private contracts went primarily to party loyalists.[5] However, for those Rwandans who lived through the civil war and genocide, the RPF's talk of democracy fell on deaf ears. They had first-hand experience of the ill effects of multi-party politics, which many people saw as a partial cause of the 1994 genocide.

Consensual Democracy

For many Rwandans who lived through the genocide, democratization meant violence, fear and insecurity as political elites jockeyed for pole position. Initially, the RPF leadership appeared to acknowledge the general population's fear of and reluctance for democracy and campaigned to allay their concerns. The RPF proposed a uniquely Rwandan-style consensual democracy built on inclusive government as the only model that could return the country to the social and political harmony of the precolonial period. It swore it would not allow foreign donors to impose a Western form of democracy, as it had in 1990. Through the end of 1997, both RPF leadership and local government representatives actively sensitized Rwandans on democracy, RPF-style: a political environment without voice, controlled by a single dominant political party.

As the country moved toward local elections in 1999, and national elections in 2003, the RPF restricted political party activity, coopted or suppressed civil society organizations, and curtailed freedoms of speech, press and association.[6] For all these controls, Rwanda was still home to almost a dozen parties. Their proliferation gave the appearance of an emergent democracy, much to the delight of donors. Few realized that the opposition parties operated in a coalition with the RPF. Independent or alternative political platforms were (and are) forbidden. Instead, under the guise of the National Consultative Forum of Political Organizations, party leaders met to build consensus and promote national cohesion.[7] The goal of the forum was to develop political leadership skills, particularly for women and young people. At all times, consensus was deemed essential; and consensus meant total agreement with RPF policies. Dialogue and debate were not on the table, nor was there any consideration of alternative policy proposals.[8] According to the RPF, there was but one path to the new Rwanda: the one it paved for itself. Within this carefully ordered environment, the RPF could rest assured of its success at the polls it stage-managed; with seats populated by party loyalists, democracy could proceed.[9]

Coopting Critics

By 2000, the RPF had consolidated a strategy of cooptation and coercion toward its opponents—real and imagined—including representatives of churches, women's cooperatives, survivor self-help groups, human rights organizations, local and foreign journalists and aid workers, as well as political opponents. The only individuals and organizations that appeared to operate freely were those whose mandates aligned with the government's national unity and reconciliation and Vision 2020 goals. The RPF's position was clear, and in direct opposition to the ideals of democratic systems the world over: civil society was not a counterweight to government, nor would it influence policy outcomes. Rather, civil society was conceived to act as the development branch of the government. Johnston Busingye, secretary general in the Ministry of Justice, reaffirmed this, publicly stating: "When civil society sees itself as something different to government, as almost opposed, then it is a problem."[10]

Control, not criticism and confrontation, defined the RPF's relationship with civil society. A telling example is the case of the Tutsi survivor group Ibuka (the Kinyarwanda word for "remember"). Since its inception in late 1994 the leadership of Ibuka, an umbrella organization of survivor groups working across the country, had become increasingly critical of the government, perceiving many of its policy choices as hostile to its survivor membership. Some of the policies it singled out included the government's release of prisoners before their cases could be evaluated for trial, the lack of homes and land for survivors, and notably, the RPF's willingness to allow new-caseload returnees to appropriate their property.

A key Ibuka sticking point was the RPF's politicization of the national week of official mourning activities.[11] Beginning on April 1, 1995, the RPF declared a week of national mourning, culminating with a national address by Vice President Kagame on April 7. For survivors, forced public duties to remember the genocide were offensive on multiple fronts. The government's portrayal of the civil war and genocide created stark distinctions between victims and perpetrators that did not match the individual, violent experiences of many, lumping diverse experiences of violence before, during and after the genocide into a largely false and single story of Hutu perpetrators and Tutsi survivors. This forced dichotomy meant that those who died at the hands of RPF soldiers were erased from public memory. Many Ibuka members had an additional, simpler complaint: they objected to the start date of the national mourning ceremonies. For them, the genocide started on April 6, not April 7. It was a small but important distinction. The RPF may not have appreciated the criticism, but it was not entirely deaf to it. A few years later, in 2003, the government put the date debate to rest, and mandated national mourning during the entire month of April.

Most troubling for Ibuka members was the requirement of communal labor known as *umuganda*. On the last Saturday of each month all Rwandans were (and are) expected to contribute their time to the state. *Umuganda* activities include cultivating fields, planting trees, cleaning up litter, street sweeping, and building houses for genocide survivors. National instructions for the work to be done during *umuganda* are often communicated to local leaders the night before or the same morning, leaving people with little time to plan how best to accomplish the task, or to ensure the proper tools are available.[12] During *umuganda*, no cars are allowed on the road, and shops are closed until at least 10 a.m. Those who fail to participate are fined; those who cannot pay the

US$10 charge (a prohibitive sum for the average Rwandan) may be detained until the fine is paid. Wealthier Rwandans, particularly those in urban centers, prefer not to do the work of "poor people" and will often pay the fine.

In the weeks leading up to the mourning period, the government uses *umuganda* to exhume and identify the bodies of people killed in the genocide, so they can receive a proper reburial. Many Ibuka survivors questioned this practice, wondering in private if the exhumed were truly victims of the genocide. By 2000, the same survivors questioned the legitimacy of the recovery of bodies, querying whether the corpses might be victims of RPF crimes, or whether the government was digging up the same graves year after year. Not all survivors felt this way; years later, many still hoped to recover the remains of a loved one, which would provide a much-needed sense of closure. For Christian survivors, being able to properly bury their dead ensured their eternal salvation, while those with traditional beliefs sought private burial to ensure their relatives' safe passage into the spirit world. Exhumations were ongoing through 2014 as part of government-led initiatives to honor and remember lives lost, through reburial at local government offices and national memorials alike.[13]

Ibuka's leaders, including its Vice President, Josué Kayijaho, and founding member, Bosco Rutagengwa, would meet regularly with local representatives to discuss issues of importance to the general membership. Time and again, their common grievance was the government's politicization of mourning week and the forced work of *umuganda*. When Kayijaho expressed these concerns with representatives of the Ministry of Local Government (the agency responsible for monitoring NGOs), asking them to consider the emotional and spiritual needs of Tutsi survivors of the genocide, he was coldly rebuffed. In late 1999, the government had become riled by Ibuka's leadership. It threatened to depose those at the helm and replace them with a known Hutu *génocidaire*, Elisée Bisengimana, who was also a member of the RPF.

Bisengimana was one of many Hutu representatives from the former government whom the RPF integrated into the local administration.[14] For strategic reasons, the RPF wanted to place Hutu leaders in charge of largely Hutu populations, particularly in the northwest. This policy was met with utter shock by Tutsi survivors, many of whom saw such government appointees as an affront to all they had lived through and lost. Survivors who spoke against the proposal were jailed for slander.[15]

The RPF began a full-scale purge of the Ibuka leadership in March 2000, with the assassination of Kayijaho's brother, Assiel Kabera. Kabera had been an advisor to President Bizimungu, and an ardent advocate for survivors. His death signaled that the RPF would not tolerate dissent from any quarter, and sent chills through Ibuka's membership. Many senior founding members, including Kayijaho, soon fled into exile. A few weeks later, a party faithful and long-time member of the RPF's central planning committee, Antoine Mugesera, was "elected" Ibuka's president. Underlining the risks of speaking out against his candidacy, RPF *abakada* worked within the organization prior to the vote to be sure that all members knew for whom to cast their ballots.[16]

An Undemocratic Ascension

March 2000 was an eventful month in Rwanda. Amid the liquidation of the Ibuka old guard, Paul Kagame became president. With people and place under RPF control, Kagame came out of the shadows to regularize his role as Rwanda's leader.

Pasteur Bizimungu, an ethnic Hutu, served as Rwanda's figurehead president from 1994 to 2000. Immediately following the end of the genocide, Kagame was widely considered the de facto power holder in his role as vice president, head of the military and, from 1998, chairman of the RPF. Depending on the source, Bizimungu either stepped down or was forced out of office after being accused of corruption in 1999.

His downfall was assured in March 2000 when he delivered a stinging attack on parliament. In thinly veiled references to Kagame's increasing control over the political process, Bizimungu accused his fellow parliamentarians of allowing the future president to control the executive branch of government. Bizimungu also denounced senior members of the RPF's inner circle, highlighting that he—the son of a Hutu born to a Tutsi mother—had joined the RPF to overthrow the oppressive rule of former President Habyarimana. He had no interest in working with a new parliament that engaged in more of the same.

Bizimungu's denunciation of his fellow politicians followed similar remarks from the speaker of parliament, Joseph Sebarenzi, and the forced resignation of the Prime Minister Pierre Célestin Rwigema. A Tutsi who survived the 1994 genocide, Sebarenzi spoke out about the RPF's human rights record and President Kagame's firm grip on all branches of government—the executive, legislature and judiciary. Sebarenzi hoped to reform parliament into something it had never been: an independent body able to challenge the government and limit political power. Kagame, however, wanted parliament—along with political parties, churches, civil society organizations and the press—to follow his lead, not contradict him. After Sebarenzi pushed through a bill that gave parliament stronger powers of oversight, Kagame forced him out of office, much to the dismay of moderate RPF politicians like Bizimungu. Fearing for his life, Sebarenzi fled Rwanda in mid-2000, eventually landing up in the United States, where he lives today. Upon his departure, senior RPF officials, led by President Kagame, continued to denounce Sebarenzi before international audiences, a common tactic in authoritarian regimes where character assassination is used to discredit opponents.

The newly appointed Ibuka leadership also denounced the now-exiled Sebarenzi, simultaneously accusing him of financial mismanagement and of being a monarchist who sought the return of the Rwandan king, Kigeli V Ndahindurwa, from his home in exile in the United

States. Both allegations were false, but effective. This tactic of public condemnation revealed the RPF's efforts to eliminate the political middle ground. Older Rwandans had witnessed this same approach at the end of colonial rule, from 1958 to 1964, when then President Kayibanda consolidated his rule. Recently arrived returnees from Uganda and elsewhere knew little of this historical tradition of marginalizing political opponents; they did not recognize the RPF's sidelining of former supporters as something of concern. As many new returnees were benefiting from their position of strength and proximity to the RPF-led government, few saw any reason to question the RPF's central and natural role in controlling politics since the genocide.

Government accusations of Sebarenzi's latent monarchism were intended to denounce him as a Tutsi extremist who wanted to restore the hierarchy and oppression that characterized daily life under Belgian rule. Central to such regime rhetoric was the notion that all that was wrong with Rwandan society was rooted in the lingering effects of colonial rule. An unintentional outcome of this rhetoric was that it served to remind ethnic Hutu that the monarchists sought to subjugate them all over again.[17] Nonetheless, senior RPF officials slapped the monarchist label on their critics to discredit them as individuals who would allow colonial powers once again to dictate Rwanda's fate. This tactic was deeply ironic, as Habyarimana had formerly accused the RPF of seeking to overthrow his government to reestablish monarchical rule and Tutsi hegemony when it first entered Rwanda in 1990. All the same, the tactic was effective. It situated the RPF as the sole entity able and willing to steer Rwanda away from the immoral leadership and corrupt politics that led to the 1994 genocide. It also signaled to Rwandans that it was business as usual among political elites, who would shore up their own positions with little regard to the wellbeing and concerns of ordinary people.

Many Rwandans, particularly survivors of the genocide, considered Sebarenzi to be a man of principle who risked his own life to speak out on their behalf. Such people are known as *ibipinga* (those with deep-rooted ideals), and are held in high esteem by ordinary Rwandans.[18] The RPF's scapegoating of Sebarenzi, and other political elites who dared to question the ruling party, revealed a predictable pattern— first silence then elimination from public life. In Rwanda's tightly controlled and closed political system, despite his impeccable political credentials as a Tutsi who had survived the genocide, Sebarenzi was still unable to defend himself. Kagame reminded other *ibipinga* that his grip on power was absolute when he ousted six RPF ministers in his first cabinet shuffle as president in March 2000. Kagame's actions served to warn other elites that their fate lay in his hands alone, and to tread lightly lest they end up excluded from power like Bizimungu and Sebarenzi.

Bizimungu was soon the target of another RPF smear campaign. He eventually spent time in prison, in solitary confinement, after a public falling out with Kagame. Feeling betrayed after giving so much of himself to the RPF from its earliest days, in 2001 he started a new political party that was banned almost immediately upon registration. In 2004, Bizimungu was found guilty of trumped-up charges of embezzlement, attempting to form a militia, and inciting public violence. Unexpectedly, Kagame commuted Bizimungu's sentence in 2007, but he was no longer a political force of any remark.[19]

Bizimungu's exit from public office, subsequent incarceration and eventual pardon is emblematic of the way elites circulate in Rwandan politics. As the government aggressively and efficiently marginalized moderate Hutu (those willing to share power with Tutsi), Tutsi genocide survivors, Francophone old-caseload Tutsi refugees and dissident RPF Tutsi, it was evident that internal struggles for power would not be tolerated.[20] To this day, individuals with political aspirations, or those who express criticism, are targeted. Real or perceived rivals are dead, in jail, or have fled the country. In Rwanda, politics is a dangerous life-or-death game.[21]

Stylized Democracy

During his tenure as vice president (1994–2000), Kagame's rhetorical commitment to national unity and economic development meant that he had already garnered glowing praise from international and regional observers as a new kind of African leader—one who respects the rule of law, rails against corruption, protects human rights and is willing to listen and learn from his opponents. Kagame's many admirers include former US President Bill Clinton, former British Prime Minister Tony Blair, American religious leaders such as the evangelical pastor Rick Warren and Rabbi Shmuley Boteach, and business icons, including Bill Gates of Microsoft and Howard Schultz of Starbucks. This veneration gives Kagame a veneer of respectability and esteem, eclipsing his less savory attributes. By the time Kagame was sworn in as president in April 2000, his style of leadership made it clear that "Rwanda has made a transition from one type of authoritarian regime to another."[22]

Kagame's ascent to the presidency was met with a collective shoulder shrug in the rural hills. Rwandans already felt the dual tension of RPF rule. The language of unity and reconciliation did not align with the RPF's strict social controls and the murder of tens of thousands of citizens. For many, the ways that the RPF consolidated its power were characterized by many of the same waves of exclusion practiced by previous regimes. The Rwandan state has always been the primary driver of national change, whether under the watchful eye of the king, the Belgians in colonial days, or postcolonial presidents.

All the same, the RPF frames Kagame's leadership as distinctly different from the discriminatory and ethnocentric rule of his predecessors. Particular emphasis is placed on distancing Kagame from Rwanda's pregenocide president. Invariably, Habyarimana is portrayed as an underhand, corrupt politician who hatched the genocide, while Kagame is an ascetic, principled and selfless leader. In words and deeds, however, Kagame's authoritarian leadership is not fundamentally different from that of the man who came before him. Rwanda has always been governed by a strongman and his narrow clique of political, intelligence and military cronies. Kagame's reign is marked by a single distinguishing feature: vast informal spy and surveillance networks, at home and abroad.[23] Gideon, a professor at the National University of Rwanda, summed up the ordinariness of this presence: "If ten young men walk down the street, six of them are from military intelligence."[24] The RPF's liberation vision was now in plain sight: a uniquely Rwandan democracy that would be able to provide the safety and security that so many Tutsi who grew up in Uganda craved.

1. Belgian paratroopers guard a group of alleged Hutu arsonists during Rwanda's Social Revolution in September 1960. In many parts of Rwanda, bands of Hutu insurgents regularly set fire to Tutsi homesteads in efforts to chase Tutsi out of the country.

2. Rwandans of all ethnicities fled the violence of the Social Revolution, taking up residence in neighboring countries. Here, in Goma, a patron (center) is shown with his clients in 1961.

3. Some Rwandans lived in makeshift grass homes in RPF-controlled camps during the civil war, like this one near Byumba, 1992. The RPF expected to be gratefully welcomed by a Hutu population who supported their liberation struggle. Instead, most met the RPF "invaders" with a mixture of fear and skepticism.

4. A group of mostly Tutsi civilians, seeking protection against Hutu militiamen, sit in the Sainte-Famille Catholic church listening to a member of the security services in May 1994. Many Tutsi were taken from Sainte-Famille and killed by Hutu militants who maintained checkpoints around the church during the genocide.

5. Rwandan children huddle, in shock, after their orphanage was shelled in Kigali during fighting between RPF rebels and government troops in May 1994, despite ongoing UN-brokered peace talks. The genocide created some 100,000 orphans; most live today in poverty, compounded by lack of access to education and high rates of HIV/AIDS.

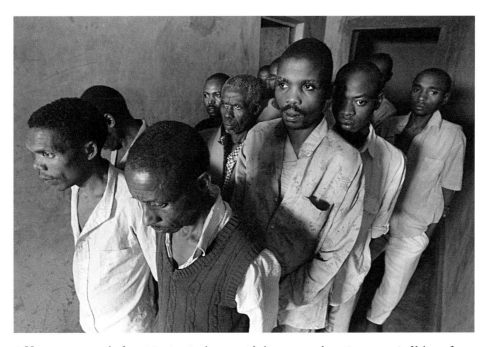

6. Hutu men accused of participating in the genocide line up at a detention center in Kabuga, June 1994. Most killers were ordinary men—fathers, husbands and farmers—who killed for reasons beyond ethnic animosity. Most participated in the carnage "because they feared punishment from other Hutu if they refused to take part in violence" (Straus, *The Order of Genocide*, p. 96).

7. Canadian Major-General Guy Tousignant of the United Nations Assistance Mission for Rwanda discusses prison conditions with the RPF warden in Kirambo, northern Rwanda, April 1995. Seeking to control the northwest region of the country, the RPF subjugated ethnic Hutu residents.

8. Internally displaced Rwandans wait outside a hospital complex in Kibeho camp, May 1995. Medical supplies and hospital staff were non-existent, leaving most citizens to fend for themselves in deplorable conditions. The RPF explained that military action in the camp was necessary to root out potential *génocidaires* intent on continuing their killing of Tutsi.

9. Exhausted Rwandan Hutu refugees rest on the side of the road next to the old Muginga refugee camps near the Zairean town of Goma, November 1996. Seasonal rains made already squalid conditions even worse. The UNHCR bungled the repatriation effort, leaving the RPF to forcibly return fearful, war-weary civilians back to Rwanda.

10. Many of Rwanda's genocide memorials feature hundreds of exhumed bodies, preserved with powdered lime, appearing as they did at death. This graphic display of remains, photographed in 2006, is at the Murambi Genocide Museum in southwestern Rwanda. Survivors of the genocide consider the raw display of the remains of their loved ones an offence to their memory and an affront to government-led reconciliation initiatives.

11. Women are central to Rwanda's postgenocide reconstruction efforts. Many work in unsafe conditions in low-skill jobs such as road construction, as photographed here in 2007. Widows of the genocide, particularly those who lost their land in the absence of male relatives, earn much-needed income at these menial jobs.

12. An RPF soldier stands watch as voters queue to cast their ballot in local elections in Kigali, February 2011. Armed observation is the order of the day at most civic activities designed to build ethnic unity, including the *gacaca* courts, *ingando* reeducation camps and *umuganda*.

13. The government's commitment to universal primary education for all Rwandan children has yet to translate into adequate facilities, as seen in this primary school classroom in Western Province, 2014.

14. Kigali's central roundabout, photographed here in 2016, is the epicenter of modern Rwanda: clean, safe and efficient.

15. Kigali's roads are kept clean by a veritable army of female road sweepers. Public cleanliness (*isuku*) is a virtue in the new Rwanda.

PART III

Setting Up for Success

8

STATE, PARTY, FAMILY

In the early 2000s, the RPF began to roll out multiple programs intended to educate and mobilize Rwanda's citizenry. The government's aim was the smooth delivery of public services, including postgenocide justice in the form of the community-based *gacaca* courts. Ever systematic, the RPF set out its parameters for success, making it clear to all Rwandans what was expected of them, including their participation in unity and development initiatives. Speaking at the official launch of the *gacaca* courts in June 2002, President Kagame succinctly outlined his vision: justice is the backbone of national unity, which in turn is a foundation for peace and security; all are required for economic development.[1] Foreign donors welcomed the government's emphasis on economic development as the basis of security. At last, the development phase of Rwanda's transition from genocide to democracy could begin—it was something they had hoped for since the civil war ended in July 1994.

Empowered citizens are central to the RPF's version of democracy. According to the RPF, an empowered citizenry will be able to resist the vices of poor leadership and break the cult of obedience that they believe

was a major factor behind mass Hutu participation in the 1994 genocide. In fact, critics claimed that unity and development projects were
designed to manage and control Hutu, particularly men and boys, who
were assigned collective intent to murder Tutsi.[2] Boniface, a prominent
Tutsi businessman and member of the RPF who returned from Uganda
in 1995, summed up this sentiment: "We would rather be conscious of
our enemy than naively pretend, like you foreigners, to think we have no
enemy out there planning to exterminate us but instead to hopelessly
fantasize about a utopian Rwanda."[3]

The RPF's vision required all hands on deck—ready and willing to
bring to life its policies for economic growth and development, as well
as national unity and reconciliation. Founded in 1999, the National
Unity and Reconciliation Commission (NURC) was tasked with implementing a series of local and national initiatives designed to broker
reconciliation between Tutsi survivors and Hutu perpetrators. The
RPF's broader goal was to transform Hutu and Tutsi into Rwandans
who would no longer think, act or vote along ethnic lines. At the same
time, Vision 2020, drafted by the Ministry of Finance, aimed to transform and modernize the economy. The policy states: "Rwanda's ongoing
development will have, at its core, the Nation's [sic] principal asset—its
people."[4] The RPF intended to make Rwanda a middle-income country
by 2020, with a median household income target of US$1,240 and a life
expectancy of fifty-five years (up from the 2000 baseline of US$290 and
forty-nine years).

A focus on people is a practical must in a place with few natural
resources. Rwanda's primary resource remains arable land, most of
which has long been used by subsistence farmers, on plots averaging
about half a hectare in size. Resources that could be exploited for
economic development are few and far between, excepting limited
deposits of gold and tin. For a while, Rwanda's mineral exports were
healthy: a product of clandestine extractions by Rwandan, Burundian
and Congolese traders in the neighboring Kivu regions of Congo. As

export trails were difficult to trace, for a short time these traders, along with senior military officials from Rwanda and Uganda, benefited handsomely from the ongoing conflict in eastern parts of Congo. In April 2001, the United Nations Panel of Experts issued an embargo on all Rwandan mineral exports until their origin could be determined. Domestic manufacturing produced what the local market could bear: cement, roofing sheets, housing shingles, and other industrial supplies intended to fuel infrastructure repairs. By 2001, manufacturing output had inched upward to 80 percent of 1993 levels.[5]

Based in Kigali, and rarely venturing out to the rural hillsides to visit the projects their governments fund, donors played a major financial and moral role in RPF plans to develop Rwanda. Led by the US, donors turned a blind eye to the RPF's domestic human rights abuses and repressive political climate, as well as its ongoing military involvement in Congo. Only the Dutch (in 2003) and British (in 2004) suspended aid when the government stated its intent to renew its military presence in Congo. The RPF later reversed its decision, choosing to maintain the status quo in Congo rather than engage in a full-fledged military intervention.

Although not always plain to observers, in the early 2000s the RPF's plan was simple and straightforward: focused development to extend the RPF's reach into the hearts and minds of Rwandans.[6] According to the RPF, the slightest perception of political instability was not conducive to private sector and foreign investment, two key goals of the Vision 2020 policy. By 2006, it was considered unpatriotic to question the RPF's vision or to complain about its policies.

Becoming Modern

The military concept of Rwandanicity or Rwandanness is central to the RPF's vision for ethnic unity. Rwandanness prioritizes the importance of the army (*ingabo*) in development.[7] Individuals are taught to suppress their own needs in service to the greater patriotic good of loyalty. In exchange, the RPF promised national security and social services. This social contract is rooted in precolonial state structures, in which the state and military were overlapping entities, each reinforcing the authority and legitimacy of the other.[8] It is also a predominantly male space, where masculine traits of courage and virility are rewarded. Both the Kinyarwanda word for male (*umugabo*) and army (*ingabo*) have the same root (-*gabo*), highlighting the relationship between the protective role of the military in public life and men in private life in Rwandan society.[9] Masculine military values served, then and now, to distinguish elites from everyday people, but also to provide guidance on social values and to remind all that good citizens ought to exhibit military-like moral rectitude, as well as incorruptibility, a willingness to serve, and an over-arching commitment to "the Truth" with a capital T. Since the genocide, Truth was defined, of course, as the RPF's version of precolonial ethnic unity, where divisions wrought by colonial rule were replaced by Rwandan unity and its former glory was restored by the RPF.

Political indoctrination in the guise of citizenship reeducation (*ingando*) and civic leadership training (*itorero*) became commonplace. Reeducation is a common feature of post-conflict reconciliation and reconstruction initiatives the world over; Rwanda was no exception. Donors like to fund such programs, even as they recognize them as a form of victor's justice. As the winners of their war, the RPF decided who would be educated, and to what social and political ends. Launched in 2007, long after *ingando* was introduced in 1998, *itorero* remains at the heart of government efforts to create model citizens, from schoolchildren to the CEOs of private companies. By 2012, there was a special emphasis on those in leadership positions—government and military leaders as well as teachers, professors, social workers, journalists, doctors, lawyers and others in civil society and the private sector.[10]

Both *ingando* and *itorero* set out the expectations of model citizenship. The RPF celebrates graduates of both programs with elaborate military-style passing out ceremonies, hailing them as catalysts for

148

social and economic change. President Kagame often gives commencement speeches to *itorero* graduates, in person or by video link, reminding them of the responsibility of civic life. Having the president speak at such events makes clear the perks of model citizenship—good jobs, houses, nice cars and connections to other wealthy and educated Rwandans. The message is subtle yet direct: those loyal to the RPF do well in the new Rwanda, while those who question the government will be dealt with harshly.[11]

Itorero produces a special class of militarized citizen called *intore*. In precolonial Rwanda, the title of *intore* was given only to soldiers who served and protected the king as patriots and war heroes.[12] Contemporary *intore* learn military values as the foundation of modern culture, including songs and poems celebrating Rwanda's precolonial golden age and praising the country's renaissance under the RPF. This narrative of redemption is best found in the song "Victory to the Children of Rwanda" (*Intsinzi bana b'Urwanda*), the refrain of which regularly rings out in public gatherings and across the hills. Its chords hailed the RPF capture of State House in July 1994, and it was sung during each of Kagame's presidential campaigns and at other liberation-themed events, including the Kigali Peace Marathon, the cycling Tour du Rwanda and the twentieth anniversary of the genocide commemoration.[13] When the song plays, good Rwandans know to sing aloud or sway along lest they be labeled divisionist or be accused of denying the genocide.

The privilege of becoming *intore* comes with multiple responsibilities, notably as an extra pair of eyes and ears to monitor the daily activities of the general population. Upon graduation, they are tasked with one job—supporting the RPF's broader goal of undoing "genocidal mentalities" while working to reform administrative structures and ethnic identities. According to RPF philosophy, a functioning bureaucracy and Rwandanness combine to deliver peace to Rwandans. Key tasks to build and sustain peace included the ongoing decentralization of government functions and ensuring widespread citizen participation in local decision-making, namely choosing local officials and managing limited resources. These strategies provided the necessary institutional framework and mechanisms of social control that would, by 2006, come to define the Rwandan developmental state, a topic examined further in Chapter 11.

Individual tasks related to rebuilding lives and livelihoods came second to the more fundamental work of participating in government-led unity, reconciliation and development initiatives. Olive, a Hutu girl who returned from the refugee camps along the Zairian border in 1997 at the age of sixteen, laments the new rules. Having lost her parents in the camps, she cares for her three surviving siblings and two orphans of the genocide. Sitting cross-legged on the dirt floor of her single-room *umudugudu* (village) home in northeastern Rwanda, her chin resting on her hands, Olive considers her future: "I am an orphan of the genocide, so I know about pain. But these rules! How can I afford to eat, to send everyone to school and just make sure we survive? It's impossible because I have no adult support, and when I go to my local official to seek help, he gives me a fine for breaking some rule or another. I am also not a real survivor so getting support is hard. Becoming modern is a real challenge."

For others, the government's vision was enticing. For many wealthier and educated Rwandans—particularly those Tutsi who grew up abroad—it represented the end of a long journey of political exclusion and economic marginalization. The promise of belonging as a full-fledged citizen was a heady reward after long suffering. The opportunity to participate in the development of their Rwanda was met with a mixture of glee and determination. It was a welcome challenge—the fruits of being part of the new Rwanda would accrue to those who put in the work. In exchange for the promise of sharing in the economic gains and improved status in society, the government's expectation was loyalty, which broadly meant loyalty to the RPF as a political party.

Mary is in her late forties. She has lived in Kigali with her husband and three children since April 1995. President Kagame appointed her to the Senate in 2003. On a cool and rainy evening in July 2005, we shared drinks at the Hôtel des Mille Collines. The hotel is (in)famous as the subject of the well-known 2004 Hollywood film *Hotel Rwanda*, starring American actor Don Cheadle as general manager Paul Rusesabagina during the genocide. Western audiences embraced the film for its heart-wrenching portrayal of Rusesabagina's efforts to save the lives of more than 1,200 Tutsi holed up in the hotel during the 1994 genocide. Over a glass of Chinese wine, Mary leaned across the table to recount how, as a child, she longed to enjoy the perks of hobnobbing with "other important people." Having been born and raised in a refugee camp in Uganda, she recalled desperately wanting to live in Rwanda, and how fortunate she felt to be able to contribute to her country's development since her return. By her own estimate, Mary had achieved more in her life since returning in 1995 than she ever thought possible. She has a degree from the National University of Rwanda, her husband holds a prestigious senior rank in the military, her children are educated at an English-language private school, while she possesses a government job that "lets me improve myself and my country. I joined the RPF in 1995, grateful for the opportunity to be part of the 'family.'"

Mary waxed lyrical, her clasped hands resting on her heart: "It's truly a blessing to be part of something big. To contribute to something that builds Rwanda and makes our country more peaceful." From our perch on the top-floor balcony, we looked across the capital city, over the hills and valleys leading to the airport on the outskirts of town and farther east toward Tanzania. "Look at our country," Mary implored. "The hills were bare. We [the RPF] have developed them. Now locals [rural Rwandans] have homes and health centers; they have peace. We have provided. The way forward is the RPF way."

Mary failed to mention that many infrastructure improvements were the result of unsafe, low-paid and unskilled labor. Between 1994 and 2000, it was common to see women and men without proper tools, shoes or other safety equipment digging roads, repairing war-damaged buildings and fixing pit latrines. Some of the laborers were prison inmates. Detainees worked from dawn until dusk in their pink prison uniforms at a variety of tasks, such as tilling, terracing, building bridges, repairing health centers and schools and cleaning up churches across the country. As part of their sentence through a unity and reconciliation mechanism known as TIG (the French acronym for "works in the public interest"), prisoners worked to rebuild government-owned buildings and schools, build new homes for genocide survivors and repair roads in Kigali and other town centers.

Leveraging the State

In the minds of Rwandans, the state and the government are one and the same. The directives of the government are implemented by state officials, including senior officials such as Senator Mary, civil servants and the military, as well as individuals who technically appear to be outside the state system, such as civil society leaders, church officials and journalists. The state is omnipresent through Rwanda, and as such is an emotional entity, producing hope and fear, conformity and control. This "community of affect" represents a dual tension for the population: a promise to reduce household poverty and advance ethnic unity, while also ensuring—through credible threats of harm—compliance with government directives.[14] As a result, the state is a source of both self-empowerment and self-preservation, as individuals work to meet the many demands of the RPF, whose rules and regulations bear the full force and weight of the state.

The RPF uses the state's machinery to standardize the implementation of government policy.[15] Standardization is dismissive of the role of individual rural Rwandans and belittles their private realities. RPF officials treat them like children, in need of guidance about the right way to do things. This message is often delivered in patronizing ways. Eric, a newly appointed executive secretary, sums up this condescending, elitist perspective: "I do not like to look at poor people and deal with them. In fact, when I worked in the Ministry, I did not have to look at the poor. That was the level of policies and decisions. It is now in this new function that I am directly confronted with the poor."[16]

A mixture of government incentive, demographic density and Rwanda's hilly terrain combine to explain the impressive ability of the RPF-led government to command authority, mobilize the masses and prompt compliance. By 2002, population density had grown to 345 per square kilometer. More people lived on Rwanda's rolling hills than in 1993, when 255 people occupied a square kilometer.[17] In contrast to the vast expanses of open land that characterize most African countries, Rwanda's densely inhabited hilly landscape has a fishbowl quality. The population density means an absence of private space in rural and urban areas. Rural farmers work every available centimeter of land for food production or grazing livestock. There is a feeling that anyone who wishes can see and know anything, placing considerable power in the hands of local officials, and providing incentives for friends, family and neighbors to betray them in exchange for favors or preferential treatment.[18] The University of Bath African Studies scholar Andrea Purdeková explains this "sphere of vision" as the "experience of being seen—whether real or suspected—[affecting] the performance of those under state watch."[19]

Many Rwandan citizens claim to feel watched, and they are. The government aims to produce individual compliance through its many legal rules and cultural codes, including a vast surveillance network. The RPF oversees "local life through administrative presence."[20] Respect for authority and hierarchy is everything. Political and military elites dictate policy, programs and practice down to local government officials, who then ensure that the rural masses carry out the orders as instructed. Local leaders, in turn, monitor the activities and speech of individuals within their bailiwick. Compliance with government directives is paramount, as is knowing and respecting one's spot in the hierarchy. It is common to see poor, rural Rwandans supplicating before local officials in hopes of securing much-needed social benefits, and then to observe those same local authorities deferring to their higher-ups. Naturally, President Kagame is at the top of the pyramid. Rwanda's hierarchical political structure has its origins in precolonial monarchy: the pecking order has merely been refined by successive political leaders. The RPF and President Kagame are but the most recent beneficiaries of this centralized and stratified system.

Class Status

Individual ability to anticipate and cope with the many demands of government is shaped more by socio-economic class than by ethnicity. For the average Rwandan, class is a structural reality more than a marker of identity. A person's class is informed by the degrees of inequality experienced as a result of economic position, social status and access to networks of persons of prominence. Your location in the hierarchy further shapes how you are likely to exploit degrees of difference. Knowing your station in life and understanding who is more or less important than you is central to successfully navigating Rwandan social and political life. Lesser or low-status Rwandans understand "being important" or "being a high person" as code for people who are more powerful than they are, just as important people know their equals and superiors. Poor people—Tutsi, Hutu and Twa—call those in positions of power over them *abaryi* (eaters), highlighting their awareness that they are unable to make ends meet, while officials appear to get fat at the trough of government.

In 2001, as part of the Vision 2020 policy, the Ministry of Finance and Economic Planning (MINECOFIN) formalized Rwanda's class structure, with the goal of providing evidence for funding the RPF's poverty reduction policies to foreign donors.[21] The logic is simple: understanding economic class allows authorities to work with Rwanda's poor to address their poverty. In addition, having government officials at the lowest levels of the bureaucracy makes service delivery more efficient. Making poverty visible is the first step in reducing poverty. It is a laudable goal, but one that comes with increased government presence in the lives of Rwandans.

Vision 2020 sets out six categories of class. The peasantry is made of four categories of differing degrees of poverty. In 2002, some 80 percent of Rwanda's population lived in rural areas, as subsistence farmers or peasants. Lowest in the hierarchy are those living in abject poverty (*abatindi nyakujya*); next highest are the destitute (*abatindi*); above them are the poor (*abakene*). Taken together, these three categories represent the poorest of the poor, making up the majority of rural residents: *abatindi nyakujya, abatindi* and *abakene* represent approximately 66 percent of Rwandans. The fourth and highest category of the proletariat is the salaried poor (*abakene wifashije*), which is the socioeconomic class of many elected local officials, representing about 14 percent of the population.[22] The rich without money (*abakungu*) and rich (*abakire*) represent the educated urbanites at the top of Rwanda's class hierarchy.[23]

One's proper place in the hierarchy determines personal access to often scarce resources, which, in turn, depend on one's social, political and economic networks. The abject poor, for example, are universally

---

Table 3. Postgenocide Socio-economic Hierarchy in Rwanda

Umutindi nyakujya (*abatindi nyakujya*, pl.)	Abject poor
Umutindi (*abatindi*, pl.)	Destitute
Umukene (*abakene*, pl.)	Poor
Umukene wifashije (*abakene wifashije*, pl.)	Salaried poor
Umukungu (*abakungu*, pl.)	Rich without money
Umukire (*abakire*, pl.)	Rich

shunned, save for when there is an unpleasant or risky task at hand. Espérance, an elderly ethnic Twa woman, saved the lives of a handful of destitute and poor Tutsi she knew during the 1994 genocide. Her marginal status combined with her Twa identity allowed her to safely help them and avoid being found by the Hutu killing squads. "Before the genocide, almost everyone ignored me," spat Espérance. "So hiding Tutsi was easy because no one came to see if I was okay, or to ask my sons to join in the killing, so I could easily save them." Since then, Espérance has been able to forge loose ties with the friends and family of the Tutsi she helped save. Even so, these only go so far. Espérance notes, with tears in her eyes, that when the crops fail to produce enough for everyone to eat their share, she and her family are the first to be excluded.

Rwandans in the destitute, poor and salaried poor categories work to maintain their often tenuous grip on critical resources—land, food and housing. Social mobility is unlikely, although it is common to hear mothers urging their children to study hard in hopes that education can break the poverty cycle. The salaried poor provide a ready pool of volunteer local officials, as working with the government (even in an unpaid capacity) can boost an individual, and his or her family, into the coveted rich without money class.[24] Those in the rich without money category experience a double bind: they are closest to the power, prestige and privilege of the elite rich with money, but still struggle to maintain a sometimes slippery grip on their "important" social status. As the category from which most appointed and paid government officials emerge, the rich without money are most likely to be caught between receiving central government directives and ensuring their implementation in the categories of poor below them.[25] In Rwanda's image-conscious and rule-based society, being rich without money is stressful; individuals are aware of how close they are to the top, and how easily they could tumble down. They also know that those lower down the ladder will likely let them fall, as their tenuous status makes helping someone who has slipped a risky proposition.

The burden of success or failure is placed squarely on the shoulders of individuals with little regard for the emotional or physical legacies of class. Consider the rule that forbids walking barefoot in Kigali and other towns. Since rural producers must go to government-mandated markets to sell their wares, being unable to wear rubber flip-flops and open-toed shoes or to be barefoot in public places in urban centers furthers their economic exclusion. For those who cannot afford to go to market to provide for their families, RPF invocations to participate in economic life appear contradictory. As Boston University political scientist Timothy Longman notes: "Rather than fighting poverty," these laws "fight signs of poverty."[26] The official narrative is that covered shoes improve hygiene, but the result is that the need to own covered shoes becomes politicized— for many of Rwanda's poorest citizens, not having them becomes a barrier to access to the economic centers of the country. Sunny, a 43-year-old destitute Hutu man who was released from prison in 2006, notes drily: "I heard that Jeannette [President Kagame's wife] owns the new Bata shoe factory in Kigali. Bata makes covered shoes, so now we all wear them."[27]

Being so poor that one cannot afford shoes is more than a barrier to public life: it results in feelings of insecurity, anxiety and stress for Rwandans who struggle to meet the many demands of development. Eugenie, a 24-year-old Tutsi survivor of the genocide, whispered her displeasure: "I swear this government passes rules to make it impossible to live. They tell us to feel proud to be Rwandan. The words are inspirational and I admire the efforts of my government. But it's like those who make decisions don't really know how things are at the grassroots. The exact situation is difficult to explain, but there is no way to really talk about it without feeling pressured."

In time, the structures and hierarchies of the RPF—as the dominant political party, the Rwandan Defense Force, and the administrator of the state—ran into and over one another, making it difficult for people to avoid the exacting demands of good citizenship. It was within this tightly interlaced framework that the government sought to mobilize the population for development and unity via activities such as *ubudehe* (community mobilization for poverty reduction), *umuganda* (communal public works), *urugerero* (national service), *umushyikirano* (national leadership summits), *ingando* (citizenship solidarity reeducation camps) and *gacaca* (community-based genocide courts).[28] Local government officials were charged with implementing these initiatives, which made them the most powerful individuals in the lives of those who were expected to fulfill the new requirements of citizenship.

Institutional mobilization to force individuals to serve the state is nothing new. The idea of customary labor is rooted in Rwandan social and political structures. The practice of communal work (*umuganda*) is a good example. President Habyarimana reintroduced *umuganda* to Rwandans in the mid-1970s. His version was not identical to precolonial and colonial expectations, when rural people had to provide their labor in service to their local chieftain or colonial official (known as *akazi*). Instead, Habyarimana's MRND established communal labor as a Rwandan development tool.[29] The *umuganda* tradition continues under the RPF. Citizens are now expected to attend monthly *umuganda* meetings, with the broader goal of nurturing a shared national identity.

The Family

By 2005, the RPF had expanded its reach through to "the soft and encompassing language of family."[30] Families are Rwanda's smallest political unit. The home is where children learn how to behave in public and private, what is expected of them in society, and about ethnic identity.[31] The home is where a person must unlearn ethnic hatred, a message directed primarily to non-Tutsi families, as it is thought mostly Hutu need educating on the values of ethnic unity and being part of the Rwandan family. Newly released prisoners are especially targeted for indoctrination and repeatedly reminded of the need to set a good example, best demonstrated by answering immediately when authorities call, obeying orders and not "causing trouble."[32]

The family is responsible for the proper upbringing of children and the RPF is now front and center in this process. President Kagame is positioned as the father of the nation, a role with deep historical meaning, since the prosperity of the nation is tied up in the physical and spiritual health of the Rwandan leader.[33] It is Kagame's duty to provide for Rwanda, in the same way that fathers are expected to provide for their families in societies characterized by patriarchal gender norms. In precolonial Rwanda, the king assured the fertility of the land and livestock through agrarian rituals. The powers of the king extended to a small group of royal ritualists (*abiru*) who helped him assure the health of the nation by preventing invasions, curbing natural disaster, and maintaining a war footing to repel invaders.[34] The idea of the president as father of the nation is hardly a new feature of Rwandan political culture. Governance has always been shaped by a cult of leadership. This tendency extends back to precolonial times, when the orders of the king were the law of the land, just as they were under postcolonial Presidents Kayibanda and Habyarimana. By the end of 1973, all Rwandans were required by law to be card-holding members of Habyarimana's MRND; indeed, anyone born during his regime was automatically registered as a party member. This all-encompassing approach to governance continues under the RPF, albeit with a slightly different tone and a more intense tenor.

Ranking RPF officials, including President Kagame in his many domestic speeches, use the language of family (*umuryango*) to shame Rwandans into becoming party members. The message is clear: good citizens are members of the RPF family. Those who do not join are unreliable "outsiders" who want to destabilize Rwanda's security. Non-family members are suspect, and must be reported to military and political officials as people who are against national unity or "divisionist." Outsiders cause "instability" as they refuse to "build the country together."[35] Ever the reprimanding parent—whether speaking to senior government and

159

military officials, or the rural masses—Kagame typically adopts a professorial stance, carefully admonishing Rwandans to do what is expected of them so national development can take root and flourish.

In the time the RPF has held power, the list of expectations in the name of national unity and development has lengthened. In 2001, the RPF introduced an "oath-of-oneness," a civic pledge that requires all civil society leaders, university staff and student leaders, local administrators and others in leadership positions to publicly pledge allegiance: "I solemnly swear before the [RPF] men that I will work for the RPF family, that I will always defend its interests, and that, if I divulge its secrets, I will be decapitated like any other traitor."[36] Although there are rare instances where enterprising individuals have avoided the demands of party membership, usually anyone who tries to avoid taking the pledge is harassed and intimidated into submission.

Government ministers and other senior officials also take the oath, doing so directly at the Office of the President. Their pledges are recorded as evidence of their accountability to the party. The RPF perceives failure to take the oath as a vote against it, which makes it difficult to avoid membership. Public pressure to show governmental support triggers stock answers that only bolster the RPF's official narrative of unity and development. Party membership equally determines one's access to the perks and promise of political power. During a walk in his Kigali neighborhood, Mohammad, a twenty-something graduate of the RPF's militarized *itorero* program, said: "Staying out of politics is hard. Even when you try to keep from entering politics, politics enters you."[37] Spéciose, a 54-year-old widow of genocide and a volunteer *gacaca* judge, reflected this view: "To survive politics in this country is to know how to walk on eggs without breaking them. If you break the eggs, trouble is around the corner."

Unsurprisingly, RPF party loyalists and members of aligned political groups have an overall rosier perception of Kagame's rule than do poor rural residents or those elites who have fallen out with the government. This "captivated minority" of government supporters generally believe in and indeed directly benefit from RPF rule, just as those loyal to former President Habyarimana benefited from his rule until the dying days of his regime.[38]

Loyalty First

Captivated elites are most likely to act as government cheerleaders, benefiting as they do from their enthusiastic support for RPF policy and practice. As the 2003 presidential and parliamentary elections drew near, RPF handlers—government spokespersons and RPF-vetted journalists—set the scene. The RPF's pitch to voters was simple: a democratic mandate to remake Rwanda would allow the RPF to focus exclusively on the task of promoting ethnic unity and economic development. By the time the elections were over, the RPF had successfully consolidated national power, with Kagame winning 95 percent of the presidential vote. The RPF's resounding victory was a foregone conclusion. In the preceding decade, Rwanda's political opposition had been cowed, journalists silenced, and civil society coopted or eliminated. Nonetheless, the 2003 elections gave the appearance of civic and political rights; in other words, democracy without substance. Some donors expressed disappointment with the outcome while still considering Rwanda a special case deserving of their continued financial and moral support.

Behind closed doors, the US, the UK and the Netherlands raised concerns about the ban on political activity, highlighting a contradiction in the RPF's rationale: if national security was fully under control, why not open up the political sphere to competition? However quiet, President Kagame tolerated no external criticism, particularly from an international community that failed to stop the 1994 genocide. In his usual fashion, the president linked criticism of his government to genocide denial: "Those who have divergent interpretations of how and why the genocide occurred are revisionists and/or proponents of the theory of double genocide [of Hutu by Tutsi]."[39]

Equating criticism to genocide denial has been an effective RPF tactic since 1994. The RPF adroitly denied all criticisms about the lack of political competition before international audiences, and asserted to domestic ones that restrictions on party activity were necessary to assure national unity, given Rwanda's history of violence. When donors pushed the RPF to clarify its position, the government portrayed its authoritarian tendencies as benign, declaring that it was committed to a democratic transition. Opportunities for any political opposition to operate freely and on an equal footing with the RPF in both urban and rural areas evaporated. As a result, the 2010 and 2017 parliamentary and presidential elections were also uncontested.[40]

The 2003 elections did not permit input from Rwandans. Only two candidates challenged Kagame; the MDR fielded Faustin Twagiramungu who returned from exile in Belgium to campaign. Despite the MDR's best try, it was hardly a contender. The National Electoral Commission (NEC) banned the party before campaigning had begun; still Twagiramungu attracted almost 4 percent of the vote, running as an independent candidate.[41] The remaining parties threw their support behind President Kagame. Alternate visions for Rwanda's political future simply did not exist. The RPF leadership read Twagiramungu's meager vote tally as evidence that some Hutu were voting along ethnic lines. This interpretation allowed them to double down on efforts to root out anyone perceived as holding genocide ideology in their heart. Even as the RPF cracked down on free speech, journalists and other observers continued to wholeheartedly venerate the president.

Weeding Out Deniers

By 2001, talking about ethnicity had become the equivalent of supporting the genocide. Good citizens spoke only of being Rwandan. The revised 2003 Constitution made public references to ethnic identity illegal (article 33) and criminalized "ethnic divisionism" and "trivializing the genocide" (article 13). New laws against "ethnic sectarianism" and "genocide ideology" were passed. Used to police language in public and at home, the laws were vaguely defined yet broadly applied by judges.[42]

Constitutional provisions reinforced a 2001 criminal law on sectarianism that punishes public incitement to ethnic discrimination or divisionism by up to five years in prison, heavy fines or both. In the run-up to the 2003 elections, the RPF formalized the idea of "genocide ideology" as a rhetorical weapon to control the contours of political speech. Literally meaning the ideas that lead to genocide (*ingengabitek-erezo ya jenoside*), genocide ideology would come to limit more than freedom of expression. Genocide ideology and negationist laws presume that all Hutu men participated in the 1994 genocide, despite a glaring lack of "evidence that most ordinary perpetrators subscribe to these views."[43] Consequently, the laws served to remove ethnic Hutu from the public sphere. Everyday usage of the term *itsembabwoko* (genocide) became suspect, and it all but disappeared from the official narrative, eventually making its usage both subversive and punishable by law.[44]

The RPF had legitimate concerns about genocide denial. There is, particularly among Rwandans in the diaspora, including some Hutu political elites, a thriving culture of genocide denial. According to their ethnocentric views, the events of 1994 were the product of Hutu self-defense in the context of civil war. Ironically, the RPF's strict use of genocide ideology as a tool to control free speech has served to prompt extremist positions, minimizing or denying the genocide, among Hutu political opponents.

From the perspective of many ordinary Rwandans, the use of the language of genocide ideology is the RPF's way to control what people are thinking and how they relate to one another. Former prison inmates feel this acutely; they shut up to fit in. Thomas, who was released from jail for lack of evidence in 2002, laments the challenges of participating in public life:

> When we go to *umuganda* everyone knows which of us [Hutu] is a
> released prisoner. Tutsi neighbors tell [officials] that they are too
> afraid to work next to us, particularly when we work with machetes.
> Then you see them later and they laugh because we had to do their
> labor. I was released for lack of evidence but that does not matter. I
> am Hutu so I am guilty.

The government also targeted independent journalists, labeling them
purveyors of divisionist opinion, and strictly controlled women's groups
and self-help cooperatives as well as churches and mosques. When
asked in 2001 about this overarching control, Minister of Foreign
Affairs Charles Murigande explained that the RPF could not leave the
elections to chance, as it was not yet clear that "the population should be
left alone to elect competent leaders."[45]

It was all more of the same. Few doubted that the ruling RPF would
fail to handily capture the parliamentary and presidential majority.
Campaigning was nothing but veiled coercion. Local officials lectured
Rwandans in pre-election sensitization meetings about voting for the
"right" candidate. In the wee hours of the morning before the election,
local officials and party loyalists went door to door rousing sleeping
Rwandans to get to the polling stations. Mobile provider MTN delivered mass text messages reminding people of the need to vote correctly.
In all corners of the country, individuals were cajoled to vote, then
queued to vote for the "right" candidate under the watchful eye of armed
soldiers.[46] President Kagame officially won re-election with 95 percent
of the vote. The ruling party claimed the extraordinary majority to be a
sign of reconciliation, noting that majority Hutu had voted for the RPF.

The NEC, a government body stacked with RPF loyalists, was
responsible for all aspects of the campaign and balloting, including
setting up electoral infrastructure, voter registration, regulating candidate nominations, and ensuring civic and voter education. The RPF
revised the constitution before the polls to reserve a certain number of

seats for women, youth and the disabled. The combination of reserved seats and party-list quotas gave Rwanda the highest percentage of women (48.8 percent) in parliament in the world at the time, something for which Rwanda won hearty approval from international donors and admirers.[47]

Rwanda's many fans failed to appreciate the extent of the RPF's political savvy. In fact, the RPF merely gave the appearance of a substantive parliament staffed by competent, hardworking and dedicated women and men.[48] Instead of a stronger democracy, the electoral result revealed a political system designed for control rather than dialogue. By the end of 2003, the higher echelons of power were firmly in the hands of a few men, notably President Kagame and his inner circle of political, military and business advisors. Political moderates, male or female, had been purged from the public sphere, giving the RPF near total control of all aspects of daily life. Uncontested authority allowed the government to concentrate on its commitment to remake Rwandan society in its singular vision. With its goal of maximum economic growth in the shortest amount of time, the government sought to mobilize all Rwandans to the work of developing the country.

9

GOOD CITIZENS

As soon as the elections were over, President Kagame returned his party's attention to growing the economy. With political control, the RPF could now begin to sow the seeds of liberation. Producing good citizens who would focus on development while eschewing politics required mass socialization into the rules of postgenocide political life. The goal was to a create a marketplace for political goods—jobs, health care and other perks for ordinary citizens, Hutu in particular—in exchange for unquestioning loyalty. Donors, unaware of the punitive side of crafting good citizens, welcomed this approach, consolidating the RPF's status as a donor darling, with Vision 2020 the emblem of Kagame's leadership acumen. The policy attracted considerable foreign praise as a model of how post-conflict governments in Africa and elsewhere should remake their economies.[1]

The government's first Poverty Reduction Strategy Plan (PRSP), in 2002, outlined the macroeconomic, structural and social policies of developing economies to reduce poverty. Periodically updated and revised in 2008 and 2013, Rwanda's PRSPs are a roadmap, informing its progress reports on meeting development goals, while courting donor aid through clearly articulated policy goals. The anti-poverty goals of Vision 2020 and Rwanda's first PRSP conveniently overlapped with the United Nations Millennium Development Goals.

Rwanda's first PRSP included the government's iconic education policy—free primary schooling for all. At first glance, the RPF's education policy appeared to be a striking success. By 2014, the official primary school attendance rate had soared to 96.7 percent. A closer look reveals a less impressive reality.[2] Only 36 percent of primary students enter secondary school. For girls, the primary school graduation rate is a meager 28 percent. Mandatory costs for uniforms, textbooks and other expenses make schooling a luxury for many families. Public school classrooms are so crowded that the school day is split into two periods, meaning one group of students attends classes in the morning and the second in the afternoon.[3]

Agnes, a sixteen-year-old aspiring student, lamented her inability to go on to secondary school: "We are told how to develop ourselves, how to put unity before all else. The government says Vision 2020 can help us thrive. If we don't thrive, it is because of our poor mentality. This government wants us to change, but the path is not easy. How can I be flexible for development when I can't enroll for lack of space?" Agnes' experience, like that of many Rwandans, highlights the tension between the RPF's development aspirations and local realities.

The real outcome of Rwanda's education policy is a low-quality education that does not yet produce "a large cohort of primary and secondary school leavers with a basic set of skills."[4] In fact, both before the genocide and since, Rwandans average just 3.3 years of schooling, despite RPF claims that by 2015 Rwandans received on average almost 11 years of education. Access to higher education and the lifestyle choices that go with it are largely a pipedream.

Promises of access to education ring hollow for many young Rwandans. For them, rural life is relatively isolated, where people are just trying to get by, as they did before the 1994 genocide. Income inequality is a painful reality for many Rwandans—young people in particular—as their inequality of opportunity is deeply felt. Environmental degradation, including shifting rainfall patterns, hotter and drier weather, as well as diminishing soil quality, further shapes individual and family choices for Rwanda's rural majority. GDP numbers do not capture the local barter and self-help economies where Rwandans share food, help each other during planting and harvest cycles, and provide care to children, widows, the elderly and other vulnerable individuals. Despite the government's lofty policy promises, rural people still live life on the margins. There are few opportunities to improve their standard of living or quality of life.

All the same, the RPF claims that youth and women are central to Rwanda's imagined future, where Hutu and Tutsi live in harmony, and where the spoils of economic development mean that everyone has enough to eat, can access government services, and is safe and secure. Young people are a government policy priority: 42 percent of Rwandans are younger than fourteen, and an additional 19 percent are under twenty-four years of age.[5] Rwandan women over the age of thirty-five make up a disproportionately high percentage of the population, as fewer men than women survived the genocide, and of those who did, many ended up in prison, which meant they did not actively contribute to the economy.[6] Contributing to GDP is a must in the new Rwanda.

Farmers whose livelihood depends on what they grow are understandably risk-averse: crop failure can spell disaster for them and their families. Even so, the government's drive to develop shows little regard for rural realities. The national land policy, introduced in 2000, is one example of this indifference. With an aim to "modernize agriculture" and encourage the "rational use of land," the national land policy has, in fact, increased the vulnerability of rural families.[7] Rwanda's mountainous terrain, combined with variations in soil quality, means that few families have enough arable land to provide for their basic nutritional needs. Dispersed plots, while less productive, are often shared in alliances with other families, and serve as a form of collective insurance for peasants—enough crops are harvested to provide sufficient food for basic survival. However, the national land policy considers usage for basic survival irrational and makes it illegal for families to work together to tend their fields as local growing and climatic conditions allow. The RPF ordered local officials to appropriate "irrationally" used land and gave large plots to "senior government and military officials and important businessmen" who now use the land for commercial purposes.[8]

Displaced rural Rwandans experienced the double insult of not being compensated for their expropriated land and not being hired to work for a daily wage for the new rich (*abakire*) landowners. Many complained that individuals from outside their communities were brought in to work the fields. Joseph B., a destitute Hutu man, said: "We don't even benefit from their employment. How are we supposed to eat without land?" Janvier, a poor Tutsi man, further lamented: "The new landowners have brought their own people to work their land; they live here now and have changed everything. First they take our land, then they bring their own people to cultivate it? How can we eat? How can we exist? We cannot afford most things. It is very hard."[9]

Local officials read Joseph's and Janvier's comments as laziness or opposition to Vision 2020. Their words are better interpreted as resistance to a policy that works against their interests as rural producers. Again, the government has little concern for the peasantry. By 2006, according to the RPF, rural poverty had decreased by nearly 12 percent. The RPF explained its success to satisfied donors as the result of wise policies to improve agricultural production, slow population growth, and ameliorate infrastructure. No explanation was offered for Rwanda's rising Gini coefficient, a measure used by economists to assess income inequality.[10] Operating on a scale from zero to one, Gini numbers closer to one represent greater inequality. According to the World Bank, Rwanda's Gini had risen to 0.53 in 2013, up from 0.29 in the mid-1980s. Increased income inequality did not deter the ruling RPF, and the government continued to rigidly implement the various elements of the Vision 2020 policy.

Unity as Conformity

Not unlike Vision 2020, the policy of national unity and reconciliation is an ambitious social engineering project that seeks to control the population through coerced consent. Its primary task is to forge a unified Rwandan identity while fostering reconciliation between genocide survivors and perpetrators. The National Unity and Reconciliation Commission is charged with overseeing the top-down implementation of unity activities. There are two substantive programs—Civic Education, and Conflict Management and Peace Building—staffed by young Anglophone returnees, mostly from Uganda. Regular consultative meetings are held, including a biannual National Summit, to ensure that government agencies, political parties, local officials and Rwandans "from all walks of life respect and observe the policy of national unity and reconciliation."[11] Staff organize community festivals to promote unity and reconciliation, provide funds for students' clubs, and consult with other government bodies to ensure full compliance with the policy of national unity and reconciliation.[12]

To counteract the presumed ingrained ethnic disunity learned during the postcolonial period, the RPF dedicates significant state resources to educating the population on the importance of unity. Among the government's primary tools for "reeducation" are mandatory citizenship reeducation camps known as *ingando*. For periods ranging from several days to several months, politicians, church leaders, ex-combatants, released prisoners, *gacaca* judges and incoming university students all attend *ingando*, to study government programs and Rwandan history, and learn how to unify and reconcile.[13]

Ingando lecturers, most of whom are RPF party members, teach participants the government's official interpretation of history, as presented in the policy of national unity and reconciliation.[14] To many participants, notably Hutu who experienced the events of 1957 to 1962, the history taught at *ingando* camps is offensive. Unsurprisingly, the camps also teach pupils not to question the RPF's vision of national unity. Augustin graduated from *ingando* after being released from prison in 2005. He sees reeducation as something designed to exclude Hutu from public life: "I am a former Hutu. This means I am a source of shame for this government. They think only Hutu killed. *Ingando* is just a way for [the RPF] to make sure we don't think for ourselves. The message is clear: we are not full citizens."

For all its inherent repression, reeducation is a crucial step to climb before demobilized soldiers, and other combatants who fought along-side the genocidal forces, are allowed to return home. Contrary to donor expectations that the RPF would mistreat demobilized combatants during reintegration, most returned to their home communities without much fuss or fanfare following sensitization training. Indeed, RPF efforts to disarm, demobilize and reintegrate soldiers are broadly recognized as a success, with *ingando* providing a direct path back to civilian life with minimum resentment from genocide survivors.[15] Through *ingando* newly demobilized Hutu men rejoined their home communities or settled in *imidugudu* villages, with the blessing of the RPF leadership.

Tutsi survivors of the genocide did not always welcome demobilized Hutu, as the presence of a possible killer in the neighborhood was unsettling. Even so, most survivors accepted their presence as everyone knew there was nowhere else for these men to go. As demobilization was voluntary, many of those who returned had not participated in genocide and were not worried about being falsely accused of crimes they did not commit. The RPF understood the necessity for demobi-lized men to make a smooth and expedient transition to civilian life; they were needed in the countryside to take up roles as productive, tax-paying members of society.

Instruction on how Rwandans should become unified came down from the top of government. The RPF introduced new national holidays—Heroes Day (February 1), Day of Hope (April 7), Liberation Day (July 4) and Patriotism Day (October 1)—to chime with its vision of ethnic unity, and serve as platforms for leaders to remind Rwandans of the need to fight genocide ideology. It adopted new national symbols in 2001—flag, anthem and emblem—as the existing ones symbolized the genocide and encouraged an ideology of genocide and divisionism. According to a senior Ministry of Culture official, "the old [symbols] are stained with Tutsi blood. We need a fresh start with new symbols to represent Rwanda as it is: peaceful and prosperous."[16]

The old flag was based on the Belgian flag and was made up of three vertical bands, one red, one yellow and one green with the letter "R" in the middle. For the RPF, updating the flag was important because of its association with Hutu domination over Tutsi. The new flag is made up of three horizontal stripes: green on the bottom, yellow in the middle and light blue on top, with a beaming sun on the right side. Green represents the promise of prosperity through the "modern and rational use of the country's resources"; the yellow band, the sun's rays, represents the hope of economic development and the "awakening" of the Rwandan people from "old tendencies of hatred"; blue represents "peace and stability for all."

Some were baffled by the introduction of new national symbols. Emmanual, a Tutsi survivor of the genocide, noted that the new symbols "seemed to be designed for those who returned after the war" rather than "to facilitate peace and security." Tharcisse, a Hutu who was released from prison in 2004, thought that the new symbols were an effort to "remind those like me that Rwanda no longer belongs to us."

Beyond new national holidays and emblems, the RPF encourages collective memory of the genocide through vast memorial sites and mass graves that double as museums to illustrate the end-result of ethnic divisionism. In sites across the country, victims' lime-drenched skulls, bones, clothing and personal items are on display, exposed on shelves, in semi-open tombs, or in the schoolrooms or on church benches where the killing occurred. The message is clear: never again will there be genocide, thanks to the watchful eye of the RPF.

For many viewers, and particularly survivors, the crude display of human remains is a reminder of the government's politicization of the genocide, and its overall lack of concern for individual emotional healing. Bernadette is a Tutsi survivor who owns a thriving restaurant in Gitarama town. She offers harsh condemnation:

> I survived the genocide and so did my husband. Our children died. To see bodies that might be theirs on display is sickening. It is also clear to me that they do it for *abazungu* [white-skinned] visitors. Rwanda's story is meant to shock, to show them that the RPF is doing everything to train us to be better human beings. But they show no concern for us. When it comes to memorials and mourning, affecting outsiders is more important than caring for locals.
>
> This language of "never again" is just a way to market the genocide if you ask me. It brings in tourists who want to see what happened here. I make a good living because tourists come to visit memorials here. It feels like blood money because I know that many of them leave here thinking the RPF is doing a good job.
>
> You would not believe the kinds of questions *abazungu* ask us about the genocide—did your relatives die? Did you participate in the killing? You must feel so safe in the new Rwanda they say. You must be impressed with justice and reconciliation they say. It's absurd. They don't know that we Rwandans are tied together by secrets.

Secrets permeate Rwanda's most extensive instrument of national unity, the *gacaca* courts, established in 2001. Opting for maximal justice, the RPF chose community-based courts over other post-conflict reconciliation mechanisms, such as amnesty for crimes committed, or a truth commission. Some post-conflict efforts at justice and reconciliation endorse amnesty as a legal tool that either bars or nullifies prosecution of war crimes, crimes against humanity and other heinous crimes. In so doing, amnesty aims to bring enemy combatants into the new political and military order and preempt a return to hostilities by including key opponents in the post-conflict system. Truth commissions are government-led bodies tasked with discovering and revealing past wrongs and abuses by all parties to a conflict so that a common historical record can be established. Like amnesties, truth commissions presume truth-telling to be the backbone of justice and reconciliation efforts. They allow victims to talk about what they experienced and provide perpetrators a space to atone for their actions, often in exchange for reduced criminal and civil prosecution.[17] The RPF chose neither; an airing of crimes committed before, during and after the genocide was never a priority. Instead, the leadership chose to revive traditional *gacaca* courts as the best way to prosecute genocide crimes while assuring government control of the process.

Traditionally, the courts were not designed to try serious crimes like genocide.[18] Literally meaning "grass," *gacaca* was once a process through which male elders navigated disputes on small patches of grass inside traditional homesteads. The entire community was not involved, as they now are since the genocide. Instead, wise elders, known as *inyangamugayo* (literally, those who detest disgrace), resolved conflicts within and between families over mundane matters including marital issues, conflicts over property and inheritance rights, as well as personal grudges. The goal was restitution in order to maintain harmony at home and social order in the community. Sanctions were likely the responsibility of the family. Resolution of the dispute was marked with sips of banana beer through a single straw, as a show of reconciliation. Unlike modern *gacaca*, the purpose was not to determine individual guilt or to apply state law.

Initially, the RPF had no intention of rolling out genocide grassroots justice akin to traditional *gacaca*. But the Ministry of Justice soon realized the magnitude of the task of bringing as many genocide perpetrators as possible to justice. By 1998, the RPF had selected *gacaca* as the best way to assure accountability while also providing an avenue to sensitize the rural masses to the virtues of democracy. Furthermore, the courts would allow the RPF to link the provision of justice to its decentralization of political and economic structures, which had begun in 2000. The government's policy of maximal prosecution also meant mass participation in rendering justice. For the RPF, the genocide was a collective offence. As such, genocide justice required a collective solution in the form of updated and improved *gacaca* courts.

Justice through *gacaca* was only possible in the early 2000s, as the RPF wanted first to ensure control over the process. How genocide crimes would be tried had been under discussion since 1995, when the government first hosted high-level meetings with donors on the topic. Like other mechanisms of national unity, the *gacaca* courts operate on an unspoken but convenient premise that censors what can be said about the 1994 genocide while invoking the specter of future ethnic violence to silence government critics and ordinary people alike. The result is that people speak about the violence they or their loved ones experienced in hushed tones or not at all.

However, initially, the *gacaca* courts, which ran from 2005 to 2012, appeared to offer an exception to such silences. Proponents of the courts claimed Rwandans would be able to speak about what they experienced and witnessed during the genocide in these community-based, open-air courts whose primary task was to provide justice and reconciliation for all who participated.[19]

Under the *gacaca* system, local communities came together to witness, identify, corroborate and prosecute those responsible for perpetrating the genocide. The *gacaca* courts had jurisdiction over genocide and crimes against humanity committed between October 1, 1990 and

December 31, 1994. Atrocities such as the Kibeho massacres and perceived revenge crimes perpetrated by soldiers and civilians aligned with or loyal to the RPF were not openly discussed.

Like other RPF endeavors, it was an ambitious undertaking. The courts put most of the population on trial—as perpetrator, victim, bystander, rescuer or judge—to make accusations and evaluate confessions. There were over ten thousand *gacaca* jurisdictions throughout the country, one for each administrative cell and sector. Community members lined up to vote for RPF-vetted lay judges, 250,000 modern-day *inyangamugayo*, whose task was to ensure that the accused perpetrators tell the truth of what they did during the genocide. Once the truth had been established, survivors were to forgive.

Postgenocide justice was an expensive project. Consequently, the RPF leadership carefully and systematically laid out its justice strategy for donors, with the *gacaca* courts at the center.[20] Donors expressed concern about whether the courts would respect basic legal principles of due process while also providing defense lawyers and judges adequately trained in legal procedure. The government met criticisms of the *gacaca* process and procedure with stories of its restorative role in precolonial Rwanda. Human rights considerations were quickly swept aside in service of the greater good of political stability. The primary qualification for judges was loyalty, or at least the promise of it, to the RPF.[21] Most judges were Hutu men who had been coopted into local RPF party and state administrative structures. Judging offered a way to wield power and gain social status at the local level in a system with few such opportunities. The trade-off was the promise of jobs and other perks for otherwise marginalized Hutu men and women in an RPF-dominated state structure. Largely unaware of the compromises needed to deliver *gacaca* justice, donors also realized there was no alternative way to try over 100,000 individuals for genocide crimes—a monumental task for even the most developed of court systems. Moreover, the government's ownership of the process gave donors the impression the courts would fundamentally support the national unity and reconciliation process, a goal of *gacaca*'s primary donors, the Americans, Belgians, Canadians and Dutch.

Gacaca began as a pilot project in June 2002, was refined in 2004, and launched nationwide in January 2005. It operated in three key phases: the pilot phase from 2002 to 2005, which launched an ongoing public sensitization campaign, lasting from 2002 to 2012, to educate Rwandans on *gacaca*'s goals; the information-gathering phase from 2005 to 2008; and the judgment phase from 2006 to 2012.[22] The courts wrapped in June 2012, having heard almost two million cases in communities across Rwanda.[23]

The courts took an adversarial and prosecutorial approach that prioritized the appearance of justice. It established what the University of Antwerp anthropologist Bert Ingelaere calls "a forensic truth."[24] He means that the RPF prioritized the retelling of its sanctioned truth about what happened during the genocide over actual or sincere expressions of truth, telling of what happened, how and by whom. For many Rwandans, the expectations of performing before the *gacaca* courts in ways that were acceptable to government monitors was an additional burden at a time when most citizens could barely find enough food to eat. As Jeanne, a poor middle-aged widow of the genocide said wistfully: "There can be no peace in the heart if there is no peace in the stomach."[25]

For many Tutsi survivors of the genocide, women in particular, *gacaca* became yet another place where the RPF rules of how to behave prevailed. Young women explained that they offered their forgiveness to their Hutu brothers either to avoid disappointing male Hutu relatives or simply to comply with the RPF's reconciliation agenda. Others, particularly middle-aged men and women, offered forgiveness as it provided them with some measure of physical safety in their home communities. Few survivors believed that reconciliation in any form was possible, given the serious nature of genocide crimes. Most felt that punishment in any form was insufficient, even as some understood that their Hutu brothers had been put in an impossible situation of kill or be killed. Empathy was in short supply, as Hutu perpetrators—accused and confessed—tried to recount their crimes in ways that minimized their responsibility.

Whatever one's role before the court, the general consensus is that the *gacaca* process did not produce a rich account of who did what to whom during the 1994 genocide. Ultimately, *gacaca* short-circuited individual truths in favor of a government-sanctioned "Truth." Social repair became secondary to government control. For all the lofty rhetoric about justice and reconciliation, in practice the courts were a formal, state-managed space that served to reinforce government authority. There was no space for Rwandans to tell their truth about what happened to them and their loved ones during the genocide.

Managing Threats

RPF officials considered the heartaches of rural people as natural growing pains resulting from the implementation and delivery of national unity and economic development. In Kigali, the government was supremely confident. Bureaucrats, soldiers and private-sector entrepreneurs seized the many opportunities that Vision 2020 presented to them. The capital was abuzz with a sense of promise, and no one embodied that optimism more than President Kagame. His tireless commitment to Rwanda's forward momentum was infectious to all in his orbit. In his 2006 State of the Union address, the president urged Rwandans to hold their heads high now that their country was known around the globe for its professional model of development. To the RPF, there was nothing that could stop Rwanda from achieving its goals of becoming a modern country where all citizens worked hard to put the shameful legacy of the 1994 genocide behind them.

The RPF's enthusiasm was not fully infectious. Some regions were experiencing famine; already vulnerable households struggled to grow enough food to meet even modest caloric needs. The southern region was hit hardest, by widespread drought caused by unusually low rainfall.[26] Heavy rains in other parts of the country yielded the same unfortunate results. For all the government's claims of improved economic growth, many Rwandans remained vulnerable to nutritional shortfalls. In some areas of the country, the poorest of the poor subsisted on grass and weeds. Meanwhile, out-of-touch local and central government officials insisted that famine was not possible in well-managed and self-sufficient Rwanda.

Implementation initiatives of the Vision 2020 policy yielded mixed results. Urban areas benefited significantly more than rural ones. The quality and availability of infrastructure were uneven. Most communities lacked roads, bridges, electricity lines and sanitation facilities. Those who did not live within walking distance of a town remained most vulnerable, notably widows, orphans, people with disabilities, and households headed by minors. Rural poverty was exacerbated by the government's monocropping policy, which made it illegal to grow produce for subsistence needs. Instead, rural farmers were told by local authorities to grow coffee, tea and other foreign-exchange producing commodities. Some local officials were sympathetic to the practical hardships of their rural compatriots, but most forged ahead, implementing the orders they had received from Kigali without considering their impact. Action was the order of the day.

For RPF officials, good citizens were to be apolitical, primed and ready to contribute to development. More importantly still, they had to be willing to trade in civil and political freedoms in exchange for free education, affordable health care, internet connectivity and food security. Louis, a district official in Southern Province, summed up the challenges officials like him face in developing the population: "You talk to them, and you think they listen but the people do nothing with the good advice you give them. They say 'yes' because they are tired of you and your [sensitization] speeches, but they are not convinced. They are resistant. They are really difficult."[27] This push-and-pull between the demands of government and an insufficiently acquiescent population characterized governance in Rwanda both before and after the 1994 genocide.

From the perspective of RPF officials in Kigali, barriers such as famine and poor crop yields were to be overcome with a combination of hard work, self-sacrifice and ingenuity. The decentralization of local governance structures that began in the year 2000 meant that there was little opportunity to escape top-down demands for all Rwandans to "get unified" and "lift themselves out of poverty." President Kagame set the pace. For him, "development is a marathon that must be run as a sprint."[28] Vestine, a middle-aged Twa survivor of the genocide, lamented that the president's sprint did not take into account the fact that not everyone had the resources to keep up. She said: "I know why we have to rush to get unified. The genocide caused everyone harm. But this idea that development can also be quickly gotten? This is naive thinking in a country where the land is tired and people like me are even more tired." Eugene, a recent secondary school graduate whose Tutsi parents were both born in refugee camps in Uganda, sees Kagame's challenge in a different light: "I mean, to be able to participate in development? To see it actually happening with new roads and buildings? This is an honor and I am glad our president is setting the pace."

Ambition, resilience and personal responsibility were essential to "be worthy" of living in, and contributing to, the new Rwanda.[29] As Eugene's words make clear, young Rwandans more readily exhibit such attributes. By 2010, it was a patriotic duty to live life as an entrepreneur. There was no space to question what it meant to be a patriot, or whether or not the RPF's model of a good citizen was anything other than another way to control the hearts and minds of Rwandans.

10

CONFORMITY OR ELSE

The RPF was nothing if not determined and systematic. The government ensured absolute compliance from its citizens through public shaming; individuals submitted to state requirements lest government officials, family and friends see them as "bad." Any so-called "bad" citizen is socially shunned, as well as excluded from unity and development programs. More worryingly still, he or she may be labeled a "genocide denier," "ethnic divisionist" or as someone holding "genocide ideology" in their hearts.[1]

The use of such labels was now commonplace. In 2008, the RPF revised the constitution to legally call the events of 1994 "the genocide against the Tutsi" (*jenoside yakorewe abatutsi*), replacing the everyday language of *itsembabwoko* (genocide).[2] This renaming formalized Tutsi as the sole victims of the genocide and Hutu as its lone perpetrators. In so doing, another layer was added to the collective guilt of Hutu. The renaming of the genocide made symbolic sense, as activist Hutu-led political groups operating outside of Rwanda continued to deny the 1994 genocide or to accuse the RPF of double genocide (of Hutu by

Tutsi). Some foreign academics also subscribe to these hypotheses; government critics use their research to explain the RPF's murderous intentions to eliminate Hutu.[3] As Oxford University political scientist Will Jones notes, the thesis "despite lacking credibility continues to be a fertile source of Rwandan genocide denial."[4]

Also on the agenda was control of the political sphere in the run-up to the 2010 presidential elections. For all the adroit manipulation and subtle control of political space, the authoritarianism of the RPF is ever intact. Competitive elections in such systems are designed to contain threats to the dominance of the ruling party, while eliminating presumed electoral radicals who dare challenge Kagame's preeminence. Rather than allow a level playing field, the RPF prevented the United Democratic Forces–Inkingi (FDU), the Democratic Green Party of Rwanda (DGPR) and the Social Party-Imberakuri (PS) from fielding candidates by preventing them from registering as political parties.[5]

Following Kagame's 2010 presidential electoral victory—claiming 93 percent of the vote—tolerance of the RPF's verbal attacks and harassment of its political opponents briefly wore thin. The RPF's colossal win was later revised down to 78 percent, in response to European Union allegations that Rwanda's elections were not as free and fair as its delegates would have liked. The audit of poll numbers did not result in a more democratic Rwanda, as ballots were allocated to parties already operating in alliance with the RPF.

Throughout the 2010 campaign, the FDU's presidential candidate, Victoire Ingabire Umuhoza, and other senior FDU members proposed that the genocide affected all Rwandans, not just Tutsi. This, unsurprisingly, drew the ire of the RPF. Both Ingabire and the party's general secretary were arrested at different times early in 2010. Ingabire's troubles began at her very first rally. In a January 2010 speech at the Gisozi Genocide Memorial Centre in suburban Kigali, Ingabire implored the government to recognize Hutu lives that were lost in 1994. Ingabire's suggestion was politically tone-deaf, not because it was incorrect—

indeed, her words resonated with many who were unhappy with how RPF-led reconciliation efforts were progressing—but because, by equating Hutu lives lost during the 1994 genocide with Tutsi lives lost, Ingabire essentially denied the genocide. Her statements showed a naive and almost farcical understanding of ethnic relations in Rwanda under the RPF, indicating to many domestic and international observers that she was not a legitimate contender for the presidency.

In view of a government structure that efficiently deploys "a combination of espionage, threats, and violence" to maintain its political and military primacy, Ingabire's words were not well received.[6] In short order, Ingabire became the object of recognizable RPF tactics to control who can say what to whom and when about the 1994 genocide. The RPF stymied FDU efforts to register for the 2010 elections and aimed to weaken its appeal in the countryside without raising negative comment from donors. At first, the RPF engaged in subtle obstruction. Bureaucratic hurdles were raised to prevent party registration. RPF-controlled media outlets denounced FDU leaders. Party activities were placed under perpetual surveillance. In time, these tactics gave way to more direct forms of intimidation and harassment at rallies and organizational meetings. The RPF publicly denounced Ingabire and the FDU by linking her and the party to the now terrorist FDLR—a claim lacking evidence. Even so, it was an easy task to make such a connection: after all, the FDU had previously encouraged the government to allow the FDLR to participate in Rwanda's reconciliation efforts. For Ingabire, the proposal made sense: FDLR fighters participated in the genocide, which meant they deserved a seat at the reconciliation table. However, for the RPF leadership, the thought of negotiating with the FDLR was absurd, as was negotiating with Ingabire. Soon after, Ingabire was arrested on allegations of genocide denial, as well as for terrorism and having genocide ideology. Following her trial, in 2012, Ingabire was found guilty of conspiracy to undermine the government and genocide denial, and sentenced to eight years in prison.[7] Her case was appealed before the Rwandan Supreme Court, whose judges increased her sentence to fifteen years. Despite international donor pleas for an impartial retrial, Ingabire remains in jail at the time of writing.[8]

Surveillance Society

The RPF's treatment of Ingabire and her FDU compatriots is emblematic of how it manages all its political opponents, at home and abroad, monitoring even the most mundane of human interactions. In Rwanda, public gatherings of more than five people require prior permission from local police and government officials, making gatherings difficult and risky, even when the stated goal is apolitical, like hosting a wedding, funeral or graduation celebration. Abroad, the RPF sends security officials from the Ministry of Defense to track Rwandans living in the diaspora and monitor opposition political activity. When Rwandans assemble in cities or towns in other African countries, or in Europe or North America, the RPF sends operatives to infiltrate the crowds and track those in attendance. These young men and women make their presence known by continuously taking photographs of everyone. Agents from the Department of Military Intelligence (DMI) also slip into public meetings or opposition protests, where they take photos and report on those in attendance, as well as what was said.

Critics at home and abroad have tried to mount online forums to encourage discussion about Rwanda's political present and future, but to little avail. The same intolerance for dissent and discussion is found online. The RPF has an army of social media warriors who flood the Facebook pages and Twitter feeds of domestic and foreign critics and observers with RPF narratives of success. This mode of online image management is so well known and so often employed that the censorial formulas of paid social media gurus are easy to identify. Such attacks are devoid of substance. Instead, masses of RPF devotees will chastise foreign critics for their naïveté and racist understanding of Rwanda.[9] There are very few domestic critics who have been able to use pseudonyms to voice their online dissent. They are routinely attacked by RPF trolls online, always with personal insults, often intimidating family and friends, and occasionally, using thinly veiled threats of disappearance or death.[10]

Both the government and its opponents rely on blogs, listservs, private chat rooms and social media sites to make their views known to wider audiences. The result is an online presence that either denigrates or glorifies the policies of the RPF, often leaving outsiders unaware or confused about political realities on the ground. Foreigners living in Kigali are not exempt from surveillance, which makes them unable to openly talk about politics. The RPF monitors the speech of development workers, foreign journalists and other foreigners through an unspoken "24/20" rule. A health specialist living in Kigali explains: "You say something wrong and you get 24 hours to leave the country with 20 kilos worth of stuff."[11]

The RPF regularly taps landlines and mobile phones. As the joke goes, "the government is like MTN [the national mobile service provider]—everywhere you go."[12] Rwandans living abroad know to communicate their news sparingly or in code to family and friends back home. Political talk, with far-away relatives by phone or at the dinner table, is rare. The costs are too high.

Information gathered by surveillance networks managed by the DMI is used to identify those who threaten national security. The political activities of these enemies of the state are closely monitored, sometimes resulting in a person's disappearance, torture or assassination. The DMI offers rewards or payment of up to US$1 million for the assassination of RPF critics and former allies by way of casual accident or happenstance, just as if it was "bringing on workers for a plumbing job."[13] To international audiences, speaking in English, President Kagame and other ranking officials deny or minimize the use of assassination plots to eliminate critics. At home, speaking in Kinyarwanda, the president and his peers openly target political opponents as a means to remind Rwandans of the government's willingness to use violence to maintain control of the public realm.

Since 2008, Rwanda has been a de facto one-party state.[14] Alliance parties do not have independent platforms and their candidates must be vetted through the RPF party executive. All the same, the 2008 elections broke new ground, particularly with respect to gender parity. Women gained forty-five of eighty seats, securing a majority 56 percent of parliamentary seats. The proportion of female parliamentarians climbed to 64 percent following the 2013 parliamentary elections. Speaking to reporters following those elections, Kagame gushed that women were shaping his country's future.

Women Pave the Way?

Presidential enthusiasm has yielded dramatic increases in women's political and social presence in the public and private spheres, but whether visible female representation has resulted in real power advances is debatable. Since the 2003 elections, the RPF has passed landmark legislation providing women with equal legal rights, has implemented gender-sensitive legal reforms, and created new government entities designed to protect women and promote their interests. These include a Gender Monitoring Office and the Forum of Rwandan Women Parliamentarians. Considering that before 1994 women "held no subnational political office, lacked the legal right to inherit property or open bank accounts, and were prohibited from joining profit-making organizations, the structural progress has been remarkable."[15] These social, institutional and symbolic changes have made Rwanda a leader in the global movement for gender equality.[16]

Some Rwandan women, particularly those who are urban, educated Anglophones, have benefited from the RPF's broad-based commitment to gender equality. However, rural women, many of whom are appointed into low-level, women-only positions in government, have only seen their unpaid workloads increase and their economic security threatened as the men in their lives begrudge their presumed influence in society.

Historically, Rwandan women have relied on men. Husbands worked outside the home and made all important decisions while wives managed the home front and were financially dependent on men—fathers and brothers before marriage, husbands and their male relatives thereafter. Female survivors of the genocide found that traditional structures were no longer possible and they sought changes to reflect the new demographics of postgenocide society. As the University of Wisconsin political scientist Aili Mari Tripp notes, advancing women's rights is a positive by-product of war and conflict.[17] Rwanda is no exception. And, as in other post-conflict societies, those men who benefit from traditional gender norms remain resistant to change.

Mireille is a gregarious student at the American high school in Kigali. Recently, she hoped to become president of the debate club. When she stepped forward to run, Mireille found that her female teachers and the boys in her class thought this position of leadership to be a naturally male domain. Her classmates chastised Mireille for being "too American," meaning her aspirations to lead were too aggressive, too independent and, ultimately, unpatriotic to the Rwandan way.[18] The insult highlights current gender relations across the board.

Female parliamentarians are expected to do it all—be active public leaders, while also successfully managing domestic life. Rwandan sociologist Justine Uvuza found that the husbands and male relatives of even the most powerful women in Rwandan politics still expected them to do the cooking, laundry and other household chores.[19] For some women, outsourcing domestic tasks to a paid housekeeper is not an option as male relatives expect "their" women to take care of them.

The irony is that while some women appear to hold much public cachet, their private lives are still governed by traditional gender expectations. Even if you legislate during the day, you must fold socks in the evening. The presence of prominent women in the public sphere and the possibilities for younger women and girls have come at a cost: domestic violence in Rwanda is at an all-time high. Men and boys from all walks of life—young and old, wealthy and poor, educated or not—have struggled to accept women's public roles. Traditional gender norms of the strong male provider have not caught up with the social and demographic realities of daily life since the genocide ended. According to the United Nations Development Program, one in every three Rwandan women has experienced or continues to suffer violence at the hands of her male relatives—notably her father or husband. The RPF's Gender Desk estimated in 2011 that up to 93 percent of all victims of reported physical and psychological abuse are women.[20]

Women continue to negotiate their place in the new Rwanda. Hindering the development of a Rwanda-specific feminism is the inability of women leaders to build a social movement for gender equality. RPF control of the public sphere and its reach into the private realm make the emergence of a women's movement unlikely, particularly since female political leaders are not yet willing to stand under the banner of feminism. Such attitudes are good reminders of the difficulty of transforming cultural codes from the top down. As the Rwandan proverb goes: "Hens don't crow where there is a cockerel."

Feminist organizing is a future possibility, however, as more women and girls become educated and enter the workforce. Georgia State University anthropologist Jennie Burnet has written about Rwandan women's increased presence in politics and their limited policy influence. She believes having more women in public life will one day pave the way for their meaningful participation in governance, while also creating "change in cultural and social conceptions of gender roles."[21] Some of these changes are already taking place. For example, urban women have seen their socio-economic mobility increase as Rwanda's new gender paradigm grants them formal access to salaried jobs, including positions within government at the legislature and ministries, along with the resultant purchasing power. President Kagame has also appointed numerous women to senior government posts, including the agriculture, health and foreign affairs portfolios. The president considers women to be "steadier and more honest," saying too: "I would be very happy for a woman to succeed me."[22]

Notwithstanding this, female visibility has yet to translate into real opportunity to shape Rwanda's future. The president and his closest advisors maintain their tight grip on political power. In reality, parliamentarians—male or female—actually have little authority to legislate on behalf of their constituents. Consulting ordinary people is not part of Rwanda's political culture. Women elected to seats reserved for women were nominated or at least vetted by the RPF via the Forum of Political Organizations. Most of these women owe allegiance to the RPF, rather than the constituencies who elected them.[23] Indeed, representatives of the government "have vetted candidates in elections at every level since 1998, and in most communities, the population was informed in advance of the 'correct' candidate for whom to vote."[24]

In Rwanda's authoritarian system, party loyalty always trumps the rhetoric of gender equality. Rwanda's elites are skilled at keeping the ruling class on its toes to consolidate their power. Parliamentarians, like other public figures, learn to parrot the party line. Those who do not are quickly relegated to the sidelines. Loyalists are rewarded with plum posts, are insiders to government tenders, and benefit from other perks that come from glorifying or praising RPF rule and Kagame's vision for the country. At the same time, real or perceived critics are demoted or ejected from government, whether on allegations of being divisionist, or, in the case of RPF party loyalists, of corruption or poor job performance. At any time, members of government can also lose their political standing and perks through frequent cabinet shuffles.

Unmasking Ethnic Politics

Central to the RPF's management of the public realm is maintaining the image of Rwanda as a place committed to progress for all of its citizens. This includes convincing Hutu to abandon their ethnicity to work to implement the RPF's forward-looking vision for Rwanda.[25] For RPF intellectuals, Hutu identity is not the private assertion of ethnic identity, but the basis of Hutu nationalism. This threat of political organizing around ethnicity must be banned to protect Rwanda's present and future security and development.

A history curriculum approved by the Ministry of Education in 2006 is now on offer to secondary school learners following prolonged disagreement within the RPF on the "proper version of Rwandan history and our historical unity before the colonizers arrived."[26] Within the Ministry of Education, how to teach the causes and consequences of the genocide remained a hot topic for a decade. A definitive curriculum had to be approved, leaving many history teachers and professors in a bind about how to balance teaching the complexity of the genocide, while respecting the official narrative of its causes and consequences.[27] Angie, an American secondary school teacher at a private school, summed up the challenge of teaching history from her office in the upmarket Kimihurura neighborhood in Kigali:

> The struggle is to communicate to students the gravity of the genocide without having them ask too many questions. Our goal is to teach critical reading and writing. When high schoolers begin to ask too many questions about the genocide, we have to be very careful. Some parents are politicians and senior government officials so our students have heard a particular version of events their whole lives. And I'm sure in some families that the genocide isn't even being discussed. Historical sources and sources critical of the government cannot be introduced let alone critically examined without raising the attention of the authorities.[28] I don't know of a foreign teacher who has been accused of denying the genocide but it is a weight and responsibility that many of us feel.

The RPF continued to focus on identifying and reeducating those who it felt held divisionist or genocide ideology values. In 2008, the

RPF created a new agency to manage the presence of genocide ideology in Rwandan society, the National Commission for the Fight against Genocide (Commission nationale de lutte contre le génocide). Known by its French-language acronym, the CNLG is responsible for all matters related to the history, memory and commemoration of the genocide, including monitoring the population for having genocide ideology and denying the genocide. Its director and other senior officials are all members of the ruling RPF, giving President Kagame a direct line to influence its activities if he wishes. Despite the official switch to English as the language of commerce and school instruction, the CNLG is a predominantly French institution, which allowed the RPF to reward comrades who had returned from French-speaking countries such as Burundi and Congo with their own positions in government.

The RPF targeted individuals of all ethnicities educated in French during the Habyarimana years in NURC- and CNLG-organized reeducation programs, the assumption being that their education in the 1970s, 1980s and early 1990s had radicalized them to believe in Hutu Power. Little is known about "the extent to which Hutu subscribe to 'genocide ideology' or to values that can be seen as 'divisionist' or even racist."[29] Take Aloys. In his own words, he is a "former Hutu" as it is now a crime to use ethnic labels. He is also destitute (*abatindi*), earning less than US$1.25 per day, the minimum income to qualify as poor under government poverty guidelines. As a rural farmer in his late forties, Aloys is among the most marginal of individuals in Rwanda today. In 2001, he was accused of acts of genocide in his home community and incarcerated. Aloys was later released in 2006 for lack of evidence, but suspicion still hangs over him. Released prisoners rarely benefit from government programs to support non-Tutsi survivors. Despite government demands that individuals must find paid employment, securing a job as a released prisoner is not easy, particularly since most owners of high-production farms are recent Tutsi returnees with little interest in employing individuals outside of their own economic networks.[30] Destitute men like Aloys are merely part of the rural masses to be governed; they are not worthy of consultation about their place in the new Rwanda. Consequently, we know little about what men like Aloys think about their place in society and even less about their hopes and dreams, fears and frustrations.

A rhetorical double standard emerged as the CNLG launched its work. Tutsi, particularly Tutsi-identified individuals loyal to the RPF or working for the government, were encouraged to proudly own their ethnicity. Many elite Tutsi, including children born since 1994, were able to hold their heads high as ethnic Tutsi. Given Tutsi dominance of public life, it was easy for individuals to claim their ethnic identity without much risk of stigma or attack for being divisionist or holding genocide ideology. After all, Tutsi could not have such ideas; they were the victims of the genocide, not its perpetrators. Soon, social etiquette around ethnicity emerged, with wealthier and politically connected self-identified Tutsi able to talk about their Tutsiness as a badge of honor and pride. Ethnic Hutu, on the other hand, whether politically connected or not, had to exercise more discretion, for Hutuness remained a trait that the government sought to expunge.

For the RPF leadership, the logic was simple: the majority Hutu population needed to be monitored for their presumed commitment to genocide ideology. The government justified its claims through a series of Parliamentary Commission reports from 2003 to 2008. The research found within these reports warned of the presence of genocide ideology, and its nasty cousin, genocide denial, in nearly all sectors of society—families, schools, churches, local NGO and development organizations as well as among political opponents, journalists and human rights defenders.[31]

The reports' findings were presented to donors as evidence of the presence of ethnic hatred in Hutu hearts and minds, to explain the policy choices of the RPF. Few were convinced, given the RPF's overt targeting of Hutu men. In a meeting with a CNLG official, a Dutch donor questioned the reports' evidence, suggesting that methodology had been skewed to support what he considered to be intrusive ways to tackle the "yet unproven" presence of genocide ideology in Rwanda.[32] The Rwandan official would have none of this line of questioning, and accused the Dutchman of being a Hutu sympathizer. She went on to chastise the Dutch government, saying that its development projects in the countryside were not worth enough euros for her administration to waste its time working with outsiders willing to deny the genocide.[33]

Central to RPF efforts to eliminate genocidal ideologies was its continued campaign to contain the Hutu Power FDLR through an active military presence in eastern Congo. In 2008, a United Nations panel of experts on Congo linked senior members of the Rwandan Defense Force to the National Congress for the Defense of the People (CNDP), a Tutsi-led anti-Congolese government militia. The report showed evidence that Rwanda had provided support to the CNDP and its leader, Laurent Nkunda, despite strong denials from President Kagame's office.[34] Critics of the RPF outside of the country used the publication of the report to accuse the government of using the FDLR as a pretext to conceal its illegal mining activities in Congo. In a typical show of defiance, Kagame bragged that if the RDF were actually in Congo, the conflict would have ended because of the superior discipline and tactical skill of his soldiers.

Renewed war in Congo raised the ire of international human rights groups. They claimed that the now rump FDLR was unable to mount a military threat to Rwandan national security. The RPF forcefully rejected what it considered spurious claims from foreigners bent on meddling in Rwanda's affairs. Meanwhile, it continued to monitor the behavior of numerous citizens, particularly that of young Hutu men and women living in communities along Rwanda's western border with Congo. The political equation was a simple one: Hutu politicians and their loyalists are, by their ethnic association with Hutu extremists linked to the previous government, extremists themselves. The RPF has relied on this logic to justify and legitimate its policy choices for two full decades.

Managing Hutu

By 2010, the disappearance of those perceived to be FDLR loyalists or presumed political opponents of the RPF had become commonplace, with young men and women in their late twenties and thirties bearing the brunt.[35] Just old enough to have experienced the genocide but young enough to represent Rwanda's post-1994 present, their patriotic duty is to undergo reeducation, found families, and become contributing members of society, not aid and abet the RPF's sworn enemy or practice Hutu nationalism. Caught between the majority of Rwandans, who are under the age of fifteen, and those past their forties, whom the RPF considers as too old to contribute to Rwanda's emergent knowledge-based economy, these young men and women are the country's future. They are also considered those most likely to fall into the grip of genocide ideology, making them most subject to the watchful eye of the DMI, community members and family alike. For these young Rwandans, "getting unified" is paramount: any activity or behavior that appears to be a refusal to unify results in swift punishment, usually without judicial verification or the presumption of innocence. Making a public accusation against someone for holding genocide ideology is sufficient to have their social benefits, job or religious ties severed. Social isolation and economic hardship are usually the result, even when charges are politically motivated, because the speaker criticized the government or its policies.

The RPF's watchful eye reveals a tension in its national unity project. By 2010, the government considered unity initiatives to be progressing well in the countryside and in urban Kigali, evidenced in its first "Reconciliation Barometer" report.[36] Government policies were deemed to be on the right track in the report, with evidence of success in getting Rwandans unified. However, the report noted 25 percent of Rwandans still held genocidal ideologies. Conducted by RPF-vetted staffers at the NURC, the government commissioned national unity and reconciliation surveys again in 2012 and 2015. Interestingly, certain aspects of these surveys indicated that some Rwandans, Hutu and Tutsi alike, saw the RPF as comprised of ethnic radicals, seeking to restore the precolonial glory, power and privilege of the Tutsi monarchy.

Rather than consider these perceptions, the RPF doubled down on its efforts to unify Rwandans on its own terms. For fifteen years, the government had committed itself to crafting an aesthetically pleasing narrative about Rwanda as a hopeful and forward-looking country that had recovered from the horrors of the 1994 genocide. To maintain this positive message, notably before international audiences, it was plain to ordinary citizens and RPF loyalists alike that regime rhetoric must focus on Rwanda's status as an African success story and a good development partner. As such, the RPF has sought to control what is said about Rwanda in print—whether through the reports of donor partners or the work of foreign academics. This management of how Rwanda is spoken and written about informs what outsiders know about Rwanda as publishing on governance, justice, reconciliation and development is politicized.

Any research that concludes that life in Rwanda is not as the RPF purports is quickly discredited, including reports from the African Peer Review Mechanism, the Mo Ibrahim Foundation, the United Nations and the World Bank.[37] The findings of such studies are either suppressed, or discounted as the product of poor research methods or foreign researchers bent on undermining the RPF's efforts to remake Rwanda. What circulates instead are polished RPF-sanctioned reports proclaiming that the citizenry is reconciled, justice is being served, citizens are pleased with service delivery projects, and they love the RPF and President Kagame.[38] These same reports are also used to demonstrate that genocide denial, ethnic divisionism and genocide ideology still exist in society.[39]

Reports that do not accord with the RPF's image of a self-sufficient Rwanda dedicated to economic growth and service delivery are degraded as "biased and misleading."[40] For example, a foreign researcher working on the UN's human development report in 2007 was blacklisted following the approval of the Minister of Local Government. When the report reached the cabinet, the finding that Rwanda needed to address growing poverty and commit to deepening democracy was rejected. Instead, the RPF distanced itself from the now published report, claiming it was filled with inaccuracies intended to derail Rwanda's development successes. The RPF way was, and is, the right and only way.

The focus is on making good citizens out of bad in dictatorial, rather than consensus-based, ways. Highlighting ideological and political differences regarding issues such as national unity, ethnic identity, genocide ideology, economic development, land and agricultural practices, judicial practices and political representation remains risky. The experience of Béatrice, a former member of the RPF, is suggestive. Béatrice joined the party in 1998, paving the way for her eventual appointment as a local government official. A Hutu woman who survived the 1994 genocide while protecting her Tutsi neighbors, Béatrice prided herself on being Rwandan and making a positive contribution to development. She wholeheartedly agreed with the RPF's goal to return Rwanda to traditional ethnic unity. However, by 2004, she felt government efforts to undo ethnic identity were merely masked forms of political and social control. Béatrice became uneasy about the repressive and aggressive ways that the RPF sought to ensure that all citizens conformed to its vision of society. In a meeting with other appointed local government officials, she raised the question of justice for the crimes committed by the RPF before, during and after 1994. Her fellow executive secretaries sat silent. Some left the room. Others rocked back and forth on their chairs. Finally, a fellow Hutu colleague who also lived through the genocide reminded Béatrice that the RPF stopped the genocide, and noted, "talking about such things is against the law. It is divisionist."

Things soon turned sour for Béatrice and her family. A mother and widow who lost her husband in the genocide, Béatrice considered herself a patriot and model Rwandan citizen. She knew she had erred in raising the issue of RPF crimes. In her heart and soul, justice was something Béatrice believed in: "But dread has a taste, you know?" she said plaintively. Frustrated, shunned by her colleagues, and fearing economic hardship and social isolation, Béatrice sought political asylum in Belgium in 2009. The basis of her claim was commonplace: she was politically persecuted for questioning RPF ethnic unity and identity initiatives. Her desire for understanding of who did what to whom during the genocide is, in her opinion, not only valid: it needs to be discussed and debated among Rwandans to allow national and individual healing. She continued:

> When I work to educate and sensitize those living [in my community], the talk turns to forgiveness and justice as part of reconciliation. At *gacaca*, talking about real issues is not allowed as the government has its observers to make sure the population does what it is told to do. Reconciliation without justice for all and justice without truth is a hoax. But this government believes in a vision against a population that is unsure. Working together is an option but is difficult to imagine when we are told what to do, how to do it, and what to think. Trust is low, even within families, and suspicion is high. Talking is needed. Not all Hutu are guilty despite ideas in society that all we did [in 1994] was kill. Are we not human too?

In Béatrice's community in southeastern Rwanda, as in others across the country, participation in *gacaca* trials remained mandatory. Those who did not attend were subject to intimidation, harassment and fines until they presented themselves to fulfill their socially mandated role as perpetrators. Their collective task before the courts was to tell the truth of what they had done during the genocide, while survivors had to forgive those who killed their loved ones. Human rights organizations continued to criticize the *gacaca* process as a form of rough justice that fell short of minimum legal standards.

The courts presented ethnic Hutu with a no-win choice: testify to denounce the crimes of fellow Hutu, or confess while exposing others in the process. Either way, Hutu were on trial without much regard for what they may have done (or not done) during the genocide. In cases where Hutu sat on the judging panels, there was pressure not to appear too lenient or accommodating to their ethnic brethren. Genocide ideology and ethnic divisionist laws also affected any testimony made before the *gacaca* courts, as anyone expressing such views, whether as victim or as perpetrator, was liable to be punished.

Holding genocide ideology could result in a prison sentence of up to twenty-five years (or life for repeat offenders), meaning that speaking one's truth or challenging the RPF's official narrative of Hutu killing Tutsi was akin to looking down the barrel of a loaded gun. Béatrice lamented the maximal prosecution of Hutu, noting that this approach would only serve to create that which the RPF was trying to avoid: a return to ethnically motivated violence. She continued:

> The problem I see is that we are not allowed to talk about the geno-cide as it happened. To question the RPF's truth, well this is a death sentence. I know there was a genocide in this country—Tutsi died in high numbers and they were targeted because of their Tutsi identity. And there was civil war that the RPF launched! The genocide was a decision of Hutu politicians who held extremist views to eliminate our Tutsi brothers and sisters. Some Hutu killed, but not all did. Even some Tutsi and Twa killed! After the genocide ended, many Rwandans spoke of the civil war and genocide. Many of us have lived in violence for a long time.
>
> This government thinks the violence we experienced only happened between April and July 1994. No, this is not true, but of course there is no way to talk about such things without serious consequences. We used to speak of the genocide and massacres as a way to respect all lives lost. Now we must speak exclusively of the

genocide against the Tutsi. How will Rwanda heal and move forward if some of us cannot speak of our harms? Without frank conversation, how can a middle ground be found? It can't exist because the government won't allow it. Instead, those of us who question the official narrative are considered [Hutu] extremists. This is what will radicalize young people. The hopes and dreams of the new Rwanda are not for Hutu. This injustice is what will mobilize and perhaps even radicalize Hutu. Peace based on coercion and fear is not sustainable. This is why so many Rwandans, not just Hutu, question this government's commitment to justice and reconciliation.

As a local official, appointed by the RPF, my safety is compromised as I question the policies of my bosses. This is why I went to Belgium. I reject the golden cage of being part of the RPF machine. I want freedom for me and other Rwandans. It's not possible to fight for it in Rwanda.

Béatrice's lament is one shared by many Hutu, particularly those who lived through the genocide and those who have had children since. The bitter aftertaste of injustice that had crept into Rwandan political life in the late 1990s and early 2000s was out in the open by 2008. Some Rwandans saw and were willing to challenge—albeit carefully and cautiously—the one-sided nature of RPF governance, its justice and reconciliation projects, as well as its agricultural, land and other policies. Hutu—ordinary citizens and government officials like Béatrice—felt the sting of RPF rule, made sharper by age-old fears about a return to oppressive and unforgiving political rule. Nonetheless, Béatrice's thoughts on postgenocide justice highlight that former ethnic Hutu recognize and indeed sympathize with their ordinary Tutsi friends, neighbors and relatives. Moreover, Hutu can distinguish between elite and ordinary Tutsi, and indeed, are consistently mindful to do so.[41]

The grievances of once-loyal local officials like Béatrice fell on deaf ears as the RPF continued to cajole and coerce social reconciliation and political harmony. Before international audiences, President Kagame lauded his government's achievements in rebuilding the country following the devastation of the 1994 genocide and promoted Rwanda as a positive place to live, work and invest. The president noted that since RPF-led efforts to reconcile and unify Rwandans were progressing according to schedule, his government would shift its focus to fighting genocide ideology. According to the president, such a fight is the only legitimate basis of political harmony, continued economic growth, and the creation of a Rwanda-specific version of democracy according with traditional Rwandan values, not Western ones. This political rhetoric kept the symbolism of the democratic rule that foreign donors require alive and well, while also revealing Kagame's soft-authoritarian tendencies. Such a rhetorical turn is not unexpected: authoritarians, including Rwanda's postcolonial presidents, have long used the language of democracy and inclusivity to mask their dictatorial tendencies.

PART IV

The Fruits of Liberation

11

RULES, RULES AND MORE RULES

The RPF has an impressive reach into the everyday lives of all Rwandans. This reach is a product of "clear hierarchies and an intricate organization" that appoints government officials to positions with overlapping administrative roles.[1] Official restructuring in 2006 decentralized state bureaucracy under the guise of better grassroots service delivery (see Map 2). Units of governance are divided into six levels: 5 provinces, including Kigali City, 30 districts, 416 sectors, 2,146 cells, 14,774 villages and *umukuru* (village committees). As of this writing, local government officials represent fully half the government's payroll.[2]

The sixth and lowest level of government is not an administrative unit per se, but rather an appointed presence with roots in the Habyarimana regime: a *nyumbakumi* is a non-salaried government official, responsible for approximately fifty people.[3] It is unclear how many *nyumbakumi* there are. In 2006, during the administrative restructuring, a senior Ministry of Local Government official noted that "there are as many as the population requires to meet the development needs of their locale."[4] The RPF abolished the *nyumbakumi* post in 2006 in

Table 4. Hierarchy of the Rwandan State, 2006 to 2011*

Entity	Number	Responsible Official
National Government	1	President (elected, paid)
Province (*intara*)	5	Governor (appointed, paid)
District (*uturere*)	30	Mayor (appointed, paid)
Sector (*umurenge*)	416	Executive Secretary (appointed, paid)
Cell (*utugari*)	2,148	Coordinator (volunteer, unpaid)
Village (*umudugudu*)	14,837	Coordinator (volunteer, unpaid)
Nyumbakumi (head of ten houses); dissolved in 2006		*Nyumbakumi* (appointed, unpaid)
Umukuru (four-person village-level committees, heading 50 to 200 households); since 2006	One per village	*Umukuru* (appointed, unpaid)

* Ministry of Local Government (MINALOC), *The Republic of Rwanda after Territorial Reform* (Kigali: MINALOC, 2006).

favor of *umukuru,* four-person village-level committees responsible for governing between 50 and 200 households. Even so, *nyumbakumis* continue to hold sway in their communities as representatives of the RPF.[5] The government also considers Rwandans living in the diaspora to be a separate administrative unit, managed by the Diaspora Directorate General in the Ministry of Foreign Affairs.

RPF-appointed, paid executive secretaries govern each sector (*umurenge*), the beating heart of local government. Much like the mayor under Habyarimana, their primary function is to coordinate and fund sector- and cell-level activities. Executive secretaries work alongside an elected sector committee made up of bureaucrats who are responsible for implementing policies at the local level. Also at the sector level is an elected but unpaid council that acts in an advisory capacity to the executive secretary and the sector committee. These non-elected executive secretaries are accountable to the central authorities in Kigali (who appoint and pay them) rather than to the citizens they serve. Sector-level officials take few, if any, decisions on their own. Their primary task is to implement decisions made in Kigali. As a result, local governance is "paralysed and ineffective because it waits for vital information to make it down the tree-like 'plumbing' of the state."[6]

Paradoxically, rather than transfer power or devolve influence to ordinary people, decentralization has allowed the RPF to expand. Officials at the cell level look to Kigali for policy instructions as well. Working as the heads of cell committees, these unpaid, elected volunteer coordinators are responsible for the daily administration of the people in their jurisdictions. Together, the sector and the cell represent the immediate source of state power at the level of the individual. It is at these levels that the control and authority of government play out in daily life. Reports on individual behavior, as well as requests for benefits or privileges, start at the local level. As Gaspard, a *gacaca* judge, cautioned:

> There is no one level that is more important than the other. Each has its purpose and a specific task and that is something Rwandans know how to respect. But at the lowest levels, it can really feel heavy. If you are having an affair, they know. If you are drunk or if your house is in disrepair, they know. If you fail to attend sensitization meetings, they know. If you want to join a cooperative, you must get a signature from someone like me who might ask for the signature of your village coordinator who might also ask for the signature of your *nyumbakumi*. So there are a lot of people watching you, checking on your actions and the people you are with. Without signatures, nothing happens. If you are not a good citizen who supports national unity and reconciliation, you will rot at home.

Top-down administration is institutionalized and incentivized in the form of performance contracts termed *imihigo*. *Imihigo* requires local government officials, be they appointed or elected, to publicly swear

under oath to implement national policy goals as instructed by government superiors in Kigali. Any deviation from these directives is a breach
of contract. The threat of breaking *imihigo* commitments puts a lot of
pressure on local government officials. Those who fail to meet their
contractual requirements may be fired, jailed or disappeared. As one
local official sighed, "*imihigo* is the engine of everything," before
lamenting, "it is killing us, no one can escape it."[7]

In 2006, only district-level mayors signed *imihigo* contracts. They
were then responsible for ensuring that officials down the line at the
sector and cell levels implemented policy directives as instructed. In
2007, James Musoni, then minister of local government, announced
that all local government officials would sign *imihigo* contracts with the
president from that time onward. Kagame further decreed that individual household heads must sign *imihigo* contracts with their local officials, as a promise of good citizenship and loyalty to the RPF.[8] Citizens
who fail to meet their *imihigo* commitments are fined; local officials
who blunder are fired. Today, sector and cell authorities are among the
socially weakest and most politically vulnerable individuals in Rwanda.
They are caught between the often impossible demands of national
policy directives and a local population that does not always respect
their authority.

Through *imihigo*, the RPF can assign to local officials forbidden and
mandated tasks in the name of development. Such tasks include
ensuring that all citizens wear covered shoes, making sure certain trees
are not cut or wood sold without permission, preventing livestock care
in public places, or informing on those who refuse to participate in
nocturnal neighborhood security patrols. These tasks, formalized
through *imihigo*, give the appearance to non-Rwandans of a government that is serious and committed to economic development. In
practice, stressed and under-resourced local officials regularly skimp
to meet their *imihigo* commitments. In 2009, the international non-
governmental organization Global Integrity reported in its "Notebook

on Corruption" that local officials often cut corners to meet unrealistic policy goals. Global Integrity found that schools and hospitals built under *imihigo* contracts sometimes became unsafe and unusable, as local leaders did not take the necessary time to build durable structures.[9] The University of London development scholar Benjamin Chemouni noted the same: "The lack of popular participation in planning and evaluation means that targets can be irrelevant and/or unrealistic, but also that accountability flows upward only. This paves the way for 'cooking' numbers, harsh implementation and undermining local ownership."[10]

The RPF, under Kagame's leadership, is consolidating this inverse democracy as a uniquely "Rwandan" one that relies on speaking for Rwandans rather than listening to or consulting them. President Kagame now tells Western donors and foreign investors that Rwanda's violent history makes a transition to Western-style liberal democracy impossible, saying democracy must be homegrown in a way "that must adapt to the wearer."[11] Boston University political scientist Timothy Longman calls this strategy "performance legitimation."[12]

Rwanda Incorporated?

At the heart of performance legitimation is self-sacrifice, a duty that is rewarded, particularly when individual needs are suppressed for the greater good. Rwandan government rhetoric rewards a strong work ethic, making military efficiency a pillar of its neoliberal economic development and national unity policies. The result is that political business in Rwanda has become a market economy—the commodities are allegiance and cooperation, their supply and demand regulated by violence and threat. President Kagame is the CEO of Rwanda, running the country like a private corporation.[13]

Using the language of empowerment, the RPF mandates new rules to modernize and upgrade everyday life. New rules are enforced with

Table 5. Fines in Francs for Forbidden or Compulsory Activities, 2006*

		RWF
1	Tending livestock on "public land"	10,000
2	Cultivating on riverbeds	10,000
3	Refusal (when asked by authorities) to dig anti-erosion canals	10,000
4	Absence of roof gutter and water receptacle near home	10,000
5	Having a second wife	10,000
6	Churches without a chapel	10,000
7	Religious group praying at night	10,000
8	Refusal to participate in nocturnal security patrols	10,000
9	Parents failing to send their children to school	10,000
10	Teacher or other adults dismissing child from school for failure to pay school fees	10,000
11	Consulting traditional healer without permission	10,000
12	Cutting trees without permission	10,000
13	Heating wood to make charcoal	10,000
14	Selling wood products without permission	10,000
15	Refusal to make or use a "modern" cooking stove	10,000
16	Selling homemade produce (cheese, milk, etc.) without permission	10,000
17	Home without compost bin	2,000
18	Home without clothesline	2,000
19	Home without closed toilet	2,000
20	Home without table for cooking utensils	2,000
21	Home without storage facility for drinking water	2,000
22	Person without clean clothing and body hygiene	2,000
23	Teacher without clean clothing and body hygiene	10,000
24	Drinking beer at home or in a bar (cabaret) with a straw	10,000
25	Commercial center without a toilet	10,000
26	Restaurant without toilets or not clean	10,000
27	School compound not clean	10,000
28	Health center with poor sanitation	10,000
29	Market with no toilets and/or not clean	10,000

* Table reproduced from Bert Ingelaere, "Do We Understand Life After Genocide? Center and Periphery in the Construction of Knowledge in Postgenocide Rwanda," *African Studies Review*, 53, 1 (2010), p. 52.

steep fines. Levies average 10,000 francs, or approximately US$11 per transgression—an extraordinary sum in a country where the average daily income is US$2 per day. Among the many new prohibitions imposed by the RPF to improve rural life, which are subject to financial penalties, are having a second wife, consulting a traditional healer, drinking beer with a straw, making charcoal and refusing to use a modern cooking stove.[14] Such rules may appear to make sense in a fast-moving, modernizing society. In practice, they are out of step with how rural Rwandans live, ignoring things like the need for solidarity, trust and cooperation among poor people who must rely on one another for the basics of life, whether they like it or not.

The RPF's rules are designed to do more than control individual behavior, particularly behavior that the RPF leadership considers "unmodern"; they also permeate and control social interaction. Citizens are praised for reporting the personal shortcomings and failures of others in their community. Making personal disclosures public is easily justified when compulsory or forbidden activities are open to broad interpretation by local officials and neighbors alike.

At the center of such surveillance are ordinary people trying to understand how to incorporate new rules into their daily routines. Marie-Ange is a young Tutsi woman who was twelve years old at the time of the genocide. She was raised in rural Rwanda, just outside the town of Byumba, some 67 kilometers to the north of Kigali. She and her immediate family survived the genocide because they were able to find protection in RPF-controlled areas before the killing began. In the years following the genocide, Marie-Ange, like many of her neighbors, felt grateful to the RPF and its efforts to provide physical safety and basic services to all Rwandans. She recalls the experience of having clean water made available at a communal stand in 1998, and how the provision of this basic service quickly became political. Ultimately, access to basic services became linked to genocide ideology, and citizens were monitored for evidence of deviant behavior:

We all felt like this government would provide the basics so we could get healthy and begin to feel like the terror of the genocide was over. I wanted to focus on my education so I could help heal and rebuild my country. Living during the genocide was like clinging to death—I could have died at any moment. But I didn't and no one in my family died. So that was a blessing.

Soon though, there were squabbles over water. A neighbor died trying to get water because a young Hutu accused her of taking more than her share. I don't know if she did, but there was no justice in the government's solution. Our local official punished them both! And the woman was a [Tutsi] survivor! A widow whose children were left behind to suffer! And the boy was just a child during the genocide! They locked him up, saying he was a *génocidaire*, that he had geno-cide ideology in his heart. But he wasn't; he was just a boy trying to survive like the rest of us!

Soon, they closed the tap to us and we had to get permission to get water. To get water to cook and clean! I felt bitterness because I believed the RPF would provide like they promised. Sure, they provide. You can see so much development. New [electricity] poles, new water stands, new houses, schools and [health] clinics.[15] But those of us who survived, we feel a lot of pain because of this govern-ment. A Hutu boy going to prison without justice? Controlling access to water to make sure genocide doesn't happen again? What kind of logic is this? What kind of respect for survivors is this? Is it illegal to be poor, to have needs? It is now 2008, and we have a government that treats us like little children who don't know what to do or say. "Get developed," they preach. "Get modern," they cry. "Get unified," they say.

Of course we want these things. But to be led what to think and how to think it? This is an insult to survivors like me. It is also an insult to our Hutu neighbors, for few of them [in Byumba] killed. How can we reconcile when the government doesn't understand what we need? When they don't listen to us? Instead, we have a situation where we are rewarded to report on our friends and neighbors. If I see someone using the water without permission, it is my duty to report [to local officials]. If I don't and someone sees that I see the theft, I can get in trouble. There is this circle of observation that we live in now. You watch me, I watch you, and the local official gets rewarded because we are all watching each other, and everything appears peaceful and modern. The government explains such a system as necessary to root out those with genocide ideology in their hearts. But I see what is going on—our duty is to get developed, get modern, and not criticize.

Marie-Ange's experience illustrates that the sheer number of administrative and military personnel involved in monitoring individual mindsets makes it difficult to opt out of unity and development activities. From 2001, Rwanda's youth have been a particular focus of government efforts, as 61 percent of Rwandans are under the age of twenty-four.[16]

The RPF cited jobs for youth as a critical priority in 2012 when it released its second World Bank-approved Economic Development and Poverty Reduction Strategy (EDPRS II). The policy added manufacturing to its Vision 2020 pledge to create a knowledge-based economy. The goal was to promote foreign investment in the nascent manufacturing sector, a curious choice in a country where local output was lower than it had been in the 1980s.[17] Nonetheless, the decision pleased the International Monetary Fund, since the responsibility for job creation and shame for failing to do so was shifted onto the shoulders of Rwandans. The political message inherent in the government's strategy was clear: good Rwandans are entrepreneurs who take personal "responsibility for the situations in which they live" and who do not rely on the government to support them.[18]

Meanwhile, the RPF trumpeted its efforts to increase rural income through household living conditions surveys. Designed to evaluate the poverty of Rwandans, four government-led surveys were administered between 2000 and 2014.[19] By 2011, the RPF was touting the success of its economic policies, noting that rural poverty had decreased by 12 percentage points since 2006. In just five years, some 660,000 Rwandans (out of 11.5 million) had been lifted out of extreme poverty.[20] The figure masked the pressures felt by local officials to meet *imihigo* performance targets. Ministry of Finance officials clashed with foreign donors over government claims that extreme poverty was in decline. The government pointed to its consistently high rates of macroeconomic growth (around 8 percent per annum since 2000), while donors began to question Rwanda's growing income inequality and the resulting social vulnerability of the country's poorest citizens.

Rural farmers faced numerous difficulties in meeting the government's quotas for forced crop production and land commercialization initiatives. Consider, for example, Rwanda's commitment to boost coffee production. High-altitude hills in western parts of the country are rich with volcanic soil; with warm days and cool nights, the region produces some of the best tasting coffee in the world. In 2012, the government touted it as a miracle crop, responsible for countless rural jobs, boosting small farm revenues, and making up 30 percent of Rwanda's foreign exports. Coffee was also hailed for promoting reconciliation between Tutsi survivors and Hutu perpetrators as they worked together to grow, harvest and wash Rwanda's specialty beans for global consumption.

Nearly half a million Rwandans are involved in the coffee industry, most as smallholder producers.[21] The government has invested in cupping and washing stations to maximize the export value of coffee in a competitive world market. For some, like Immaculée and her family, planting coffee bushes has been a veritable economic boon. Since 2008, her three children have been enrolled in private secondary schools and she was able to build a new four-room house.

Rural farmers are not all reaping the same rewards as Immaculée. Instead of allowing farmers to grow crops for daily household consumption, local officials induce subsistence farmers to uproot their patches of sorghum, sweet potatoes and other vegetables to plant and grow coffee that is sold exclusively via government-run cooperatives. Not all cooperatives are fairly run, meaning the price paid per kilo of coffee can vary wildly. Wronged farmers rarely find an avenue for recourse, but they still cannot opt out of growing coffee. Didier summed up the pressures: "We must grow as we are told. Those who don't can really suffer. Sometimes you spend a few days in prison. Other times, the officials come and just pull up your plants. Either way, we work hard and are still hungry."

In parts of the country, the RPF's unrelenting drive for economic growth has resulted in tense community relations. The effects of new land registration and land use laws passed in 2008 were deeply felt. There was little room for innovation or adaptation to weather patterns and other non-negotiables like seed availability or fertilizer quality. Shared scarcity was the result, with families sometimes struggling to feed themselves, let alone take surpluses to market to barter for or earn cash to buy food they are no longer able to grow themselves. Despite calling on Rwandans to be entrepreneurial, the RPF made getting to local markets more complicated. Rules calling for improved hygiene resulted in increased hardships, as local officials monitored individual compliance with rules requiring the wearing of covered shoes, banning plastic bags, organizing the renting of market stalls and mandating paying sales tax in advance. It is now near impossible to sell one's own produce and other wares informally.[22]

Informal economic activities like selling vegetables, phone credit, cigarettes and other sundry items remain unacceptable economic activities, labeled by the government as unmodern, dirty and contributing to a culture of tax evasion and petty corruption. Still, ordinary Rwandans sell and trade basic necessities and luxury items on the black market, including meat, vegetables, milk, cooking oil, antibiotics, traditional beer, clothing, mosquito nets, refrigerators and televisions. Faustin, an eighteen-year-old street vendor, summed up the risks and rewards of the informal sector:

> Selling outside of legal markets is tricky because officials know that we do it. You have to be careful to trade and sell to people you know and trust so no one turns you in. If you get caught, the penalties are high—fines, prison, beatings and they make you destroy your goods. I've even seen those selling plastic bags get forced to destroy them with their teeth! So, yeah, there is a black market that no one really talks about.
>
> We don't even complain about high taxes in case someone decides to turn you in for questioning the government. But the rates are high! One mama told me she had to pay advance taxes of 1500 francs to set up her stall. She only sold 1000 francs of product that day! When she went to cash out her tax account, the official was gone and she had no way to get her money back! You can't even talk about this kind of corruption because the government says there isn't any. If you ask me, the black market is a kind of reconciliation initiative. We sell to those we really trust. They trust us to sell them a good product and we trust them not to turn us in for selling outside of official markets.[23]

Dignity for Whom?

Since 2007, the RPF has become increasingly committed to weaning Rwanda from foreign aid. Dignity and self-reliance became government policy in August 2012 when President Kagame announced the Agaciro [dignity] Development Fund (AgDF). The government's rationale behind this policy was to encourage Rwandans to "think big" and realize that nothing is impossible with hard work and ingenuity.[24] The AgDF aims to reduce Rwanda's dependence on foreign aid while increasing domestic revenue to allow Rwandans to develop in line with government priorities, not the whims of donors.[25] By the end of the year, government agencies, private sector companies, cooperatives and church groups were all fundraising for the AgDF. The heavy hand of the government made it difficult to avoid contributing to the fund, regardless of ability to pay. Those who were too poor to contribute were viewed with suspicion.

Following the president's lead, *acagiro* became a personal mantra for Rwandans, urban elites in particular. Signs of it appeared on stickers and posters stuck to the side of buses, in storefront windows and on the back of motorcycle helmets.[26] The government stance was clear to all: dignity must be homegrown; it cannot be bestowed by foreigners. President Kagame soon heralded *agaciro* as a way of life, as well as a source of inspiration and necessary sacrifice for all.

The concept of *agaciro* served as the ideological framework for the upcoming Rwandan commemoration of the twentieth anniversary of the genocide, an event of monumental importance in the post-1994 era. The anniversary was conceived as more than a commemoration of Tutsi lives lost. It was also a chance for the RPF to showcase its service delivery and national unity policies to the world. No stone was left unturned and no expense spared as the government worked to ensure a responsive and loyal population to show the world what tiny Rwanda had accomplished since 1994.

The government sought to fund self-sustainability, at least in part, through taxation. Speaking to Parliament on the release of the 2011–12 national budget, Finance Minister John Rwangombwa accentuated the importance of "good citizens" who paid taxes to increase domestic revenue to reduce dependence on foreign aid.[27] For weary rural Rwandans, the directive was but an additional burden to an already heavy load of obligations. Rwandans had little choice but to live with the contradictions of meeting government demands to develop in a resource-poor environment. The RPF dangled a carrot of social mobility and dignity for those who toed the party line, while wielding a stick of foreclosed opportunities and hardship at those who failed to comply.[28]

The gift of social mobility had become the domain of cell and village officials, as part of their *imihigo* contracts. Parliament passed a law that created yet another government agency to oversee low-income and local-level economic activities.[29] In joining Rwandans together in economic cooperative and livelihood associations, the law aims to make Rwandans work together in the formal economy, through shared decision-making and access to credit and savings schemes designed to leverage shared resources for economic growth.

Depending on their age and demographic, rural dwellers received the idea of cooperatives with measured optimism or skeptical resignation. Epimaque, a young former Hutu accused of genocide crimes, who was released for lack of evidence in 2003, thinks cooperatives act as an important social lubricant: "The problem is that Rwandans don't share easily. We hide our emotions. Cooperatives don't allow for hiding how you feel about rules like which crops to cultivate or how to sell at market. Getting a fair share out of cooperatives means you have to debate and discuss. This is a good thing, I think. We learn compromise and how to share with one another." Evariste, an elderly ethnic Twa who lived through the violence of 1959 and 1994, is less optimistic: "Cooperatives decide for us. How we will spend our time and spend our money. Some [members] don't even have money to spare but not contributing is a form of disloyalty. Not joining is not really an option."

By 2011, resentment of the cooperative model of market growth was widespread, even among youth. Even those with paid employment felt the pressure. Some low-income rural Rwandans went so far as to criticize the demands of membership, as they had nothing to give to mandated cooperatives and other local development initiatives. In 2009, the government instituted mandatory saving schemes at the sector level, known as Umurenge SACCO.[30] Rwandans were to place their savings in a bank or savings cooperative, which they could in turn leverage in the form of loans and grants. A fine idea in principle, the saving schemes were in practice difficult to justify as few people had sufficient surplus to warrant a savings account. As government efforts for economic self-reliance intensified in 2012, participation in SACCOs and other cooperatives became coercive rather than suggestive. David, a middle-aged businessman who returned from Zambia in 2004 to live in his native Nyagatare town, reveals the anxiety-inducing aspects of local saving schemes:

> [The official] comes with a police officer or member of the Local Defense Force. He tells you put 5,000 francs in the SACCO. He explains that if you don't deposit, there will be problems with his *imihigo* commitments. He points out that his police escort has a gun and can put you in prison. He hints that police can come back day or night. All is said is a calm manner, quietly with courtesy. There is no raising of voices or arguing.
>
> The pressures to save are burdensome. I had to sell some land to pay my SACCO deposit. When I went to get the signature [of the local official], he told me the minimum deposit is now 10,000 francs. What kind of system is this? I save to avoid prison? I sell my land to save? Where is the benefit?

According to the RPF, entrepreneurship, discipline and innovation are skills that can be taught to those willing to learn. Despite the practical challenges, the president continued to highlight entrepreneurship and individual drive as the qualities most able to propel economic growth and gain dignity. By 2012, some 60 percent of Rwandans defined themselves as self-employed, a figure that was regularly mentioned in government speeches and reports as proof of Rwandan initiative and entrepreneurial drive.[31] The reality of this figure was clouded by the growing numbers of un- and underemployed Rwandans reporting their self-employed status to local officials. While enterprising Rwandans tried to develop, many new businesses floundered under the weight of tax tariffs, while other ventures collapsed because they could not raise necessary capital.

Among the businesses that failed were numerous rural hotels that the government incentivized to accommodate foreign tourists.[32] Countless hotels and other tourist venues had been built through loans and grants to accommodate millions of projected tourists, all vying to see Rwanda's gorillas in their natural mountain habitat, visit genocide memorials and go bird-watching and trekking in lush national parks. Sites developed with foreign visitors in mind include Akagera game lodge in the east, Nyungwe forest in the southwest, Volcanoes Park in the northwest, and the Gisozi genocide memorial in Kigali (see Map 2). Since 2010, approximately one million tourists visit the country each year, with Americans, Indians, the English and Germans leading the way.[33]

Despite the impressive numbers of tourists, the hospitality industry was not well planned or managed. By the end of 2014, the hotel industry registered only 19 percent occupancy, with 97 percent of beds sold to foreigners.[34] Major hotel chains such as the Marriott, Radisson and other luxury names brought in most foreign business, while local boutique hotels, guesthouses and hostels in Kigali and the rest of the country might go for weeks without selling a room. Many owners were forced to close.

In the run-up to the twentieth anniversary of the genocide, government officials brushed off any hospitality-sector closures as typical anxieties of entrepreneurial growth and maturity, noting that most rural hotels were closed for failing to meet strict hygiene standards. Owners in Kigali and elsewhere sang a different tune, citing an absence of skilled tourism professionals, lack of demand and high taxes.[35]

Things were no less difficult in other industries, particularly in rural regions. The RPF imposed top-down technical solutions to rural production and strictly controlled who could grow what. By 2012, the country had been divided into twelve crop zones, covering everything from cash crops for export (coffee, tea, flowers and pyrethrum) to domestic food production (bananas, beans, cassava, maize, Irish and sweet potatoes).[36] In line with Vision 2020 goals, targeted zoning was developed to produce maximum yields across ecologically and topographically diverse Rwanda, and in line with the country's rainfall patterns, which invariably result in drought and flooding.

On the face of it, agricultural zoning makes good policy sense in densely populated and chronically food-insecure Rwanda. However, this approach to rural development left some of Rwanda's poorer households in the lurch as government requirements to grow according to zone meant that household food production suffered. Widespread shortages of basic foodstuffs including beans, potatoes, bananas and cereals drove prices up, putting these basic items out of reach of much of the rural poor. In 2012, UNICEF found that 43 percent of rural Rwandan children had suffered malnutrition at some point in their first five years of life.[37] These hardships are well known to the RPF, and the government has instituted several pro-poor initiatives to boost incomes. For example, the "one cow, one family" program, known as Girinka, gifts cows to poor families who demonstrate an ability to lift themselves out of poverty through household consumption and sale of excess milk at market. The initiative was ripe for petty corruption as local officials decide who might benefit. Poor households are also eligible for free or subsidized housing, health care and education, provided they meet government standards for good citizenship and entrepreneurship. Foreign agronomists and other development technicians have criticized the Girinka and other programs for showing preferential treatment to those who help local officials meet their *imihigo* contract requirements.[38]

The requirements from *imihigo* are lengthy and relentless. In 2011, the government obliged local leaders across the country to oversee the demolition of thatched roof homes as part of their *imihigo* contracts. According to the UN Development Programme, nearly 60 percent of Rwandans, notably those in rural areas, live in thatched roof homes called *nyakatsi*. All the same, the government decreed thatched houses to be a health and safety concern, and called for their destruction. The government did not assist citizens with the necessary financing to rebuild the mandated cement homes with metal sheeting roofs, as required by the decree. By December 2014, when the "Bye Bye Nyakatsi" campaign ended, at least eighty thousand rural Rwandans had been made homeless by the initiative.

Accustomed to the penury of his rural constituents, Kagame zealously pursued his pledge to reduce Rwanda's dependence on donor aid to 30 percent by 2017.[39] Weaning Rwanda off foreign aid was a tall order for a country where donors accounted for nearly half of all government spending in 2014.[40] Although Rwanda necessarily accepted outside largesse, the president remained vexed by foreign donors' previous aid restrictions, and continued to regularly and often angrily recall their failure to stop the 1994 genocide. For Kagame and the RPF, aid restrictions demonstrate foreign disrespect for his government's hard work and drive in bringing Rwanda up from the ashes of genocide.

12

FRIENDS ONLY

Rwanda's governance structure is vast, but after 2010 it was clear that all the country's rules came from one man—the president, aided by a small, influential cadre of RPF leaders. In mid-2012, the Office of the President instructed senior RPF and local officials to prepare the population for the imminent twentieth anniversary of the genocide. The message was succinct and well rehearsed: Rwanda is a peaceful and prosperous place since 1994, thanks to the skilled leadership of Paul Kagame.

For all his careful planning, the president's effort to control the event's narrative was soon called into question in an interim United Nations report alleging RPF support of a proxy militia group in the DRC known as M23.[1] The report also asserted the Rwandan government was supporting the rebellion as a means to pursue its own economic ends in mineral-rich DRC, by recruiting boys and young men to join its ranks. Just as the government readied to mark the twentieth anniversary of the genocide, donors delayed and suspended their aid, much to Kagame's dismay.

Asserting Rwanda's national imperative to provide security for its citizens, high-ranking RPF officials did not deny aiding M23. Rather, President Kagame and his Foreign Minister, Louise Mushikiwabo, evaded culpability, while complaining about the international community's condescension: "This child-to-parent relationship has to end ... there has to be a minimum respect," seethed Mushikiwabo. "As long as countries wave check books over our heads, we can never be equal."[2] Kagame also fumed: "If a country's giving us aid it doesn't give them the right to control us. I mean it. I can say thank you, you are really helpful. But you don't own me." The duo also reminded international audiences that Rwanda was a pivotal player in United Nations peacekeeping operations in Africa; Rwanda's outsized peacekeeping presence in African conflicts allowed American and European soldiers to remain at home, as preferred by their voting publics.[3]

Behind this public bravado, Kagame and Mushikiwabo engaged in telephone diplomacy with European and North American donors. The effort culminated with Kagame's conversation with Barack Obama. The then American president warned that any support for the M23 was inconsistent with Rwanda's stated desire for stability and peace. Obama's admonishment marked a subtle shift in aid rhetoric. Donor practice remained in place, however, as foreign currency soon flowed anew. The conversation with Obama indicated that, with the exception of a few diplomatic hiccups, Kagame continued to have support from major Western powers.

Behind closed doors, in their monthly coordination meeting, donors pondered if the RPF was truly committed to democracy. Following the 2013 parliamentary elections, when the RPF lost seats while retaining majority control, this charge earned further consideration. The RPF had touted its second postgenocide elections as a sign of Rwanda's maturing democracy. Instead, the results confirmed the façade of balloting in authoritarian states, where elections are "intended to show that the dictatorship can make the dog perform tricks, that it can intimidate a substantial part of the population, so that any opposition is futile."[4] Some of Rwanda's donors queried the value of funding elections if the outcome was a foregone conclusion, but none withdrew their support.

Embracing Kagame's bombastic example, senior RPF officials ended any show of courtesy for donor criticism of the RPF's version of democracy. How dare they lecture the president on human rights when he spent years suffering in refugee camps in Uganda? Kagame did not even try to conceal his hostility: "This so-called human-rights world didn't ask me what was happening for me to be there 30 years. Who are these gods who police others for their rights?"[5]

A telling example of the narrowing of the ruling class came in 2013 when Kagame angrily dismissed then Justice Minister Tharcisse Karugarama. The minister had spoken against the possibility of Kagame remaining as president after his constitutionally mandated two seven-year terms in 2017. True to form, Kagame wasted no time blasting his former friend and long-loyal member of the RPF: "Why don't you tell him to step down himself? All those years he's been there, he's not the only one who can be the justice minister."[6] Within a week, Johnston Busingye, another RPF insider, was named to the justice portfolio. The broader message to foreign meddlers or domestic critics of Kagame's reign was unflinching: if you aren't with us, then you are against us, and now, you are no longer one of us.

No Longer With Us

Anyone perceived as being against the RPF is portrayed as an enemy of the state. This tactic is well known among domestic political critics who have dared to make their grievances public. Many outsiders have concluded that Kagame is a tyrant. Indeed, there is no denying that his aggressive leadership style is repressive for many. However, Kagame's autocratic manner penetrates the lives of Rwandans in much the same way as did those who preceded him: the head of state is to lead his people toward reason and eliminate enemies by terror. The policy choices of the RPF reflect this principle, as do government responses to what outsiders believe are gentle or constructive criticisms. The strong reactions of senior officials, led by the president and those closest to him, are best understood as a blend of elite entitlement and a general acceptance in Rwandan political culture that some must die so that the body politic may live. Within a year of becoming president, Kagame was explicit: critics at home and abroad would be dealt with most fiercely, while those who supported the RPF were to be praised as model citizens of virtue.

Internal Fractures Ripple Out

The RPF was not immune to dramatic political exodus, as evidenced by the departures of former RPF Secretary-General and Ambassador to the US Theogene Rudasingwa, former Minister of Justice Gerald Gahima, former army Chief of Staff General Kayumba Nyamwasa, and former head of external and military intelligence Patrick Karegeya. The four men were once Paul Kagame's trusted friends and part of the RPF's senior leadership team. Between 2005 and 2010, they each fled Rwanda following disputes over Kagame's ironfisted approach to governance and disagreements over sharing the economic spoils of RPF rule. The self-imposed exile of these men manifested more than elite Tutsi discontent with the president. It was now apparent that at least a few RPF founding members saw the organization as "a vehicle to serve the political and economic interests of one person—the party president."[7] In August 2010, these four former confidants united to create an opposition party in exile, the Rwandan National Congress (RNC). Their objections to Kagame's leadership were carefully outlined in a sixty-page report, "Rwanda Briefing."[8] The list of shortcomings was lengthy and told with insider knowledge of human rights abuses, politically motivated disappearances and assassinations, corruption, nepotism and the policy of excluding Hutu from public life in the RPF's Rwanda.

The release of the briefing came at a time of great anxiety for the RPF leadership and, by extension, many Rwandans. Prior to the August 2010 presidential elections, grenade explosions at busy places in Kigali roused collective fears of terrorism. The gruesome decapitation of the Vice President of the Green Party frightened many, as it was widely believed that the RPF had ordered the killing, although there was no way to know for sure. Police declared the incident a botched robbery attempt; however, despite quickly apprehending several suspects, no criminal proceedings were initiated. Political opponents such as Victoire Ingabire of the FDU remained in jail, while General Nyamwasa survived a July assassination attempt outside his home in Johannesburg, South Africa.

The RPF's reaction to the briefing did little to calm a nervous public, leading some to wonder if a coup attempt from within the RPF was imminent. Politically attuned Rwandans wondered if the RPF could survive the defection of four key senior members and what a change in leadership might mean for them and their families. To this day, Rwanda has yet to experience a peaceful transfer of political power, resulting in a sense of dread for many. Marie-Pierre, a thirtysomething Hutu subsistence farmer living in southeastern Rwanda, summed up a widely shared sentiment:

I am loyal to the RPF for survival. When those in Kigali fight, it affects us all. We learned that in 1994. What happens in Kigali used to stay there. Now their upsets are ours. I want my children to grow up without knowing violence like genocide. When the big men fight, people like me fear. I'm hoping our President can regain control so we can try to continue with this life. I just invested in forty coffee bushes. I need politicians to think of people like me before they launch us into another war.

Urban elites quietly wondered whether Kagame could replace two senior military officers who had direct knowledge of the security and military operations of the RPF. The president asserted his authority by quickly adding new faces to his security detail and ordering the military to harass the relatives of the four traitors, all while wearing a bulletproof vest in public. A suffocating sense of anxiety pervaded daily life; many chose to limit their activities to daylight hours. Once again, just as in late 1993 and early 1994, people became hyper-mindful of those around them and their possible sinister intentions. Disappearances remained commonplace as arbitrary detention of potential FDLR allies or government critics—both Hutu and Tutsi—increased. At the dawn of 2012, fear was a way of life. The power of a climate of fear is its indeterminate, invisible and silent nature. It keeps everyone alert, suspicious of outsiders, and apprehensive with family, friends and colleagues.

Kagame sought to discredit his opponents and reassert his authority with one of his most tried-and-true tactics. A smear campaign was quickly mounted to denounce the four RNC founders as traitors to the cause of peace and unity. As perpetrators of the very crimes and excesses of office they now accused Kagame and others of, the "renegades" were denounced as opportunistic backstabbers seeking to cash in. This was a tricky balancing act as Kagame and other RPF leaders were unable to directly challenge the RNC's allegations without admitting to their own crimes. Too forceful a denunciation could pique the interest of the donor community, something the RPF wanted to avoid, without appearing too soft on the deserters. All four men had played critical roles in consolidating the RPF's political and military might: Gahima and Rudasingwa helped eliminate the political opposition; Nyamwasa participated in the carnage during the 1997–98 counterinsurgency in the northwest; Karegeya was involved in the disappearances or assassinations of RPF critics at home and abroad. Instead, the struggle to squash the RNC became a war of words for international, not domestic, audiences, with the publication of a fourteen-page rejoinder on the Ministry of Defense website in October 2010. Authored by Kagame's security advisor, Brigadier General Richard Rutatina, and military spokesperson, Lieutenant Colonel Jill Rutaremara, the "Response to allegations by four renegades" was a political tract designed to delegitimize the RNC while assuring donors of the RPF's commitment to economic development through technocratic governance.[9]

Meanwhile, Kagame bolstered military fealty, reminding the rank-and-file, in speeches delivered in Kinyarwanda, of their oath of loyalty to the government. Anyone with known or suspected ties to the RNC were monitored closely; even the slightest suspicion of illicit communication resulted in the firing, imprisonment or disappearance of the offending individual.

To prove that the RNC was trying to return Rwanda to "backward" ethnic politics, Kagame embraced a second favorite tactic, ordering an *in absentia* military trial of his former comrades. The January 2011 trial focused on the defendants' public criticisms of the government and the president. Unsurprisingly, all four accused were found guilty of endangering state security, destabilizing public order, ethnic divisionism, defamation and forming a criminal enterprise. Karegeya and Gahima were each sentenced to twenty years in prison, while Nyamwasa and Rudasingwa each received twenty-four years.

Rudasingwa, in his role as RNC spokesperson, scoffed at the government's rulings in a series of comments from his home in the United States in February 2011. Rudasingwa called the rulings the product of a kangaroo court. Soon after, the RNC joined hands with the Paul Rusesabagina Foundation, issuing another insult to the Rwandan government. An ethnic Hutu, Rusesabagina had become an outspoken critic of the RPF. He is well known in the Anglophone world as the hero of the popular Hollywood movie *Hotel Rwanda*. The RPF praised the film upon its release in 2004. Rusesabagina's professed political aspirations made him an object of RPF interest, then enmity, as he used his growing international presence to criticize the government.[10] Believed to command the loyalties of ethnic Hutu resident both in and outside of Rwanda, Rusesabagina became the object of his own

RPF smear campaign soon after the merger with the RNC. The RPF labeled Rusesabagina an ethnic ideologue and genocide denier. The allegations were delivered in multiple platforms, including in English-language speeches delivered by senior RPF officials, opinion pieces published in the RPF-operated newspaper, *The New Times*, and the publication of a book written by a staffer in the Office of the President.[11]

Already riled by the RNC's burgeoning partnership with Rusesabagina, the RPF was further inflamed by the September 2011 announcement that the RNC and Victoire Ingabire's FDU had joined forces to overthrow Kagame. It was almost as if the opposition in exile was actively undermining the government in the run-up to the twentieth anniversary of the genocide.

Two things were telling about these partnerships. They marked first-time efforts to form a multi-ethnic coalition to tackle the political excesses and human rights abuses of the RPF government. Cross-ethnic partnerships had yet to succeed in Rwanda's postcolonial political history, despite attempts during the Social Revolution in the late 1950s and again during the peace negotiations before the 1994 genocide. Voices of political moderation, advocating inter-ethnic power sharing and collaboration, are always among the first to be eliminated from public life. Second, just as the ruling RPF operated outside Rwanda from its base in Uganda, the coalition emerged outside of Rwanda, with the RNC directing operations from its offices in the United States. The policy platform of this coalition of unlikely allies was at once ironic and unsurprising; it was nearly identical to the ideological goals of the then exiled RPF in the late 1980s.[12] The RNC advocated the creation of a cross-ethnic transitional government to reform the legacy of the RPF dictatorship and a democracy rooted in human rights, the rule of law and repatriation of refugees.[13] This ideological continuity signaled to even the most casual observers that the RNC hardly represented a threat to the RPF's political project or to President Kagame's leadership.

The political relevance of the RNC soon receded; its influence became far less pronounced once the military court judgment was announced. Most Rwandans knew better than to discuss politics, and those suspected of supporting the RNC or other opposition parties were quickly reminded of their folly. Angelica, a Tutsi social worker who came to live in Kigali in 2001, experienced the fallout of a mundane political act, as she held out, despite repeated urging, from joining the RPF. In 2010, her Kigali home was broken into while she visited relatives living in Rubavu town in the northwest. Upon discovering the theft of electronics and some household items, Angelica went with her husband and son to report the loss to the police. Instead of opening an investigation, the officers asked why Angelica had yet to join the "family." They asked if she was a member of the RNC, insinuating that she must be if she had not yet joined the RPF. Angelica said that she joined the RPF within the week "to avoid the pressures of being independent." A representative of a Western donor country living in Kigali offered a darker assessment: "The love Rwandans have for Kagame is fearsome. It is a challenge to love someone who wants to vigorously shake you into compliance. We hear this from government officials who trust us enough to share their concerns. Rwandans really love their country and their President. Who wouldn't choose love when the alternative is death?"[14]

"Friends Speak Frankly to Friends"

Rwandans like Angelica had an additional opportunity to demonstrate their unmitigated loyalty to the RPF during the November 2011 visit of then American Ambassador to the United Nations, Susan Rice. At the Kigali Institute of Science and Technology, Rice dedicated much of her speech to praising Kagame's leadership, noting the "astonishing" economic recovery and the "remarkable" social progress Rwanda has made since the RPF took office in July 1994.[15] In the last few minutes of her presentation, citing the belief "that friends should speak frankly to friends," Rice shifted from heaping praise for Rwanda's "economic vitality" to gentle criticism, noting a lack of political rights and freedoms that threatened said growth. Advocating for increased political openness, Rice noted that "the broadening of democracy can be the next great achievement of this great country and its remarkable people." In the packed auditorium, members of the audience shifted uncomfortably in their seats. Some reached nervously to busy themselves with their cell phones. Others stopped taking notes and leaned back in their seats as if to distance themselves from Rice's words.

The entire audience were members of the country's elite urban, educated and English-speaking political class. Almost all of them had either fought in the bush for the RPF during the civil war and genocide, or had grown up in refugee camps in Uganda. They knew Rice's transgression to be egregious. There would be no cry from the gallery to assure the safety and security of those who criticize the government, whether an esteemed foreign guest like Ambassador Rice, or members of Rwanda's domestic political opposition. Within minutes, some took to social media sites like Twitter and online discussion groups to speculate on President Kagame's response. It was not a question of whether he would react, but how and when. As the head of a local cooperative remarked the next morning: "We all knew Kagame would react but we could not predict what he might do. Rwanda needs American dollars for our many [development] projects but to insult his leadership in public? In front of members of his own party? That is another matter!"[16]

Kagame waited several weeks to respond to Rice, leaving many in Kigali and the countryside on edge. Why hadn't the president responded? Was a political crisis in the offing? In carefully timed and crafted responses at his monthly press conference, Kagame first criticized Rice's indelicate suggestion that an outsider knew best what the country needed to grow its democracy. To an audience of RPF-approved journalists, the president reminded government officials, political elites and the military that he would decide the content and form of conversations about government policy and practice. Rice and her ilk were outsiders— anyone outside of the family was a traitor. Kagame went on to joke that perhaps foreigners should attend *ingando*-like reeducation before accepting an invitation to speak as a guest of the government; they too need to be sensitized to Rwandan-style democracy.

At an *umuganda* near Kigali shortly thereafter, the president used a more bellicose tone when he addressed Rice's transgression. Kagame began his address in Kinyarwanda with a soon-to-be characteristic rant about "so-called friends." Dressed casually in a button-down plaid shirt and tan chinos, with a shiny new wood-handle shovel in hand, Kagame chided Rice, then addressed her criticism in ways that Rwandans would be sure to understand:

> Every person among eleven million Rwandans can speak whenever and whatever he or she wants because we [the RPF] have continuously empowered them on freedom of speech. But I cannot accept that there are 100 or 150 people [political opponents] that we prevent from speaking, and to whom the right of reply is not allowed? What type of people are those? Why should we allow them to speak? Among them there are those who say useless things and even some destructive things. If you say things that destroy the Rwanda we are building, we shall destroy you. We won't apologize to anyone about that.

In Rwanda, language is used to reveal and conceal. Doublespeak is a powerful political weapon, with speakers using Kinyarwanda in ambiguous ways to convey levels of nuance that are difficult for non-native speakers to understand. Cultural anthropologists have studied the political qualities of Kinyarwanda to discern its political uses. Language subtly reveals the status and position of the person of the speaker. Laughter is sometimes used to express displeasure or frustration in politically charged moments, as in Kagame's reminder of Rice's profound misstep. The political uses of Kinyarwanda are best reflected in Rwanda's rich lexicon of proverbs, riddles and poetry, much of it dedicated to praising the king and his warriors. Linguists have identified at least 2,500 proverbs, cataloguing them by theme, including political authority and power, ethnic relations, gender relations, policing sexual morality, elite–nonelite relations, justice, national unity and peace, just to name a few.[17] Ordinary people also use proverbs and other metaphors to express frustration or fear through storytelling. Stories are a powerful means to share one's hopes and dreams, fears and frustrations, without overstepping the boundaries of acceptable political talk.

Kagame's words and style of delivery reflected a core value when speaking in public—*ubwenge*. A principle that guides public speech in Rwanda, *ubwenge* refers to who can say what, to whom, when and how. The interlocutor needs intelligence to speak wisely and with self-control, which makes public speech the domain of those "in the know."[18] It also accentuates the chasm between elites, as those who know, and ordinary people, who need guidance. The responsibility of knowing is something reserved for elites, meaning it is closely guarded as a form of political capital and a mechanism that reinforces the hierarchy between elites and ordinary people.

The president's words further served to remind Rwandans of Kagame's pole position as head of the government, chairperson of the RPF and military commander-in-chief. US-based, Rwanda-born political scientist Noel Twagiramungu highlights the merging of these roles and their roots in precolonial history. In the seventeenth century, the founder of the Nyiginya kingdom, Ruganzu Ndoli, introduced the concept of the leader of the country (king or president) as simultaneously "owner" of the army.[19] Unlike most other postcolonial African states, where the everyday use of multiple national languages is commonplace, Rwandans share only Kinyarwanda. In the precolonial period, having a common language helped promote political unity that in turn strengthened the growth of the state, with the geo-political entity known as Rwanda finally taking its present-day territorial shape in 1911.[20]

Rwandan culture frowns on overt or uncontrolled public displays of emotion. In contemporary Rwanda, age-old proverbs provide a useful way to understand what people are trying to communicate without explicitly saying anything that the listener might consider to be subversive, insulting or offensive. The telling and sharing of proverbs acts as a social lubricant. For outsiders, awareness of and appreciation for the political and practical purposes of proverbs is critical for understanding local dynamics. They can be used to praise or appreciate one's superior or to warn of impending calamity. Proverbs can reveal one's social or economic status, and can be used to discipline or to highlight family, clan and kinship ties, among other meanings. For example, the proverb "in a court of fowls, the cockroach never wins his case" means that individuals of lesser status rarely receive justice because they lack the necessary political connections to do so. By communicating messages that cannot be expressed openly, proverbs are the underpinning of Rwandan political life. This form of communication is open to interpretation; the success of the person receiving the message is dependent on his or her ability to correctly assess the message being conveyed.

Like any politician worth his salt, President Kagame is a master of wordplay. He uses verbal acumen to carefully inform Rwandans what is expected of them, while maintaining a carefully styled international image as a progressive African leader. When the president employs doublespeak, he uses Kinyarwanda. International journalists and other analysts are left to ask Rwandan interpreters what Kagame has communicated to domestic audiences. Rwandans, for their part, understand the importance of the president's words, having received a lifetime of socialization on the political and social uses of rhetoric. They know that their political and economic fates are in the president's hands.

The use and manipulation of language by Kagame and his closest government allies are revealed in remarks about the January 2014 assassination of Patrick Karegeya, Rwanda's former head of intelligence. Hired killers are nothing new in Rwanda.[21] Karegeya's assassination was part of a broader trend of government critics being murdered or injured, a pattern that began soon after the RPF took power in 1994, and has been intensifying since 2010.[22] Officially, the government denied any involvement in Karegeya's death. However, President Kagame came close to condoning his murder a few weeks after the fact, when he said: "Whoever betrays the country will pay the price." Both the foreign affairs minister and the prime minister pilloried Karegeya over social media; using Twitter, they declared his death a just result for betraying the government.[23] Regime insider General James Kabarebe used language Rwandans would understand in referencing Karegeya's lesser status when he said in Kinyarwanda: "When you choose to be a dog, you die like a dog, and the cleaners will wipe away the trash so that it does not stink for them. Actually, such consequences are faced by those who have chosen such a path. There is nothing we can do about it, and we should not be interrogated [by diplomats or foreign journalists] over it."[24]

References to betrayal and dogs are both linked to proverbs that RPF elites deployed to rationalize their presumed superiority and justify the loss of Karegeya's life. The proverb *Nta bushyo bw'imbwa bugere-ranywa n'ubushyo bw'inka* (A pack of dogs cannot be compared to cattle) is rooted in Tutsi superiority over Hutu, as cattle were the symbol of prestige, wealth and power in ancient Rwanda. By accusing Karegeya of being a traitor to his country, Kagame targets him as deserving death, while distancing himself from the dirty work of killing, citing the proverb *Ntihica umwami hica rubanda* (It is not the king who kills, but his followers). To be sure, Karegeya was no saint. At a minimum, it is likely that he ordered or participated in revenge killings of Hutu during and after the 1994 genocide. Even so, the victims of Karegeya's crimes will never see justice as long as Rwandan political leaders choose violence to manage political opponents. A sincere human rights approach that values all human life would see Karegeya before a court of law to account for his alleged crimes, not found dead by strangulation in suspicious circumstances in an upscale hotel room in Johannesburg.

Commemoration for Outsiders

As part of the RPF's genocide anniversary plans, the government mobilized large numbers of people in the name of national unity and economic development. Massive crowds would help shape the narrative of the event and remind foreign guests of Rwanda's spectacular recovery from the ashes of genocide. The slogan of the week-long commemoration event was "*Kwibuka!* [Remember!] But Never Again!"

On April 7, 2014, an audience of almost thirty thousand people filled Kigali's Amahoro soccer stadium, including accredited dignitaries, Rwandan government and military officials, senior civil society and church representatives, as well as school children and widows of the genocide. The ceremony had been prepared with an international audience in mind. Some five hundred heads of state, diplomats, UN and World Bank officials, and international journalists—Tony Blair, Roméo Dallaire, Samantha Power and Thabo Mbeki among them—listened to speeches by distinguished guests and stories of survivors and their rescuers, and observed a dramatization of the genocide.

To shrieks of alarm and wails of anguish, Rwandan performers acted out the RPF's version of history.[25] The play began with the arrival of a jeep full of white colonizers who swapped straw hats for the blue helmets of UN peacekeepers. Rwandan men and women in traditional dress then simulated the swift and intimate machete hacks that took the lives of so many during the genocide. The blue helmets stood passively by as the Rwandans fell one by one on the grass. As the bodies fell, the RPF soldiers swept in to save lives and restore order. The moral of the story was apparent to all: in the face of international apathy, the RPF had liberated Rwanda and led it forward for twenty years. The play's theme resonated with foreign guests, including UN Secretary-General

Ban Ki-moon. Speaking at the event, Ban proffered an apology for the failure of his organization to stop the genocide and save Tutsi lives once it had begun.

President Kagame's remarks during the commemorative week focused on Kwibohora (Liberation Day), a core theme in the postgenocide era.[26] The president highlighted the choices that Rwandans made to kill one another, while stressing that since 1994, they have made even more important choices: to stay together, to be accountable and to think big. The rhetoric of progress and success was on full display throughout the weeklong commemorations, much to the delight of visiting guests. Repeatedly, diplomats and UN officials congratulated the RPF for its vision for peace and prosperity, and apologized for their collective failures to save Tutsi lives in 1994. The government reveled in foreign praise, having long waited for a satisfying apology from the UN and other members of the international community.

Outsider commendations were particularly welcome following the decision of the Americans to cut military aid in late 2013, after another UN report alleged Kigali was sustaining the M23 militia in eastern Congo. Although the cut was symbolic (just US$200,000 from an annual military support budget of US$170 million), it signaled that Rwanda's closest allies were growing tired of its regional meddling.

Honoring Tutsi Lives

The twin themes of liberation and transformation meant that the entire country was mobilized with military-like efficiency to ensure an incident-free anniversary. Kigali, as the site of most commemoration events, was scrubbed and polished. This was a tall order for an already spotless and efficient city.[27] Still, there were a few places to cleanse and beautify.

Many stadiums across the country replaced the sod on their soccer pitches. A handful of Tutsi survivors murmured their unease with this upgrade. Stadiums had been the site of numerous massacres during the genocide. In places where bodies were piled, the grass did not grow back, leading many to conclude that pools of human blood had settled on the pitch, killing the grass and preventing new growth. These brown spots had become informal memorials for soccer fan survivors of all ethnicities, who remembered both playing on the grassy pitches in the early 1990s and cowering there in 1994 and sometimes after. Like any other civilian misgivings, the concerns of the survivors were swept aside. When the National Commission for the Fight against Genocide officially launched the twentieth anniversary commemorations in January 2014, Kigali—and the country's stadiums—had been refreshed for the main event.

The national period of mourning started at the Gisozi Memorial with the lighting of the Kwibuka Flame of Remembrance. Much like the Olympic torch, the Kwibuka Flame traveled across the country prior to the official start of the commemoration. It represented a beacon for community conversations about Rwanda's journey from genocide to peace. Never inclined to take chances, the government dispatched specially trained Ministry of Justice officials to lead these local conversations.

There was a symbolic importance to these conversations; they were the culmination of almost two decades of socialization to the RPF way, facilitated by ever-deepening government authority and presence at the local level. In 2011, the RPF appointed a series of new councils and committees to assist the sector and cell-level executive secretaries and coordinators of villages (*imidugudu*) in their work. The intention was to bring the entire population, through general assemblies of all residents, into the governance structure. The technocratic element of sector and cell governance was also placed in the hands of Kigali-appointed consultative committees. In creating a battalion of "decentralized technicians," the government has made it virtually impossible for ordinary people to question or opt out of government initiatives.[28] The abiding presence of appointed officials also makes it impossible to vote out unpopular non-elected officials. The result is a state structure that gives the appearance of bottom-up accountability, while ensuring that every person is ready and willing to meet the expectations of a model citizenry. In the run-up to the twentieth anniversary of the genocide, everyone was to be fully compliant in the name of national unity and reconciliation.

Renewed RPF efforts to liberate Rwandans from the scourge of ethnic hatred blanketed the country. Billboards to fight genocide ideology bolstered official narratives to eliminate "negative forces," "traitors," and their foreign accomplices.[29] Lest Rwandans fail to get the message, the government introduced in 2013 the Ndi Umunyarwanda (I am Rwandan) initiative. Implemented by the Ministry of Justice and NURC officials through local government channels, the program gave Hutu the opportunity to atone for crimes committed by other Hutu during the 1994 genocide. In turn, Tutsi had the chance to offer forgiveness on behalf of other Tutsi, whether or not they had been in the country in 1994. Ndi Umunyarwanda offered collective guilt for some and collective impunity for others. Those who were willing to criticize the RPF in the increasingly tense political environment before the twentieth anniversary commemorations considered the Ndi Umunyarwanda initiative to be yet another form of control. Sylvie, a nineteen-year-old National University of Rwanda student and card-carrying member of the RPF, made her skepticism plain in hushed tones:

> In Rwanda, the private world of feelings, of hopes or dreams, even falling in love to maybe one day get married, exist in the public world of apology and forgiveness. Many in my family died in the genocide. But no one cares how this might shape my life today so long as an apology is made. I am part of the new Rwanda because I am young—I didn't experience genocide directly. But I lost relatives. I don't know

much about those days because my parents won't talk about how our relatives died. And I try to keep quiet because of course I will lose my right to study if I am seen as a critic!

Ndi Umunyarwanda makes Hutu apologize for things their ethnic brothers and sisters may have done. It's absurd because it doesn't matter what actually happened. You apologize to get perks like bursaries to study or even health cards. You forgive to keep these benefits. Foreigners come and say "Wow! Rwandans know the truth." It's simple: young Hutu must apologize. Even me, I apologized to keep studying and to avoid conflict. A girl I know refused to apologize at the ceremony on campus. She said "no" several times. Finally, the police came to take her away. She is no longer in residence, and I heard she fled to Uganda to avoid getting arrested. This is so normal. You do what you are told or you suffer the consequences.

The "consequences" of not participating as required were well known to Rwandans by 2013. The performative aspects of apology and forgiveness had already been honed before the *gacaca* courts. These local courts had pursued almost every adult Hutu in Rwanda in a strategy of maximal prosecution and had wrapped up their work in mid-2012. Ndi Umunyarwanda gave the RPF a chance to remind Rwandans—especially former Hutu—of the importance of ethnic unity to national security. The initiative also pointed to cracks in the façade of government omnipotence, including President Kagame's velvet touch guided by an iron hand. Coercion to ensure conformity was the order of the day; forgiveness—but never forgetting the RPF's version of history—the backdrop to everyday life.

Tightening the Noose

Despite the resounding success of the twentieth anniversary commemorations, no rest or reprieve was forthcoming. The country shared a collective sigh of relief as the last foreign dignitaries departed from Kanombe International Airport, but President Kagame remained preoccupied with maintaining the RPF as Rwanda's rightful rulers. The RPF continued to hone its hypersensitivity to external criticism and crushing of domestic dissent.

In mid-April 2014, the government indicted internationally acclaimed gospel singer and survivor of the 1994 genocide, Kizito Mihigo, on charges of treason for threatening to overthrow the government. A few weeks before, Mihigo had uploaded a new song on YouTube that allegedly disputed the official narrative of the genocide. Mihigo's composition "The Meaning of Death" (*Igisobanuro Cy'urupfu*) called on Rwandans to honor Tutsi and Hutu lives lost during the genocide, in the name of forgiveness and reconciliation.[30] Such sentiment is illegal as a form of genocide denial.

Mihigo's case revealed the absurdity of the RPF's obsession with security and survival, as well as the extent to which it controlled the security and judicial sectors. A popular and feted singer, Mihigo thought that his fame would protect him from the wrath of the government. Before he released "The Meaning of Death," Mrs. Kagame's office had invited Mihigo to sing on behalf of genocide survivors during the official commemoration. However, Mihigo's lyrics soon raised hackles in RPF circles, and he disappeared before foreign guests arrived for the commemoration ceremonies. Mihigo reappeared after the commemorations had ended, handcuffed and dressed in pink prison attire, accused of having planned a violent overthrow of the government in collusion with the Congo-based FDLR. The Catholic Church in Rwanda remained mum, its leadership having distanced itself from the popular singer. In hopes of some leniency, Mihigo confessed to all the crimes leveled against him. In February 2015, Mihigo was found guilty of conspiring against the Rwandan government and sentenced to ten years in prison.[31] Silent shockwaves rippled across the country. The message was clear—no one was immune from the grasp of the RPF.

The Mihigo affair marked the first time that the RPF targeted an esteemed Tutsi survivor of the genocide with no obvious political or military ties yet with friends in high places, including Jeannette Kagame. Many connected elites speculated that he had been in contact with Patrick Karegeya, the former head of Rwandan intelligence found murdered in a South African hotel. Following Karegeya's assassination, disappearances and arrests among political, business and military opponents or critics of the RPF intensified, putting everyone on tenterhooks. Military intelligence had since accessed Karegeya's laptop and cell phones (he carried at least five), allowing Rwanda's security elites to track who had been in contact with the RNC co-founder before his assassination. The Kigali rumor mill has speculated that the government is systematically sorting Karegeya's contacts, and plans for them all to disappear.

EPILOGUE
The Politics of "Never Again"

Never again. These two words hover over Rwanda's collective psyche. "Never again" and its cousin "genocide ideology" are the lifeblood that sustains the country's narratives of redemption, renewal, self-reliance and dignity. "Never again" is a mantra, framing the RPF's collective perception as the hero of a dark period in Rwandan history, making it the sole arbiter of the country's genocide-free future.[1] The phrase propels government policy, setting the boundaries of acceptable public speech and action. Model citizens are socialized and sensitized to reject the ethnic ideologies that the RPF believes caused the 1994 genocide.

"Never again" is an ideology through which the RPF leadership interprets and responds to real and perceived threats. It explains why President Kagame and other Rwandan political elites seek to accumulate power and vanquish their opponents with an iron first. All powerful elements of the Rwandan state are under the president's command—the police, the armed forces, the judiciary and government officials go along with his designs. If Rwandans feel uninspired by Kagame's visionary leadership, they stand aside in the name of self-preservation rather than obedience. Others, namely rural Rwandans, struggling to make ends meet under the economic and national unity policies of the RPF, shellac their endorsement of their president with a paste of resignation and fear. For them, "Never again" means more of the same.

Even so, cries of "Never again" are a valuable history lesson, reminding us of the need to ward off mass political violence in Rwanda and elsewhere. Whatever one's assessment of the RPF's postgenocide rule, it is the only game in town. This raises a crucial question: are the policies of the RPF sufficient to avoid future episodes of genocide?

Twenty-three years of evidence suggests the possibility of more mass killing, but not imminently. As yet (openly) unopposed in its implementation of national unity and reconciliation policies, the RPF could govern Rwanda for another two decades. Such an assertion can be made with confidence since 2015. In a nationwide referendum, Rwandans voted to amend their constitution to allow President Kagame—and *only* Kagame—to stand for a third seven-year term, and then for two additional five-year terms. Kagame turns sixty in 2017. Following his reelection in August 2017, with 99 percent of the vote, in an engineered ballot that was neither free nor fair, the president is unlikely to be prevented from governing until he chooses to step down.[2]

At the time of writing there is little to indicate an immediate or even short-term return to mass violence. Nonetheless, there are sociopolitical risk factors and historical patterns of violence to consider.

This is not to suggest a path dependency guaranteeing genocidal violence in Rwanda. There is nothing inherent in the country and its people that makes genocide inevitable. Eliminating an entire people requires action on the part of many who are committed to such a project, particularly political and military leaders who ignite the vision and provide the necessary resources. We saw this commitment in action in April 1994, when hardliners within Habyarimana's MRND made a choice to exterminate Tutsi in a failed attempt to hold on to power.

The structure of the Rwandan state facilitated the mass murder of Tutsi in the context of civil war. The centralized, top-down administrative capacity of the government and its reach into all corners of the country meant that officials were able to quickly mobilize Hutu to the work of killing Tutsi. This organizational capacity was reinforced by chronic physical and economic insecurity brought on by a multi-year civil war in which popular participation in a genocide became imaginable, then possible. The government also mounted and leveraged a portrayal of the RPF as a group of Tutsi invaders returning to Rwanda to oppress the majority Hutu. This depiction served as proof that Tutsi were the common enemy, worthy of death. Simply stated, an explosive cocktail of dynamic processes made genocide the strategy of Hutu hardliner choice following Habyarimana's assassination. A similar structural shock was necessary to create a political void in which the power and authority of the RPF could flourish.

At this time, given the RPF's thorough dominance of public and private life, no such vacuum is likely to develop within the country. Instead, an external threat of the same magnitude as the rebel RPF's launch of a civil war would be needed to initiate a reconfiguration of Rwandan politics. As genocide scholars have persuasively documented, the rule of thumb is "no war, no genocide."[3] The possibility of an external shock helps explain, in part, the policy choices of the RPF and Kagame's steely approach to governance. The current conflict smoldering at the heart of the country's postgenocide evolution is a war for the hearts and minds of Rwandans, especially the Hutu majority.

The irony of the RPF's approach to containing and eliminating threats to national security is not lost on Rwandans who lived through the 1994 genocide. They know that powerful people make choices rooted in self-preservation without due regard for the rural majority. They also know that political and military elites use the machinery of the state to their own ends. The RPF leadership is no different from its postcolonial predecessors in this regard. The party has long used the institutional and administrative capacities of the state to organize

Rwandan social and political life. These are the deliberate choices of an ethnic minority government, trying to reeducate what they consider to be a recalcitrant Hutu majority with genocide ideology in their hearts.

RPF policies have yet to produce an event as dramatic or devastating as the 1994 genocide. But red coals of resentment are hot enough to create simmering tensions. Moving Rwandans away from the ethnic hatred they putatively learned under successive Hutu-led post-independence regimes is easier said than done, particularly as the diagnosis is incorrect. Despite evidence that Hutu often killed their Tutsi brethren for reasons beyond ethnic foment, the RPF leadership continues to presume it governs a seething, criminal population. Meanwhile, the RPF state, consumed with the need to eradicate those who hold genocide ideology in their hearts, is an overbearing presence in everyday life, bolstered by extensive monitoring of people and place. The assumption that Rwanda remains populated by latent murderers drives President Kagame and the RPF's policies, not a measured consideration of what people might actually need to rebuild since the 1994 genocide ended.

Despite two decades in power, the RPF's approach remains deceptively simple: in exchange for the provision of goods and services—education, health care, technocratic governance and so on—the state requires unquestioning loyalty from its people. Instead of castigation, this approach has garnered the praise of the International Monetary Fund, the World Bank and several other key donors. Not unlike in 1994, the international community is again funding violence in Rwanda.[4] Under the RPF, violence is not derived from a policy of mass extermination, but fanned from the embers of exclusion and resentment.

Support for Kagame and the RPF, or at least the appearance of it, comes in two broad forms: many in positions of political or economic influence are willing to champion an authoritarian president because their commitment to democracy is weak or non-existent in the first place, having rarely experienced its rights or obligations. They feel, perhaps rightly, that it is the RPF's turn to enjoy the fruits of power. For others, Kagame's masterful exploitation of the specter of genocide to justify the curtailment of civil and political rights is a powerful sedative. The language of "Never again" explains the harassment of domestic opponents and foreign critics. The government feels no need to justify the harsh treatment that those who have genocide ideology in their hearts consistently receive, nor does it explain the silencing of those who question the RPF's "official" history. Questioning the government's version of what caused the genocide, and who did what to whom, is enough to be charged with negating or denying the genocide. A subsequent conviction and sentence to a lengthy prison term are virtually assured. The risks of being accused of having genocide ideology make it difficult, if not impossible, to challenge the RPF's official history.

All who wish to speak a different truth quickly learn that human rights abuses allegedly perpetrated or ordered by the RPF are unmentionable. The RPF's stated commitment to accountability is but a political façade. Through selective use of the justice system, the government proclaims the crimes most worthy of prosecution are those perpetrated by its enemies, real and perceived. This denial of the experiences of millions of Rwandans is potentially dangerous, for it provides a lightning rod around which they can organize their grievances. For the moment, the politics of exclusion mean that government adversaries generally operate outside of the country. So far, they appear to lack a concerted plan to return to Rwanda, or they are supported by a fractured base that makes challenging the RPF inconceivable.

Destiny Defined

Throughout Rwandan history, winner-take-all politics has been culturally rooted in a system of dominance of the ruling group over the rest of society. The RPF is no exception to the tradition. Historical context helps us understand the RPF government's policies and actions, as it works to ensure a genocide-free future.

Representing 61 percent of the population, Rwandan youth under twenty-four stand to gain or lose the most from RPF rule. Ironically, we know the least about this generation, as they rarely have the opportunity to speak for themselves. Most, especially those growing up in former Hutu families, are "stuck," unable to imagine their future in a trying economic and social climate that makes leaving home, finding jobs and having their own families nearly impossible.[5] Of course, the same challenges confront young people the world over. However, Rwanda's legacy of genocide makes the leap to adulthood all the more tenuous. The country's vast youth population also means that Kagame retains the support of the military, notably the rank-and-file. For many young people, joining the military is one of the few paths of economic mobility available to them.

Critically, Rwanda has yet to experience a peaceful transfer of power from one ruler to the next. The RPF leadership is well aware of this vulnerability. Even so, it appears not to acknowledge this as a weighty and problematic legacy. President Kagame and the RPF elite persist in seeing the past through a romanticized lens that obscures empirical reality and the lived experience of many Rwandans.

Historians have documented the bitter and bloody power struggles of Rwanda's political elites from the late 1890s to the present, while speculating on the nature of royal rule from the late fourteenth century.[6] By the time the Europeans arrived, Rwanda had grown from a small polity comprised of competing lineages to a sizable state, under King Rwabugiri (c. 1860–95). Rwabugiri's rule introduced and then hardened political hierarchy. This paved the way for heightened awareness of ethnic identity and difference. Tutsi became associated with political power and military might under Rwabugiri's rule, which also resulted in the inferior status of Hutu and the utter marginalization of Twa. Cultural differences between Tutsi, Hutu and Twa became increasingly rigid political categories that would later define one's opportunity for socio-political mobility and access to economic wealth.

Then and now, the majority of Rwandans are subject to the self-serving decisions of political elites—whether Tutsi or Hutu. In precolonial days, the intrigues of the political class resulted in sporadic violence that targeted other elites. By the 1950s, changes implemented by the Belgians and exploited by members of the royal court resulted in broader swaths of the population being caught up in the violence of the day. For most people, the violence was not physical—it was structural, instituting a deep divide between ruler and ruled. The 1994 genocide is a product of this structural legacy; it is not an exception to the broader arc of history as the RPF government claims. The RPF's obstinate refusal to recognize this uneven historical dispensation makes clear that its policy choices are inseparable from this continuum of violence.

Rwanda's top-down and centralized state system produces physical, emotional and economic violence that is intimately related to historical ethnic, class and gender hierarchies. All societies harbor such cleavages. What matters is how they are defined and made real in people's lives. This is why civil and political rights matter; they provide recourse for people to seek redress for wrongs suffered at the hands of the government. No such custom is entrenched in Rwanda, and throughout its tenure, the RPF gone out of its way to prevent a culture of civic protection from emerging.

Contemporary Rwanda also lacks strong public institutions to check or balance the power of President Kagame and his cronies. There is no reliable mechanism to sustain the peaceful transition of power to another leader, let alone a different political model. This work will likely fall on the shoulders of Rwandan youth, provided they are given the opportunity to map their own future. A trend to watch is the role the RPF might allow youth to take in public life, to which young people will be able to offer their ideas and energy. Rwandan youth matter because they have grown up in the "Never again" era, in which ethnic identity is an outdated colonial relic.

Kagame Knows Best

There is no denying that Rwanda's charismatic president wants to do right by Rwanda. Paul Kagame is the head and heart of the body politic, where thinking and dreaming big are rewarded. Thinking big is, according to Kagame, the sole path to undoing Rwanda's legacy of violence, while producing impressive economic growth, private investment, poverty reduction and gender equality. Critics who seek to diminish these accomplishments by alluding to Kagame's blood-soaked path to power are told to mind their own business.[7] On this point, the president's response to his detractors is unequivocal: "We suffered genocide, you did not."

Outsiders who question Kagame are quickly labeled as racists, unwilling to recognize an African success story when they see one. Those who do not believe the president are invited to learn about the virtues of RPF rule at Rwanda Day. An annual event held since 2009 in European and North American cities, Rwanda Day celebrates the government's accomplishments with Rwandan expatriates and foreigners the RPF considers as friends. Attendees are treated to art, dance, cuisine and other celebrated Tutsi-centric cultural artifacts to highlight how far the country has come since the dark days of 1994. Rwanda Day is best understood as a charm offensive, designed to showcase the RPF's capital "T" truth about the country. However much Rwanda has suffered in the past, all is bright under Kagame's leadership.[8]

Western academics and journalists who question whether Rwanda is as wonderful as Kagame proclaims are invited to Kigali to see for themselves, often as personal guests of the president. Once on the ground, RPF handlers personally escort their charges around town to witness the RPF's many accomplishments for themselves—shiny buildings and new shopping centers in the morning, and the fruits of reconciliation during afternoon meet-and-greets with genocide survivors at any one of hundreds of official genocide memorials.

The government's outlook is an easy sell. After all, Kigali presents as a remarkably clean and safe city, especially to visitors who have traveled elsewhere in the developing world. There are many improvements and upgrades to see, including the new Kigali Conference Centre. Opened in July 2016, the KCC is an emblem of Rwanda's rebirth. Big and beautiful, it stands as testament to the value of national ethnic unity and the power of working together. Never mind that the government has quashed political dissent, hamstrung the opposition and coopted the media. Initiatives such as the KCC are the product of thinking big. Critics, foreign and homegrown, who question the utility or value-added of expensive vanity projects are quickly reminded that Rwanda's development results speak for themselves.

Ironically, the RPF keeps its questionable human rights records on the front burner by turning questions about alleged abuses into polemical lectures on how the gains of the country's economic growth are being used. That the government achieves impressive results matters more than its means. The president's message is seductively simple, and oft repeated by his inner circle of advisors: "Where we are going is more important than how we get there."

The idea that outcome is more prized than process permeates Kagame's rhetoric and action. The RPF's focus on development outcomes makes it little different from the regimes that preceded it. More challenging to overcome are the historical and systemic conditions that make cyclical violence part of Rwandan political life.

For the time being, the RPF, under the careful watch of President Kagame, is the only game in town. Internal threats have all but been eliminated. External threats, such as the political opposition in exile, or the FDLR rebels, represent little more than a nuisance to the government for the time being. However numerous, the tens of thousands of refugees who continue to live in exile in other parts of Africa and beyond are unlikely to organize an armed return. The majority are ordinary people trying to rebuild their lives, wary of political elites who claim to speak for them.

The RPF has no interest in waging war at home, even as it does so regionally, notably in Burundi and the DRC. Any escalation of armed violence on Rwandan soil would greatly disrupt President Kagame's global reputation for reputable, donor-worthy reconstruction and reconciliation policies. Political stability is, after all, the foundation of foreign investment and domestic growth. Armed conflict would jeopardize foreign aid, totaling over US$1 billion in 2015 alone (representing some 38 percent of the total budget).

Mass violence would also weaken the engines of the Rwandan economy—construction, agriculture and tourism—where elites collude for their own gain. President Kagame and his inner circle of trusted confidants and advisors handily control the economic sector. Those who threaten this monopoly, or question Rwanda's model of economic growth, receive the same treatment as the RPF's political opponents— no mercy. Those suspected of using their sizable private wealth to fund the opposition soon find themselves in hot water. Economic elites who operate outside of the RPF's rules of business are not tolerated. The same goes for military officers, many of whom are engaged in private enterprise.[9] They are dropped or promoted with impunity, as President Kagame carefully curates his inner circle in exchange for total loyalty. Anything less is simply not tolerated. Frequent culling serves as a reminder to other elites—including those within the RPF—that the president is not afraid to use violence to maintain his pole position.

Previous confidants who fall out with the president and the inner circle are killed in suspicious circumstances, jailed or lose status and prestige on allegations of harboring genocide ideology. Since 2012, they may also be accused of corruption. Typical allegations feature a mixture of both charges. Those who can, flee the country, choosing silence for fear of assassination, given that the long arm of the RPF can harass and intimidate former comrades in foreign lands. Two recent examples illustrate the intensification of this trend. In February 2013, Assinapol Rwigara, a wealthy businessman and one of the original funders of the

RPF, was killed in a car accident. Over the following twenty-four months, the government seized or destroyed his assets, including property in Kigali. Rwigara's wife and adult children claim the RPF murdered him to appropriate the family's sizable wealth. Conversely, the police declared Rwigara's death an accident following a "professional" investigation.[10] In May 2017, Rwigara's adult daughter, Diane, announced her intent to stand in August's presidential elections. Following her announcement, RPF-controlled news outlets promptly released doctored images of a nude Ms. Rwigara, claiming that she lacks the moral propriety to be president.[11] Yet her candidacy gained traction, particularly among Rwandans living in exile, as young Rwigara chose to challenge President Kagame at the polls—something few others dared do.[12]

Starting in 2013, the government forcibly retired several senior military officers, alleging their support of outside elements keen to challenge the RPF. By the end of 2015, more than a thousand officers, including generals and colonels, had been dismissed from the service, reminding anyone with thoughts of insurrection of the president's tight grip on the military. The RPF underscored its hardline message to the military in April 2016, when the forcibly retired brigadier general and former Kagame aide Frank Rusagara was sentenced to twenty years in prison for tarnishing Rwanda's reputation.[13] The RPF claimed that both Assinapol Rwigara and Frank Rusagara had ties to the Rwandan National Congress, the opposition party founded by former Kagame confidants in 2010. Family and friends close to the two men found themselves publicly sanctioned by the RPF for exhibiting poor morals.

Civil society, long since coopted by the RPF, offers little solace for those targeted for real or perceived political opposition. There is little in the way of organized monitoring of the policies and practices of government, and Rwandan civil society lacks close ties to international agencies that might bolster or protect domestic civil society. Even the religious community provides no relief. The RPF's surveillance mechanisms keep a watchful eye on all religious leaders, monitoring their dealings with foreign clergy as well as their interactions with their flocks. Leading religious figures of all stripes act as gatekeepers for government opinion, using their positions of authority and influence to praise RPF policy. Anglican bishop and presidential advisor John Rucyahana sets the tone for church–government interactions, acting as a cheerleader rather than counterweight to government policy. The intimacy between the church and state mimics the same symbiosis that existed before the genocide, where key members of the Catholic Church tolerated economic inequality, social exclusion and ethnic violence.

President for Life?

As Rwandans look forward to their shared future, do they believe that the RPF will deliver all that it has promised? It is hard to know what most Rwandans think as there is little space for talk beyond RPF-prescribed topics. It has become increasing difficult for foreign academics, journalists and human rights researchers to safely and ethically talk to Rwandans about politically sensitive topics. RPF officials invariably cite popular support for government initiatives, making the work of foreigners an unnecessary intrusion.

Most of what we know about Rwanda and Rwandans is carefully curated by pro-regime journalists and cabinet ministers. For example, following a mass sensitization campaign reminding Rwandans of the correct way to vote, the 2015 constitutional referendum that made way for President Kagame to stand for a third term passed with 98 percent of the vote. The military was also deployed to monitor the vote, all but assuring the outcome. Once the results of the referendum were announced, the official line was that Rwandans had spoken, delivering a resounding endorsement of Kagame's leadership. Accepting his mandate for a third term, the president reminded Rwandans that their future peace and prosperity were inextricably intertwined with his benevolent leadership. Indeed, Paul Kagame and *his* RPF will determine Rwanda's future.

In December 2016, the president indicated that his RPF plans to run the country until at least the year 2050. At the National Dialogue Council known as Umushyikirano, Kagame announced a new economic development planned dubbed Vision 2050.[14] The president mapped out his government's economic agenda for the next thirty-four years. Kagame promised to make Rwanda an upper middle-income country by 2035 and a high income one by 2050. According to the World Bank, middle-income countries have a per capita GNI (gross national income) of between US$4,036 and US$12,476; high-income countries have a per capita GNI of more than US$12,476. Raising per capita incomes to these levels will be a difficult, if not impossible, order given that Rwanda's 2015 GNI was US$700 per capita.[15]

Never one to shy away from hard work or worry about the harsh realities of the peasantry, Kagame stressed that the 2050 goals will require an average annual growth rate of 10 percent. Reaching this near-unattainable goal will fall on the backs of rural farmers, as local officials do all they can to get as much as they can out of an already exhausted population. Doing more with less is a public virtue in contemporary Rwanda, even as the government stands accused of manipulating poverty-reduction data to rationalize its hard line on economic growth.[16] For the time being, the government seems more interested in producing impressive statistics than in investing in a diversified pro-poor economy.

Grandiose planning may prove the downfall of Rwanda's charismatic president. The idea that tiny, land-locked, resource-poor Rwanda can harness a largely agrarian economy to propel the country to high-income status in three decades seems unlikely, given the vicissitudes of history and the country's socio-political legacy. Rwanda's past points to waves of mass violence, occurring every forty years or so, when the ruling class fractures and ordinary people become the targets of physical, ethnically motivated violence. The ambitious, talented and heavy-handed RPF shows few signs of bucking this trend. As the Yale University historian Dan Magaziner poignantly notes, "bodies and human suffering are the cursed currency of history, as Juvénal Habyarimana and Grégoire Kayibanda have taught and Paul Kagame regrettably continues to teach."[17] Rwandans, regardless of political affinity, socio-economic class or ethnic identity, know this all too well.

NOTES

Introduction

1. Ministry of Education, Science, Technology and Scientific Research (MINEDUC), *Higher Learning Institutions* (Kigali: MINEDUC, 2015).

2. World Food Programme, "Rwanda: Report Indicates Some Improvement in Food Security," March 13, 2013, https://www.wfp.org/stories/rwanda-report-indicates-some-improvement-food-security, accessed October 17, 2015.

3. World Bank, "Net Official Development Assistance Received (Current US$)," *World Development Indicators, Rwanda,* 2014, http://data.worldbank.org/indicator/DT.ODA.ODAT.PC.ZS; and World Bank, "% of Gross Capital Formation," *World Development Indicators: Aid Dependency,* 2015, http://wdi.worldbank.org/table/6.11, both accessed January 5, 2015.

4. World Bank, *Rwanda Public Expenditure Program: An Instrument of Economic Strategy* (Washington, DC: World Bank, 1989).

5. Aid-dependent countries are those that receive more than 10 percent of their gross national income through grants and loans. Haley Swedlund, *From Donorship to Ownership: Evolving Donor-Government Relationships in Rwanda,* PhD dissertation, Syracuse University (USA), 2011, p. 41.

6. Eugenia Zorbas, "Aid Dependence and Policy Independence: Explaining the Rwandan Paradox," in *Remaking Rwanda: State Building and Human Rights after Mass Violence,* edited by Scott Straus and Lars Waldorf (Madison, WI: University of Wisconsin Press, 2011), pp. 103–17.

7. Scott Straus and Lars Waldorf, "Introduction: Seeing Like a Postconflict State," in *Remaking Rwanda,* edited by Straus and Waldorf, p. 3.

8. According to Article II of the 1948 Convention, genocide "means any of the following acts committed with intent to destroy, in whole or in part, a national, ethnic, racial or religious group: a) Killing members of the group; b) Causing serious bodily or mental harm to members of the group; c) Deliberately inflicting on the group conditions of life calculated to bring about its physical destruction in whole or in part; d) Imposing measures intended to prevent births within the group; e) Forcibly transferring children of the group to another group."

9. Scott Straus, *The Order of Genocide: Race, Power and War in Rwanda* (Ithaca, NY: Cornell University Press, 2006), p. 96.

10. Timothy Longman, *Christianity and Genocide in Rwanda* (Cambridge: Cambridge University Press, 2010).

11. Peter Gwin and David Gutterfelder, "Revisiting the Rwandan Genocide: How Churches Became Death Traps," *National Geographic*, April 2, 2014.

12. My narration of individual experiences, such as those provided in the example of Marie and her family, are drawn from my field research, have been gathered by members of my Rwandan research team or are drawn from the ethnographic or qualitative work of other scholars. Pseudonyms are used throughout the text.

13. Republic of Rwanda, Ministry of Health (MoH), *Rwanda: Global AIDS Response Progress Report 2014* (Kigali: MoH, 2015); and Susan Thomson, "Local Power Relations and Household Gender Dynamics: Assessing Rwanda's Claim to Universal HIV/AIDS Treatment in Context," *Canadian Journal of African Studies*, 44, 3, pp. 552–78.

14. Jean-Damascène Ndayambaje, *Le génocide au Rwanda: Un analyse psychologique* (Butare: National University of Rwanda, 2001).

15. Federica Guglielmo, "Medicalizing Violence: Victimhood, Trauma and Corporeality in Post-genocide Rwanda," *Critical African Studies*, 7, 2 (2015), pp. 146–63.

16. A Kinyarwanda-language modification of the French word *cadre*.

17. Judi Rever, "What Remains Hidden in Rwanda: The Role of Civilians in Killing Hutus," *Foreign Policy Journal*, June 3, 2016, https://www.foreign policyjournal.com/2016/06/03/what-remains-hidden-in-rwanda-the-role-of-tutsi-civilians-in-killing-hutus/, accessed July 9, 2016.

18. Filip Reyntjens, "Waging (Civil) War Abroad: Rwanda and the DRC," in *Remaking Rwanda*, edited by Straus and Waldorf, p. 145.

19. By 2014, Rwanda was home to 460 people per sq. km, following a dip to 232 people per sq. km in 1994. World DataBank, "Rwanda: Population Density," http://databank.worldbank.org/data/reports.aspx?source=2&count ry=RWA&series=&period=, accessed May 20, 2016.

20. Jan Vansina, *Antecedents to Modern Rwanda: The Nyiginya Kingdom* (Madison, WI: University of Wisconsin Press, 2005), p. 193.

21. Catharine Newbury, *The Cohesion of Oppression: Clientship and Ethnicity, 1860–1960* (New York: Columbia University Press, 1988), p. 17.

22. CIA World Factbook, "Rwanda Demographics Profile 2014," June 30, 2015, http://www.indexmundi.com/rwanda/demographics_profile.html, accessed October 17, 2015.

23. Marc Sommers, *Stuck: Rwandan Youth and the Struggle for Adulthood* (Athens, GA: University of Georgia Press, 2011), pp. 25–30.
24. Natalie Ilsley, "The Dirty Secret Behind Kigali's Clean Streets," *Newsweek Europe*, October 15, 2015, http://www.newsweek.com/kigalikwa-kabu-gagikondo-transit-centerstreet-vendorssex-workershomeless-598620, accessed December 9, 2015.
25. Molly Sundberg, *Training for Model Citizenship: An Ethnography of Civic Education and State-Making in Rwanda*, PhD dissertation, Department of Cultural Anthropology, Uppsala University (Sweden), 2014, p. 15.
26. Tom Goodfellow, "Rwanda's Political Settlement and the Urban Transition: Expropriation, Construction and Taxation," *Journal of Eastern African Studies*, 8, 2 (2014), pp. 311–29.
27. Given the RPF's preeminence, the terms "government" and "RPF" are used interchangeably throughout the book.
28. Anuradha Chakravarty, *Investing in Authoritarian Rule: Punishment and Patronage in Rwanda's Gacaca Courts for Genocide Crimes* (Cambridge: Cambridge University Press, 2016), p. 3.

1 Genocide

1. Scholarly and popular efforts to understand and explain the 1994 genocide have produced a sizable literature. For a summary, see Susan Thomson, "Genocide in Rwanda," in *Oxford Bibliographies in African Studies*, edited by Thomas Spear (New York: Oxford University Press, 2016). Rwandans themselves have not written much in English. An exception is Jean-Paul Kimonyo, *Rwanda's Popular Genocide: A Perfect Storm* (Boulder, CO: Lynne Rienner, 2015). Juliane Okot Bitek's poetry powerfully documents the loss of life and innocence in *100 Days* (Edmonton, AB: University of Alberta Press, 2016). Two definitive sources document the causes of the genocide: Alison Des Forges, *Leave None to Tell the Story: Genocide in Rwanda* (New York: Human Rights Watch, 1999), and André Guichaoua, *From War to Genocide: Criminal Politics in Rwanda, 1990–1994*, translated by Don E. Webster (Madison, WI: University of Wisconsin Press, 2015). Timothy Longman proposes a set of questions to better understand and explain the genocide; see "Placing Genocide in Context: Research Priorities for the Rwandan Genocide," *Journal of Genocide Research*, 6, 11 (2004), pp. 29–45.
2. To facilitate readability, I use the English translations of French-language groups, agencies and such throughout the text. The French translation for each acronym is found in the List of Abbreviations.
3. Kambanda pled guilty to genocide before the International Criminal Tribunal for Rwanda. He is currently in prison in Mali. Sindikubwabo died of natural causes in 1998, having never faced trial for his alleged crimes.
4. Catharine Newbury and Hannah Baldwin, *Aftermath: Women in Postgenocide Rwanda* (Washington, DC: USAID, Department of Information and Evaluation, 2003), p. 3.
5. Michael Barnett, *Eyewitness to a Genocide: The United Nations and Rwanda* (Ithaca, NY: Cornell University Press, 2016); Roméo Dallaire with Brent

Beardsley, *Shake Hands with the Devil: The Failure of Humanity in Rwanda* (Toronto: Random House Canada, 2003); Alison L. Des Forges and Alan Kuperman, "Shame: Rationalizing Western Apathy on Rwanda," *Foreign Affairs*, 79, 3 (2000), pp. 141–4; Linda Melvern, *A People Betrayed: The Role of the West in Rwanda's Genocide* (London: Zed Book, 2000); Organisation of African Unity, International Panel of Eminent Personalities, *Rwanda: The Preventable Genocide. The Report of International Panel of Eminent Personalities to Investigate the 1994 Genocide in Rwanda and the Surrounding Events*, July 7, 2000, http://www.refworld.org/pdfid/4d1da8752.pdf, accessed August 9, 2017; and Samantha Power, "Bystanders to Genocide: Why the United States Let the Rwandan Tragedy Happen," *Atlantic*, September 2001, pp. 84–108. For an account from an UN peacekeeper, see Henry Kwami Anyidoho, *Guns Over Kigali* (Accra: Woeli Publishing Services, 1997).

6. Dallaire thought a fully staffed and funded UN peacekeeping force could have stopped the genocide. Lara Santoro, "Rwanda Massacres Were Avoidable, General Says," *The Christian Science Monitor*, February 27, 1998, https://www.csmonitor.com/1998/0227/022798.intl.intl.3.html, accessed July 9, 2013.

7. *Inkotanyi* is the RPF's name for its armed wing, later becoming the name of the political party, at least in official communications, around 2000. The original Inkotanyi belonged to King Rwabugiri (*c*. 1853–95), widely considered by Tutsi refugees to be the best army Rwanda ever had.

8. Des Forges, *Leave None to Tell the Story*, pp. 699–701.

9. Guichaoua, *From War to Genocide*, pp. 143–292.

10. Ibid., pp. 152–69, for the reaction of Habyarimana's family and analysis of how Hutu hardliners came to control Rwanda in the days following the downing of the presidential aircraft.

11. Scott Straus, *Making and Unmaking Nations: War, Leadership and Genocide in Modern Africa* (Ithaca, NY: Cornell University Press, 2015), pp. 304–9.

12. Guichaoua, *From War to Genocide*, p. 202.

13. Guichaoua's *From War to Genocide* analyzes the power struggles among Hutu elites before and during the 1994 genocide, as does Straus' *Making and Unmaking Nations*, pp. 273–321. On why Rwandans killed, see Lee Ann Fujii, *Killing Neighbors: Webs of Violence in Rwanda* (Ithaca, NY: Cornell University Press, 2009), and Straus, *The Order of Genocide*.

14. Straus, *Making and Unmaking Nations*, p. 311.

15. Straus, *The Order of Genocide*, pp. 95–152.

16. Ibid., pp. 113–18, 135–40, 163–9.

17. *Itsembabwoko* is a neologism that came into usage after the 1994 genocide. As the violence of the civil war and genocide was not unknown to Rwandans, the compound *itsembabwoko* was coined to refer to the killing of an ethnic group, comprising *gutsemba* (to kill) and *bwoko* (ethnicity).

18. On the RPF's military strategy, see Alan Kuperman, "Provoking Genocide: A Revised History of the Rwandan Patriotic Front," *Journal of Genocide Research*, 6, 1 (2004), pp. 61–84; Des Forges, *Leave None to Tell the Story*, pp. 652–735; Cyrus William Reed, "Exile, Reform, and the Rise of the Rwandan Patriotic Front," *Journal of Modern African Studies*, 34, 3 (1996), pp. 479–501; Alex

Shoumatoff, "Rwanda's Aristocratic Guerillas," *New York Times Magazine*, December 13, 1992, p. 34; and Straus, *The Order of Genocide*, pp. 41–64. American journalists, in extended interviews with Kagame, reveal the RPF's military goals: Philip Gourevitch, "After Genocide: A Conversation with Paul Kagame," *Transitions*, 2 (1996), pp. 162–94; and Stephen Kinzer, *A Thousand Hills: Rwanda's Rebirth and the Man Who Dreamed It* (New York: Wiley, 2008).

19. Des Forges, *Leave None to the Tell the Story*, pp. 13–15, 27, 82, 181–5, 692–73. On RPF crimes in neighboring Zaire/Democratic Republic of Congo, see UN Office of the High Commissioner for Human Rights (UNOHCHR), *Report of the Mapping Exercise*. Rwanda's September 2010 response is online: http://www.ohchr.org/Documents/Countries/CD/DRC_Report_Comments_Rwanda.pdf, accessed September 9, 2015. For context, see Reyntjens, "Waging (Civil) War Abroad," in *Remaking Rwanda*, edited by Straus and Waldorf, pp. 132–51.

20. Des Forges, *Leave None to Tell the Story*, p. 692.

21. Aegis Trust, edited by Wendy Whitworth, *We Survived Genocide in Rwanda: 28 Personal Testimonies* (London: Quill Press, 2006); Jean Hatzfeld, *Into the Quick of Life. The Rwandan Genocide: The Survivors Speak* (London: Serpent's Tail, 2005) and *Life Laid Bare: The Survivors Speak* (New York: Farrar, Straus and Giroux, 2007); Immaculée Ilibagiza with Steve Erwin, *Left to Tell: One Woman's Story of Surviving the Rwandan Holocaust* (London: Hay House, 2006); John Rucyahana with James Riordan, *The Bishop of Rwanda: Finding Forgiveness Amidst a Pile of Bones* (Nashville, TN: Thomas Nelson, 2007); Joseph Sebarenzi with Laura Ann Mullane, *God Sleeps in Rwanda: A Journey of Transformation* (New York: Atria Books, 2009); Samuel Totten and Rafiki Ubaldo (eds), *We Cannot Forget: Interviews with Survivors of the 1994 Genocide in Rwanda* (New Brunswick, NJ: Rutgers University Press, 2011). There are two online databases of survivor and perpetrator testimony: *Genocide in Rwanda* (http://www.genocidearchiverwanda.org.rw/) and *Rwanda Genocide* (http://www.rwanda-genocide.org/index.html).

22. See Jean Hatzfeld, *Machete Season: The Killers in Rwanda Speak* (New York: Farrar, Straus and Giroux, 2005). Marie Béatrice Umutesi (translated by Julia Emerson), *Surviving the Slaughter: The Ordeal of a Rwandan Refugee in Zaire* (Madison, WI: University of Wisconsin Press, 2004), offers a rare Hutu perspective on living through the genocide, as does Paul Rusesabagina with Tom Zoellner, *An Ordinary Man: An Autobiography* (New York: Viking, 2006).

23. An exception is Robert Lyon and Scott Straus, *Intimate Enemy: Images and Voices of the Rwandan Genocide* (New York: Zone Books, 2006).

24. Fujii, *Killing Neighbors*, pp. 128–79.

25. Estimates are from Scott Straus, "How Many Perpetrators Were There in the Rwandan Genocide: An Estimate," *Journal of Genocide Research*, 6, 1 (2004), pp. 85–98. See too Villia Jefremovas, "Acts of Human Kindness: Hutu, Tutsi and Genocide," *Issue: A Journal of Opinion*, 23, 2 (1995), pp. 28–31.

26. Timothy Longman, "Genocide and Socio-Political Change: Massacres in Two Rwandan Villages," *Issue: A Journal of Opinion*, 23, 2 (1995), pp. 18–21.

27. Lars Teilhet Waldorf, *Mass Justice for Mass Atrocity: Transitional Justice and Illiberal Peace-building in Rwanda*, PhD dissertation, Irish Centre for Human Rights, Faculty of Law, University of Galway (Ireland), 2013, p. 62.

28. Charles Mironko, "Igitero: Means and Motive in the Rwandan Genocide," *Journal of Genocide Research*, 6, 1 (2004), pp. 47–60.

29. Sara E. Brown, "Female Perpetrators of the Rwandan Genocide", *International Feminist Journal of Politics*, 16, 3 (2014), pp. 448–69. Women also played a role in evading the killers and rescuing neighbors: Anuradha Chakravarty, "Inter-ethnic Marriages, Survival of Women and the Logics of Genocide," *Genocide Studies and Prevention*, 2, 3 (2007), pp. 235–48.

30. Olivier's case is inspired by the work of Fujii, who writes about a man she calls Jude in *Killing Neighbors*, particularly pp. 132–7, 148–9.

31. Surf Fund, *Statistics*, n.d., http://survivors-fund.org.uk/resources/rwandan-history/statistics/, accessed September 28, 2015.

32. Clotilde Twagiramariya and Meredeth Turshen, " 'Favours' to Give and 'Consenting' Victims: The Sexual Politics of Survival in Rwanda," in *What Women Do in Wartime: Gender and Conflict in Africa*, edited by Meredeth Turshen and Clotilde Twagiramariya (London: Zed Books, 1998), pp. 101–17.

33. Amnesty International, *"Marked for Death": Rape Survivors Living with HIV in Rwanda*, April 5, 2004, https://www.amnesty.org/en/documents/afr47/007/2004/en/, accessed August 9, 2017.

34. Robert M. Press, "In Rwanda's 'Slave Ship' Prisons, Life is Grim for Suspected Prisoners," *Christian Science Monitor*, November 18, 1994, https://www.csmonitor.com/1994/1118/18011.html, accessed July 19, 2013.

35. Carina Tertsakian, " 'All Rwandans are Afraid of Being Arrested One Day': Prisoners Past, Present and Future," in *Remaking Rwanda*, edited by Straus and Waldorf, p. 212; Stephen Buckley, "Waves of Arrests Jam Rwanda's Ailing Prisons," *Washington Post*, January 29, 1996, https://www.washingtonpost.com/archive/politics/1996/01/29/waves-of-arrests-jam-rwandas-ailing-prisons/7bc29001-bfbd-4567-8a88-ceb60be474f8/?utm_term=.30056675a6b6, accessed July 21, 2013.

36. Tertsakian, " 'All Rwandans are Afraid of Being Arrested One Day,'" p. 211; and Théoneste Rutayisire and Annemiek Richters, "Everyday Suffering Outside Prison Walls: A Legacy of Community Justice in Post-genocide Rwanda," *Social Science and Medicine*, 120 (2014), pp. 413–20.

37. Donatella Lorch, "Rwanda Jails: No Space, No Food, No Justice," *New York Times*, April 14, 1995, http://www.nytimes.com/1995/04/15/world/rwanda-jails-no-space-no-food-no-justice.html, accessed September 19, 2014.

38. International Committee of the Red Cross, *Rwanda, ICRC Annual Report 2013*, https://www.icrc.org/eng/assets/files/annual-report/current/icrc-annual-report-rwanda.pdf, accessed September 19, 2015.

39. Gérard Prunier, *Africa's World War: Congo, the Rwandan Genocide, and the Making of a Continental Catastrophe* (Oxford: Oxford University Press, 2011), p. 1.

40. Vivian Stromberg, cited in Laura Flanders, "Rwanda's Living Casualties," *Ms. Magazine* (March/April 1998), p. 28.

41. I am grateful to Jennie Burnet for this point. For her analysis, see "Sexual Violence, Female Agencies, and Sexual Consent: Complexities of Sexual Violence in the 1994 Rwandan Genocide," *African Studies Review*, 55, 2 (2012), pp. 97–118.
42. Binaifer Nowrojee, *Shattered Lives: Sexual Violence During the Rwandan Genocide and its Aftermath* (New York: Human Rights Watch, 1996).
43. Ndayambaje, *Le génocide au Rwanda*, p. 46.
44. Raymond Bonner, "Rwandan Refugees Flood Zaire as Rebels Forces Gain," *New York Times*, July 15, 1994, http://www.nytimes.com/1994/07/15/world/rwandan-refugees-flood-zaire-as-rebel-forces-gain.html?pagewanted=all, accessed September 13, 2013.
45. René Lemarchand, "Bearing Witness to Mass Murder," *African Studies Review*, 48, 3 (2005), p. 97.
46. Daniela Kroslak, *The French Betrayal of Rwanda* (Bloomington, IN: University of Indiana Press, 2008), pp. 41–2.
47. Des Forges, *Leave None to Tell the Story*, pp. 682–4.
48. Andy Storey, "Non-neutral Humanitarianism: NGOs and the Rwanda Crisis," *Development in Practice*, 7, 4 (1997), pp. 384–94.
49. Susanne Buckley-Zistel, "Remembering to Forget: Chosen Amnesia for Local Co-Existence in Post-Genocide Rwanda," *Africa*, 76, 2 (2006), pp. 131–50.
50. Johan Pottier, *Re-imagining Rwanda: Conflict, Survival and Disinformation in the Late Twentieth Century* (Cambridge: Cambridge University Press, 2002), p. 109.
51. Catharine Newbury, "Ethnicity and the Politics of History in Rwanda," *Africa Today*, 45, 1 (1998), p. 7.
52. Jens Meierhenrich, "Through a Glass Darkly: Genocide Memorials in Rwanda, 1994–Present," http://www.genocidememorials.org/, accessed November 9, 2015; Jens Meierhenrich, "Topographies of Remembering and Forgetting: The Transformation of *Lieux de Mémoire* in Rwanda," in *Remaking Rwanda*, edited by Straus and Waldorf, pp. 283–96.

2 The Roots of the Genocidal State

1. Mahmood Mamdani, *When Victims Become Killers: Colonialism, Nativism and the Genocide in Rwanda* (Kampala: Fountain Publishers, 2001), pp. 160–4.
2. Gérard Prunier studied the number of Rwandan refugees living in countries neighboring Rwanda between 1962 and 1972. The majority of Tutsi refugees fled to Burundi (200,000). Some 78,000 refugees settled in Uganda, 36,000 in Tanzania and 22,000 in Zaire: Gérard Prunier, *The Rwanda Crisis: History of a Genocide* (New York: Columbia University Press, 1997), pp. 61–4.
3. Vansina, *Antecedents to Modern Rwanda*, pp. 196–8.
4. Filip Reyntjens, "(Re-)Imagining a Reluctant Post-genocide Society: The Rwandan Patriotic Front's Ideology and Practice," *Journal of Genocide Research*, 18, 1 (2016), pp. 61–81.
5. Kinzer, *A Thousand Hills*, p. 17.

6. Ministry of Education, Science, Technology and Scientific Research, National Curriculum Development Centre, *The Teaching of History in Rwanda: A Participatory Approach* (Kigali: MINEDUC, 2006); and *History Program for Advanced Level Secondary School* (Kigali: MINEDUC, 2010).

7. Chi Mgbako, "Ingando Solidarity Camps: Reconciliation and Political Indoctrination in Post-Genocide Rwanda," Harvard Human Rights Journal, 18, 1 (2005), pp. 201–24.

8. Kigali Memorial Centre, *Jenoside* (Kigali: Aegis Trust, 2004).

9. On the origins of Hutu and Tutsi as social groups, see Des Forges, *Leave None to Tell the Story*, pp. 31–7. On the politicization of ethnicity, a process unintentionally started during the rule of King Rwabugiri, see C. Newbury, *The Cohesion of Oppression*, pp. 38–52.

10. Jacques J. Maquet, *The Premise of Inequality in Ruanda: A Study of Political Relations in a Central African Kingdom* (London: Oxford University Press, 1961). First published as *Le système des relations sociales dans le Ruanda ancien* (Turvuren, Belgium: Musée Royal de l'Afrique Centrale, 1954).

11. Ibid., pp. 3–4.

12. Office of the President of the Republic of Rwanda, *The Unity of Rwandans: Before the Colonial Period and under the Colonial Rule under the First Republic* (Kigali: Urugwiro Village, 1999); and Pottier, *Re-imagining Rwanda*, pp. 109–29, for analysis of the RPF's reproduction of his interpretation of precolonial Rwanda as a timeless feudal society. On *ubuhake* contracts, see Vansina, *Antecedents to Modern Rwanda*, pp. 47–8.

13. Pottier, *Re-imagining Rwanda*, p. 110.

14. David Newbury, "Canonical Conventions in Rwanda: Four Myths of Recent Historiography in Central Africa," *History in Africa*, 39 (2012), p. 49.

15. C. Newbury, *The Cohesion of Oppression*, p. 197.

16. Ian Linden with Jane Linden, *Church and Revolution in Rwanda* (Manchester: Manchester University Press, 1977), p. 226.

17. C. Newbury, *The Cohesion of Oppression*, p. 190.

18. Ibid., pp. 191–2.

19. As well as being a numerical minority, most Tutsi lived far from the capital, working as rural subsistence farmers.

20. Straus, *Making and Unmaking Nations*, p. 278.

21. Ibid., p. 279.

22. Susan Thomson, *Whispering Truth to Power: Everyday Resistance to Reconciliation in Postgenocide Rwanda* (Madison, WI: University of Wisconsin Press, 2013), pp. 67–9.

23. Straus, *Making and Unmaking Nations*, p. 286.

24. C. Newbury, *The Cohesion of Oppression*, p. 195.

25. Ndahindurwa lived in exile, on public assistance in Maryland, US, until his death in late 2016. Ariel Sabar, "A King With No Country," *The Washingtonian*, March 27, 2013, https://www.washingtonian.com/2013/03/27/a-king-with-no-country/, accessed October 14, 2014.

26. C. Newbury, "Ethnicity and the Politics of History in Rwanda," p. 17.

27. Filip Reyntjens, *Pouvoir et droit au Rwanda: Droit public et évolution politique, 1916–1973* (Tervuren, Belgium: Musée Royal de l'Afrique Centrale, 1985), p. 503.

28. Marie-Eve Desrosiers, "Rethinking Political Rhetoric and Authority During Rwanda's First and Second Republics," *Africa*, 84, 2 (2014), pp. 214–15.
29. Filip Reyntjens, *Pouvoir et droit au Rwanda: Droit public et évolution politique, 1916–1973* (Tervuren, Belgium: Musée Royal de l'Afrique Centrale, 1985), p. 449.
30. Desrosiers, "Rethinking Political Rhetoric and Authority," p. 213.
31. Ibid., p. 206.
32. Straus, *Making and Unmaking Nations*, p. 282.
33. Ibid., pp. 501–8. See also Catharine Newbury, "Rwanda: Recent Debates over Governance and Rural Development," in *Governance and Politics in Africa*, edited by Goran Hyden and Michael Bratton (Boulder, CO: Lynne Rienner, 1992), pp. 197–9.
34. Lee Ann Fujii, "Transforming the Moral Landscape: The Diffusion of a Genocidal Norm in Rwanda," *Journal of Genocide Research*, 6, 1 (2004), p. 101.
35. Desrosiers, "Rethinking Political Rhetoric and Authority," p. 219, note 94.
36. Danielle de Lame, "Mighty Secrets, Public Commensality and the Crisis of Transparency: Rwanda through the Looking Glass," *Canadian Journal of African Studies*, 38, 2 (2004), pp. 279–317.
37. Johan Pottier, "Debating Styles in a Rwanda Co-operative: Reflections on Language, Policy and Gender," *Sociological Review*, 36, 1 (1988), pp. 41–60.
38. Occasionally, *conseillers* had more power in outlying areas, far from the burgomaster's offices.
39. Des Forges, *Leave None to Tell the Story*, pp. 71–3. Radio Rwanda's signal was strong enough to reach into neighboring countries. The RPF also launched its own station at the start of the civil war. Radio Muhabura generally glorified the RPF but did so in nationalist, not ethnic, appeals. Its broadcast signal did not cover the entire country.

3 Refugee Rebels

1. Gourevitch, "After Genocide," p. 171.
2. Kinzer, *A Thousand Hills*, p. 14.
3. Gourevitch, "After Genocide," p. 170.
4. On dynamics in Uganda, see Duncan Kamukama, *Rwanda Conflict: Its Roots and Regional Implications* (Kampala: Fountain Publishers, 1993); Mamdani, *When Victims Become Killers*, particularly chapter 6; Catharine Watson, *Exile from Rwanda: Background to an Invasion* (Washington, DC: US Committee for Refugees, 1991).
5. Rachel van der Meeren, "Three Decades in Exile: Rwandan Refugees 1960–1990," *Journal of Refugee Studies*, 9, 3 (1996), p. 261.
6. Kuperman, "Provoking Genocide," p. 65.
7. Mamdani, *When Victims Become Killers*, p. 168.
8. Yoweri Kaguta Museveni, *Sowing the Mustard Seed: The Struggle for Freedom and Democracy in Uganda*, edited by Elizabeth Kanyogonya and Kevin Shillington (London: Macmillan, 1997).

9. Mamdani, *When Victims Become Killers*, p. 170.
10. On the efforts of Rwandans to permanently settle in Uganda, see ibid., pp. 172–6.
11. Alan Rake, "Rwanda," in *African Leaders: Guiding the New Millennium* (Lanham, MD: The Scarecrow Press, 2001), p. 185.
12. See, for example, Kinzer, *A Thousand Hills*, pp. 66–7.
13. Ibid., p. 13.
14. Gérard Prunier, "The Rwandan Patriotic Front," in *African Guerrillas*, edited by Christopher Clapham (Oxford: James Currey, 1998), p. 128.
15. Noel Twagiramungu, "Rwanda, Inc: Paul Kagame's Odyssey from Rebel to Tyrant," *Political Matter*, September 2, 2015; Theogene Rudasingwa, *Healing a Nation, a Testimony: Waging and Winning a Peaceful Revolution to Unite and Heal a Broken Rwanda* (North Charleston, SC: Create Space Independent Publishing Platform, 2013). As a founding member of the RPF, Rudasingwa's book offers a rare insider perspective. For his take on the rise of the RPF and subsequent invasion from Uganda, see pp. 51–101.
16. Rwigyema's place in Rwandan history is contested. See Muwonge Magembe, "Gen Fred Rwigyemas [*sic*] Untold Story," *New Vision* (Kampala), November 22, 2015, http://www.newvision.co.ug/new_vision/news/1412032/gen-fred-rwigyemas-untold-story, accessed May 19, 2016.
17. Faustin Mugabe, "Was Rwigyema Assassinated?," *The Daily Monitor* (Kampala), October 1, 2014, http://www.monitor.co.ug/SpecialReports/Was-Rwigyema-assassinated-/688342-2470530-j6ff8qz/index.html, accessed May 19, 2016.
18. Kuperman, "Provoking Genocide," p. 68.
19. On the founding narrative of the RPF and its current policies and programs, see the party website at http://rpfinkotanyi.rw/campaign/index.php?id=23, accessed August 10, 2017.
20. Kinzer, *A Thousand Hills*, p. 56.
21. Sarah Kenyon Lischer, "Civil War, Genocide and Political Order in Rwanda: Security Implications of Refugee Return," *Conflict, Security and Development*, 11, 3 (2011), pp. 268–9.
22. Desrosiers, "Rhetoric and Authority in Rwanda," pp. 214–19.
23. Peter Uvin, *Aiding Violence: The Development Enterprise in Rwanda* (West Hartford, CT: Kumarian Press, 1998), pp. 40–50.
24. C. Newbury, "Rwanda: Recent Debates over Governance and Rural Development," pp. 193–219.
25. Cited in Jean-Marie Kamatali, "Following Orders in Rwanda," *New York Times*, April 4, 2014, https://www.nytimes.com/2014/04/05/opinion/following-orders-in-rwanda.html, accessed April 5, 2014.
26. Aidan Hartley, *The Zanzibar Chest: A Memoir of Love and War* (London: Harper Collins, 2003), pp. 364–97.
27. Filip Reyntjens, "Rwanda: Genocide and Beyond," *Journal of Refugee Studies*, 9, 3 (1996), p. 246.
28. For an authoritative account, see Bruce Jones, *Peacemaking in Rwanda: The Dynamics of Failure* (Boulder, CO: Lynne Rienner, 2001).
29. Jones, *Peacemaking in Rwanda*, pp. 130–4.
30. Anatole Nsengiyumva to Minister of Defense, July 27, 1992, International Criminal Tribunal for Rwanda archives.

31. Jones, *Peacemaking in Rwanda*, pp. 123–5.
32. For background, see Devon E.A. Curtis, "Development Assistance and the Lasting Legacies of Rebellion in Burundi and Rwanda," *Third World Quarterly*, 36, 7 (2015), pp. 1365–81; René Lemarchand, *Burundi: Ethnic Conflict and Genocide* (Cambridge: Cambridge University Press, 1996); Stef Vandenginste, "Governing Ethnicity after Genocide: Ethnic Amnesia in Rwanda versus Ethnic Power-sharing in Burundi," *Journal of Eastern African Studies*, 8, 2 (2014), pp. 263–77.
33. Military training of Burundian Hutu increased to the extent that it could no longer be ignored and the UN High Commissioner for Refugees asked the government to cease its activities. Habyarimana's officers ignored the request. Des Forges, *Leave None to Tell the Story*, p. 136.
34. Ibid., p. 137.
35. Many analysts consider the Interahamwe to be an armed wing of Habyarimana's MRND, founded in 1993 with the singular aim of killing Tutsi. In fact, the Interahamwe began in the 1980s as a club of young soccer fans. Soon, the clubs became militarized under the mentorship of MRND party loyalists and businessmen, particularly as the civil war intensified. As the scapegoating of Tutsi became commonplace, the Interahamwe evolved into a militant group attached to the ruling party. By 1993, the Interahamwe violently defended the MRND by both harassing supporters of political opponents and leading indiscriminate massacres of Tutsi that they then blamed on the RPF. See Paul R. Bartrop, "Kajuga, (Jerry) Robert (B. 1960)," in *A Biographical Encyclopedia of Contemporary Genocide: Portraits of Evil and Good* (Santa Barbara, CA: ABC-CLIO Publishers, 2012), p. 153.
36. Des Forges, *Leave None to Tell the Story*, pp. 152–3.
37. UN International Criminal Tribunal for Rwanda document KOO41427–440.
38. Des Forges, *Leave None to Tell the Story*, pp. 105–6.
39. Aimable Twagilimana, *The Debris of Ham: Ethnicity, Regionalism, and the 1994 Rwandan Genocide* (Lanham, MD: University Press of America, 2003), pp. 33–57.
40. United States Department of State Cable, "Das Bushnell Tells Col. Bagasora [*sic*] to Stop the Killings," April 29, 1994, *Unredacted: The National Security Archives, Unedited and Uncensored*, released February 4, 2015, http://nsarchive.gwu.edu/NSAEBB/NSAEBB500/docs/Document%2026.pdf, accessed May 28, 2016. Bushnell recounts her conversations with Bagosora in a 2013 interview: United States Holocaust Museum, "Prudence Bushnell: Phone Calls to Colonel Bagosora to Stop the Killings," filmed November 23, 2013, YouTube Video, 5m 11s, posted May 27, 2014, https://www.youtube.com/watch?v=5Blj8OS8kRM, accessed May 28, 2016.

4 A Semblance of Normal

1. Curtis, "Development Assistance and the Lasting Legacies of Rebellion in Burundi and Rwanda," p. 1372.
2. Peter Uvin, "The International Community in Rwanda after Genocide," *Third World Quarterly*, 22, 2 (2001), p. 178.

3. Prunier, *Africa's World War*, p. 8.
4. For analysis, see Rob Tew, "Aid Information in Rwanda: AidInfo Project Case Study (Draft Version)," *Development Initiatives*, http://www.aidinfo.org/case-studies/rwanda, accessed October 4, 2015.
5. Krishna Kumar et al., *Rebuilding Postwar Rwanda: The Role of the International Community* (Washington, DC: USAID, July 1996).
6. Quoted in René Lemarchand, "Foreign Policy Making the Great Lakes Region," in *African Foreign Policies: Power and Process*, edited by Gilbert M. Khadiagala and Terrence Lyons (Boulder, CO: Lynne Rienner, 2001), p. 95.
7. These themes feature in President Kagame's speeches, available online: http://paulkagame.com/?page_id=1273, accessed August 10, 2017.
8. Joel Boutroue, *Missed Opportunities: The Role of the International Community in the Return of Rwandan Refugees from Zaire* (Boston: MIT Press, 1998).
9. Johan Pottier, "Relief and Repatriation: Views by Rwandan Refugees; Lessons for Humanitarian Aid Workers," *African Affairs*, 95, 380 (1996), pp. 415–17.
10. Danielle de Lame, *A Hill Among a Thousand: Transformations and Ruptures in Rural Rwanda*, translated by Helen Arnold (Madison, WI: University of Wisconsin Press, 2005), p. 460.
11. Joint Evaluation of Emergency Assistance to Rwanda, *Humanitarian Aid and Effects*, vol. 3 of *International Response to Conflict and Genocide: Lessons from the Rwandan Experience* (Copenhagen: DANIDA, 1996).
12. Prunier, *Africa's World War*, p. 25.
13. de Lame, *A Hill Among a Thousand*, p. 460.
14. UNICEF, "Morbidity and Mortality Surveillance in Rwandan Refugees— Burundi and Zaire, 1994," February 9, 1996, https://www.cdc.gov/mmwr/preview/mmwrhtml/00040202.htm, accessed August 10, 2017.
15. Des Forges, *Leave None to Tell the Story*, p. 705.
16. On the American experience in Somalia, see Colum Lynch, "Rwanda Revisited," *Foreign Policy*, April 5, 2015, http://foreignpolicy.com/2015/04/05/rwanda-revisited-genocide-united-states-state-department/, accessed April 9, 2015.
17. Kumar et al., *Rebuilding Postwar Rwanda*, p. vi.
18. On RPA abuses, see Amnesty International, *Rwanda: Reports of Killings and Abductions by the Rwandese Patriotic Army, April–August 1994* (London: Amnesty International, 1994); Human Rights Watch, *The Aftermath of the Genocide in Rwanda* (New York: Human Rights Watch, 1994).
19. Lemarchand, "Foreign Policy Making the Great Lakes Region," p. 95.
20. Quoted in Gourevitch, "After Genocide," p. 169.
21. Filip Reyntjens, *Political Governance in Post-Genocide Rwanda* (Cambridge: Cambridge University Press, 2013), p. 5.
22. Ibid., pp. 1–11.
23. Gerald Gahima, *Transitional Justice in Rwanda: Accountability for Atrocity* (New York: Routledge, 2013), p. 59.
24. Ibid., p. 180.

25. Sebarenzi, *God Sleeps in Rwanda*, p. 139.
26. Reyntjens, *Political Governance in Post-Genocide Rwanda*, pp. 5–6.
27. Quoted in Howard W. French, "The Case Against Rwanda's Paul Kagame," *Newsweek*, January 14, 2013.
28. From August 1 to September 5, 1994, American consultant Robert Gersony and a team of UNHCR researchers worked throughout Rwanda, tasked to identify ways to hasten the repatriation of Rwandan refugees in neighboring countries.
29. Des Forges, *Leave None to Tell the Story*, p. 726.
30. Ibid., p. 727.
31. Quoted in French, "The Case Against Rwanda's Paul Kagame."
32. Samantha Power, *"A Problem from Hell": America and the Age of Genocide* (New York: Basic Books, 2002), pp. 329–89. On Western inaction, see Barnett, *Eyewitness to a Genocide*; and Melvern, *A People Betrayed*, and *The United Nations and Rwanda 1993–1996* (New York, NY: Department of Public Information, 1996).
33. Power, *"A Problem from Hell*," p. 359.
34. Quoted in Power, "Bystanders to Genocide."
35. Quoted in Donatella Lorch, "Rwanda Rulers Warn Against Violence," *New York Times*, October 2, 1994, http://www.nytimes.com/1994/10/02/world/rwandan-rulers-warn-against-violence.html, accessed November 9, 2013.
36. http://www.friendsofthecongo.org/pdf/gersony_report.pdf, accessed September 27, 2015.
37. Cited in Reyntjens, *Political Governance in Post-Genocide Rwanda*, p. 4.
38. Prunier, *Africa's World War*, pp. 9–10.
39. Seth Sendashonga quoted in the documentary *Chronicle of a Genocide Foretold*, vol. 3, part 3 (Ottawa: National Film Board of Canada, 1997).
40. Donatella Lorch, "Slaughter of 2,000 Leaves Haunting Scene in Rwanda," *Chicago Tribune*, April 24, 1995, http://articles.chicagotribune.com/1995-04-24/news/9504240108_1_kibeho-camp-hutus-rwandan, accessed November 9, 2013.
41. Quoted in Prunier, *Africa's World War*, p. 40.
42. Quoted in Lorch, "Slaughter of 2,000 Leaves Haunting Scene in Rwanda."
43. I am grateful to Mark Cuthbert-Brown for his account, dated April 30, 1995.
44. Immediately, during the night of the 22nd and through April 23, the RPA buried corpses—perhaps to reduce the bodycount but probably also to reduce threats to public health.
45. Cuthbert-Brown estimates between 800 and 1,600 dead: Cuthbert-Brown, "Provost Marshal's Report on the Killing in Kibeho," on file with the author. The figure of 4,000 dead comes from Paul Jordan, "Witness to Genocide: A Personal Account of the 1995 Kibeho Massacre, 1998," *Australian Army Journal*, 1, 1 (2003), pp. 127–36.
46. Jordan, "Witness to Genocide," p. 136.
47. Email correspondence with the author, June 3, 2016.
48. Gourevitch, "After Genocide," pp. 191–4.

49. Pottier, *Re-imagining Rwanda*, p. 59.
50. Jordan, "Witness to Genocide"; Terry Pickard, *Combat Medic: An Australian Eyewitness Account of the Kibeho Massacre* (Newport, NSW: Big Sky Publishing, 2008); Pottier, *Re-imagining Rwanda*, pp. 160–70; and Reyntjens, *Political Governance in Post-Genocide Rwanda*, pp. 105–9.
51. Filip Reyntjens, "Post-1994 Politics in Rwanda: Problematising 'Liberation' and 'Democratisation'," *Third World Quarterly*, 27, 6 (2006), p. 1105.
52. Guichaoua, *From War to Genocide*, p. 145.
53. For more on Nkubito's human rights legacy, see Catharine Newbury and David Newbury, "A Catholic Mass in Kigali: Contested Views of the Genocide and Ethnicity in Rwanda," *Canadian Journal of African Studies*, 33, 2 & 3 (1999), p. 293 and p. 318, ftn 1.
54. Prunier, *Africa's World War*, p. 45; US Embassy Kigali, "Ethnicity in Rwanda—Who Governs the Country?," ref. Kigali 480, August 5, 2008, https://wikileaks.org/plUS$/cables/08KIGALI525_a.html, accessed October 19, 2015.
55. Gourevitch, "After Genocide," p. 164.
56. Ibid., pp. 168–9.
57. Stef Vandeginste, "Victims of Genocide, Crimes Against Humanity and War Crimes in Rwanda: The Legal and Institutional Framework of Their Right to Reparation," in *Politics and the Past: On Repairing Historical Injustices*, edited by John Torpey (Lanham, MD: Rowman and Littlefield, 2003), p. 254.

5 Securing People and Place

1. On gender norms, see Jennie E. Burnet, *Genocide Lives in Us: Women, Memory and Silence in Rwanda* (Madison, WI: Wisconsin University Press, 2012), pp. 42–6, and Villia Jefremovas, "Loose Women, Virtuous Wives, and Timid Virgins: Gender and the Control of Resources in Rwanda," *Canadian Journal of African Studies*, 25, 3 (1991), pp. 378–95.
2. Monique Mujawamariya, "Report of a Visit to Rwanda: September 1–22, 1994," *Issue: A Journal of Opinion*, 32, 2 (1995), pp. 32–8; Filip Reyntjens, "Subjects of Concern: Rwanda, October 1994," *Issue: A Journal of Opinion*, 32, 2 (1995), pp. 39–43.
3. Soil exhaustion and erosion, as well as small plot sizes and yields, already plagued rural Rwanda before the genocide. Vadi Moodley, Alphonse Gahima and Suveshnee Munien, "Environmental Causes and Impacts of the Genocide in Rwanda: Case Studies of the Towns of Butare and Cyangugu," *African Journal on Conflict Resolution*, 10, 2 (2010), pp. 103–20.
4. Joseph Assan and David Walker, "The Political Economy of Contemporary Education and the Challenges of Switching Formal Language to English in Rwanda," in *Rwanda Fast Forward: Social, Economic and Reconciliation Prospects*, edited by Maddalena Campioni and Patrick Noack (London: Palgrave Macmillan, 2012), pp. 176–90.
5. On the politics of returned exiles, see David Newbury, "Returning Refugees: Four Historical Patterns of 'Coming Home' to Rwanda," *Comparative Studies in Society and History*, 47, 2 (2005), pp. 252–85.

6. UNHCR, *Update on Developments in the Great Lakes Region*, EC/47/SC/CRP.38 (Geneva: United Nations High Commission for Refugees, 1997).

7. Umutesi, *Surviving the Slaughter*, pp. 138–63.

8. Human Rights Watch, *What is Kabila Hiding: Civilian Killings and Impunity in Congo*, October 1997, p. 16, http://pantheon.hrw.org/legacy/reports/1997/congo/, accessed August 10, 2017.

9. Human Rights Watch, *"Attacked by All Sides": Civilians and the War in Eastern Zaire*, March 1, 1997, https://www.hrw.org/reports/1997/zaire2/zaire0397web.pdf, accessed August 10, 2017.

10. UNHCR, *Update on Developments in the Great Lakes Region*.

11. Filip Reyntjens and Stef Vandeginste, "Rwanda: An Atypical Transition," in *Roads to Reconciliation*, edited by Elin Skaar, Siri Gloppen and Astri Suhrke (New York: Lexington Books, 2005), p. 83; also "Rwanda," *World Prison Brief*, http://www.prisonstudies.org/country/rwanda, accessed May 20, 2017.

12. Peter Uvin, "Difficult Choices in the New Post-Conflict Agenda: The International Community in Rwanda after the Genocide," *Third World Quarterly*, 22, 2 (2001), pp. 177–89.

13. Alison Des Forges, "Land in Rwanda: Winnowing out the Chaff," in *L'Afrique des Grands Lacs: Annuaire 2005–2006*, edited by Filip Reyntjens and Stefaan Marysse (Paris: L'Harmattan, 2006), pp. 353–71; Jennie E. Burnet and the Rwanda Initiative for Sustainable Development, *Culture, Practice and Law: Women's Access to Land in Rwanda* (Kigali: Rwanda Initiative for Sustainable Development, 2003).

14. Rwanda Initiative for Sustainable Development, *Securing Land Rights Project: A Working Paper on Land Tenure Regularization in Rwanda* (Kigali: Rwanda Initiative for Sustainable Development, 2013), p. 6.

15. Jennie E. Burnet, "Women Have Found Respect: Gender Quotas, Symbolic Representation and Female Empowerment in Rwanda," *Politics and Gender*, 7 (2011), pp. 303–34.

16. Margot Leegwater, *Sharing Scarcity: Land Access and Social Relations in Southeast Rwanda*, PhD dissertation, Department of Anthropology, University of Leiden (Netherlands), 2015, pp. 188–91.

17. Human Rights Watch, *Uprooting the Rural Poor in Rwanda* (New York: Human Rights Watch, 2001).

18. Catharine Newbury, "High Modernism at the Ground Level: The *Imidugudu* Policy in Rwanda," *Remaking Rwanda*, edited by Straus and Waldorf, pp. 224–6, 230.

19. de Lame, *A Hill Among a Thousand*, p. 323.

20. Burnet, *Genocide Lives in Us*, p. 72.

21. Elisabeth King, *From Classrooms to Conflict in Rwanda* (Cambridge: Cambridge University Press, 2014), pp. 101–9, 137–44.

22. Des Forges, *Leave None to Tell the Story*, p. 31.

23. C. Newbury, *The Cohesion of Oppression*, pp. 53–61.

24. Ibid., p. 53.

25. Amnesty International, *Rwanda: Ending the Silence* (London: Amnesty International, September 25, 1997), https://www.amnesty.org/en/documents/afr47/032/1997/en/, accessed August 16, 2017.

26. Lara Santoro, "Echo of 1994 Genocide: Rwanda Slayings Persist," *Christian Science Monitor*, March 3, 1998, https://www.csmonitor.com/1998/0303/030398.intl.intl.3.html, accessed November 3, 2014.
27. Marijke Verpoorten, "Detecting Hidden Violence: The Spatial Distribution of Excess Mortality in Rwanda," *Political Geography*, 31, 1 (2012), pp. 44–56.
28. Des Forges, *Leave None to Tell the Story*, pp. 45–7.
29. Reyntjens, quoted in Des Forges, *Leave None to Tell the Story*, p. 47.
30. Food and Agriculture Organization, "Improved Food Situation in the Great Lakes Region but Food Outlook Bleak in Eastern DRC", http://www.fao.org/docrep/004/x0696e/x0696e04.htm#E17E5, accessed October 27, 2015.
31. Physicians for Human Rights, *Investigations in Eastern Congo and Western Rwanda*, June 1997, https://s3.amazonaws.com/PHR_Reports/congo-investigations-1997.pdf, accessed August 10, 2017.
32. In an agreement with the RPF, UNHRFOR was established in August 1994. Its primary mandate was to gather evidence to allow the RPF to begin to investigate crimes of those accused of genocide by monitoring the human rights situation in the countryside.
33. UNHRFOR, *United Nations Human Rights Field Operation in Rwanda*, April 4, 1997, http://reliefweb.int/report/rwanda/united-nations-human-rights-field-operation-rwanda, accessed August 10, 2017. International rights and media organizations relied on Rwandan researchers to document abuses in the north-west. When delegations of international consultants undertook their field missions, RPA military escorts and media handlers always accompanied them.
34. Quoted in Reyntjens, *Political Governance*, p. 116.
35. Amnesty International, *Rwanda: The Hidden Violence: "Disappearances" and Killings Continue* (London: Amnesty International, 22 June 1998), p. 11.
36. Child Soldiers Global Report 2001, *Rwanda*, http://www.refworld.org/docid/498805d326.html, accessed October 31, 2015.
37. Amnesty International, *Rwanda: The Hidden Violence*, p. 14.
38. Human Rights Watch, *World Report 1998—Rwanda* (New York: Human Rights Watch, 1999).

6 Control at Home and Abroad

1. Paul Jackson, "Legacy of Bitterness: Insurgency in North West Rwanda," *Small Wars and Insurgencies*, 15, 1 (2004), pp. 19–37.
2. Kagame quoted in Reyntjens, "Waging (Civil) War Abroad," in *Remaking Rwanda*, edited by Straus and Waldorf, p. 140.
3. Lars Waldorf, *Transitional Justice and DDR: The Case of Rwanda* (New York: International Center for Transitional Justice, 2002), p. 8.
4. International Crisis Group, "A Congo Action Plan," *Africa Briefing No. 34* (Brussels: International Crisis Group, 2005), and "The Congo: Solving the FDLR Problem Once and for All," *Africa Briefing No. 25* (Brussels: International Crisis Group, 2005).
5. The consultations resulted in two reports, published by the Office of the President in 1999. The first, *The Unity of Rwandans,* set out the RPF's version of history. The second mapped out the government's policy vision: *Report on*

the Reflection Meetings held in the Office of the President of the Republic from May 1998 to March 1999.

6. Paul Gready, "Beyond 'You're with Us or against Us': Civil Society and Policymaking in Post-genocide Rwanda," in *Remaking Rwanda*, edited by Straus and Waldorf, p. 89.

7. Herman Musahara and Chris Huggins, "Land Reform, Land Scarcity and Post-conflict Reconstruction: A Case Study of Rwanda," in *From the Ground Up: Land Rights, Conflict and Peace in Sub-Saharan Africa*, edited by Chris Huggins and Jenny Clover (Pretoria, South Africa: Institute for Security Studies, 2005), pp. 269–346.

8. Timothy Longman and Théogène Rutagengwa, "Memory, Identity, and Community in Rwanda," in *My Enemy, My Neighbor: Justice and Community in the Aftermath of Mass Atrocity*, edited by Eric Stover and Harvey M. Weinstein (Cambridge: Cambridge University Press, 2004), p. 167.

9. Isaura Zelaya Favila, "Treatment of Post-Traumatic Stress Disorder in Post-Genocide Rwanda," *Global Grassroots*, July 2009.

10. Jens Meierhenrich, "The Trauma of Genocide," *Journal of Genocide Research*, 9, 4 (2007), p. 555.

11. Amnesty International, *Rwanda: The Hidden Violence*, https://www.amnesty. org/en/documents/afr47/023/1998/en/, accessed August 11, 2017; Human Rights Watch, *Rwanda: The Search for Security and Human Rights Abuses* (New York: Human Rights Watch, 2000); United States Department of State, *Country Reports on Human Rights Practice: Rwanda* (Bureau of Democracy, Human Rights and Labor, February 23, 2000). For an account from a former regime insider, see Gahima, *Transitional Justice in Rwanda*, pp. 53–78.

12. On justice in third countries, see Reyntjens, *Political Governance*, pp. 248–50.

13. The judicial decisions and case law of the ICTR are online: http://unictr. unmict.org/.

14. Victor Peskin, "Victor's Justice Revisited: Rwandan Patriotic Front Crimes and the Prosecutorial Endgame at the ICTR," in *Remaking Rwanda*, edited by Straus and Waldorf, pp. 173–83.

15. Peskin, "Victor's Justice Revisited," p. 177. For analysis of the downing of Habyarimana's aircraft, see Guichaoua, *From War to Genocide*, pp. 143–73.

16. Leslie Haskell and Lars Waldorf, "The Impunity Gap of the International Criminal Tribunal for Rwanda: Causes and Consequences," *Hastings International and Comparative Law Review*, 34, 2 (2011), pp. 49–85.

17. Alison Des Forges and Timothy Longman, "Legal Responses to Genocide in Rwanda," in *My Enemy, My Neighbor*, edited by Stover and Weinstein, p. 167.

18. Catharine A. MacKinnon, "Defining Rape Internationally: A Comment on Akayesu," *Columbia Journal of Transnational Law*, 44, 3 (2006), pp. 940–58.

19. Republic of Rwanda, Ministry of Justice, *Organic Law No 08/96 of 30 August 1996 on the Organization of Prosecutions for Offences Constituting the Crime of Genocide or Crimes against Humanity Committed Since 1 October 1990*, August 30, 1996.

20. Amnesty International, *Gacaca: A Question of Justice*, December 17, 2002, pp. 5–7, https://www.amnesty.org/en/documents/afr47/007/2002/en/, accessed August 17, 2017.

21. Human Rights Watch, *Rwanda—Justice After Genocide: 20 Years On* (New York: Human Rights Watch, 2014), https://www.hrw.org/news/2014/03/28/rwanda-justice-after-genocide-20-years, accessed August 17, 2017.
22. James C. McKinley, Jr., "As Crowds Vent their Rage, Rwanda Publicly Executes 22," *New York Times*, April 25, 1998, http://www.nytimes.com/1998/04/25/world/as-crowds-vent-their-rage-rwanda-publicly-executes-22.html, accessed November 9, 2013; Jane Standley, "From Butchery to Executions in Rwanda," *From Our Own Correspondent*, April 27, 1998, http://news.bbc.co.uk/1/hi/programmes/from_our_own_correspondent/84120.stm, accessed November 9, 2013.
23. Human Rights Watch, "Rwanda: Human Rights Developments," *Human Rights Watch World Report 1997*, https://www.hrw.org/legacy/wr2k/Africa-08.htm, accessed December 2, 2017.
24. de Lame, *A Hill Among a Thousand*, p. 487.
25. Alison Des Forges, edited by David Newbury, *"Defeat is the Only Bad News": Rwanda under Musinga, 1896–1931* (Madison, WI: University of Wisconsin Press, 2011), p. 159.
26. Author's anonymous interviews in 2006 and 2009 with now exiled members of LIPRODHOR (Rwandan League for the Promotion and Defense of Human Rights).
27. Author's 1999 interview with a representative of the Rwandan Association for the Defense of Human Rights and Public Liberties (ADL), founded by Sibomana.
28. UNHRFOR, *Situation of Human Rights in Rwanda*, Commission on Human Rights Resolution 1998/69, April 21, 1998, http://hrlibrary.umn.edu/UN/1998/Res069.html, accessed August 11, 2017.
29. International Crisis Group, *"Consensual Democracy" in Post-genocide Rwanda: Evaluating the March 2001 Elections* (Brussels: International Crisis Group, October 9, 2001), p. 7.

7 Militarized Democracy

1. Marie-Eve Desrosiers and Susan Thomson, "Rhetorical Legacies of Leadership: Projections of 'Benevolent' Leadership in Pre- and Post-genocide Rwanda," *Journal of Modern African Studies*, 49, 3 (2011), p. 429.
2. Prunier, "The Rwandan Patriotic Front," p. 133.
3. Noel Twagiramungu, "The Anatomy of Leadership: A View-from-Within of Post-genocide Rwanda," paper presented at the 53rd Annual Conference of the African Studies Association, November 2010, p. 3.
4. Jean-Paul Kimonyo, Noel Twagiramungu and Christopher Kayumba, *Supporting the Post-Genocide Transition in Rwanda: The Role of the International Community* (Clingendael: Netherlands Institute of International Relations, November 2004).
5. Nilgun Gökgür, *Rwanda's Ruling Party-owned Enterprises: Do They Enhance or Impede Development?* Discussion Paper, University of Antwerp, Institute for Development Policy and Management, 2012, p. 32.
6. Timothy Longman, "Limitations to Political Reform," in *Remaking Rwanda*, edited by Straus and Waldorf, pp. 25–47.

7. National Consultative Forum of Political Organizations, "Historical Background of the NFPO," 2011, http://www.forumfp.org.rw/?HISTORICAL-BACK-GROUND-OF-THE-NFPO, accessed January 24, 2016.
8. National Consultative Forum of Political Organizations, "Activities and Achievement," 2011, http://www.forumfp.org.rw/?ACTIVITIES-AND-ACHIEVEMENTS, accessed January 24, 2015.
9. International Crisis Group, *Rwanda at the End of the Transition: A Necessary Political Liberalisation* (Brussels: ICG, 2002).
10. Cited in Gready, "Beyond " 'You're with Us or against Us,'" in *Remaking Rwanda*, edited by Straus and Waldorf, p. 89.
11. On mourning and memory, see Burnet, *Genocide Lives in Us*, pp. 74–109.
12. Laura G. Eramian, *Peaceful Selves: Personhood, Nationhood and the Post-Conflict Moment in Rwanda* (forthcoming).
13. Laura Major, "Unearthing, Untangling and Re-articulating Genocide Corpses in Rwanda," *Critical African Studies*, 7, 2 (2015), pp. 164–81.
14. Elisée Bisengimana was later convicted of genocide crimes in 2009.
15. Heidy Rombouts, *Victim Organisations and the Politics of Reparation: A Case Study of Rwanda* (Antwerp, Belgium: Intersentia, 2004), pp. 368–9.
16. Timothy Longman, *Memory and Justice in Post-Genocide Rwanda* (Cambridge: Cambridge University Press, 2017), p. 171.
17. D. Newbury, "Canonical Conventions in Rwanda," pp. 48–9.
18. Thomson, *Whispering Truth to Power*, p. 146.
19. For analysis, see Lars Waldorf, "A Justice 'Trickle Down': Rwanda's First Postgenocide President on Trial," in *Prosecuting Heads of State*, edited by Ellen Lutz (Cambridge: Cambridge University Press, 2009), pp. 151–75.
20. Twagiramungu, "The Anatomy of Leadership," p. 10.
21. Reyntjens, *Political Governance in Post-Genocide Rwanda*, pp. 124–62; Lara Santoro and Susan Thomson, "Why are Rwandans Disappearing?," *New York Times*, June 19, 2014, https://www.nytimes.com/2014/06/18/opinion/why-are-rwandans-disappearing.html, accessed June 19, 2014.
22. Longman, "Limitations to Political Reform," in *Remaking Rwanda*, edited by Straus and Waldorf, p. 26.
23. Lars Waldorf, " 'Thinking Big': Rwanda's Post-Genocide Politics," *E-International Relations*, April 30, 2014, http://www.e-ir.info/2014/04/30/thinking-big-rwandas-post-genocide-politics/, accessed May 9, 2014. On the surveillance mechanisms of the state, see Andrea Purdeková, " 'Mundane Sights' of Power: The History of Social Monitoring and Its Subversion in Rwanda," *African Studies Review*, 59, 2 (2016), pp. 59–86.
24. Quoted in Leegwater, *Sharing Scarcity*, p. 44.

8 State, Party, Family

1. Cited in National Service of *Gacaca* Courts, *Gacaca Courts in Rwanda*, June 2012, http://www.minijust.gov.rw/uploads/media/GACACA_COURTS_IN_RWANDA.pdf, accessed November 22, 2015.

2. Anuradha Chakravarty, "Navigating the Middle Ground: The Political Values of Ordinary Hutu in Post-genocide Rwanda," *African Affairs*, 113, 451 (2014), pp. 232–53.
3. Quoted in Thomson, *Whispering Truth to Power*, p. 83.
4. MINECOFIN, *Rwanda Vision 2020*, p. 7.
5. François Misser, "Rwanda: Economy," in *Africa South of the Sahara 2003*, edited by Katherine Murison (London: Routledge, 2004), pp. 887–90.
6. Laura Mann and Marie Berry, "Understanding the Motivations that Shape Rwanda's Emergent Developmental State," *New Political Economy*, 21, 1 (2016), pp. 119–44.
7. Frank Kanyaro Rusagara with Gitura Maura and Gérard Nyirimanzi, *Resilience of a Nation: A History of the Military in Rwanda* (Kigali: Fountain Press, 2009). On Rwandanicity, see D. Newbury, "Canonical Conventions in Rwanda," pp. 61–8.
8. Marco Jowell, "Cohesion through Socialization: Liberation, Tradition and Modernity in the Forging of the Rwanda Defence Force (RDF)," *Journal of Eastern African Studies*, 8, 2 (2014), pp. 278–93.
9. Rangira Béa Gallimore, "Militarism, Ethnicity and Sexual Violence in the Rwandan Genocide," *Feminist Africa*, 10 (2008), pp. 9–29.
10. Since its inception, almost 1.5 million Rwandans have been *itorero* trained: Rwandapedia, Twitter Post. September 27, 2016. 5:14 am, https://twitter.com/Rwandapedia/status/780697218265284608. A photo essay illustrates *itorero*'s military overtones: https://www.flickr.com/photos/rwandapedia/albums/72157673065174682, accessed September 27, 2016.
11. For a recent example, see Eugene Kwibuka, "It is Never Too Late to Play Your Part, Kagame Tells Youth," *New Times*, July 20, 2016, http://allafrica.com/stories/201607200008.html, accessed April 19, 2017.
12. Sundberg, *Training for Model Citizenship*, p. 86.
13. Maria Yohana Mukankuranga, a Tutsi who fled Rwanda in the violence of the 1960s, wrote the song in 1992. Exiled in Uganda, she urged her sons to join the RPF to liberate Rwanda from Habyarimana's clutches. Her sons died for the cause, making her *intore* through sacrifice. Christian Ituze, "The Liberation Struggle Inspired my Career—Maria Yohana," *New Times*, July 18, 2015, http://www.newtimes.co.rw/section/read/190713/, accessed February 6, 2016.
14. Purdeková, "'Mundane Sights' of Power," p. 63.
15. James C. Scott, *Seeing Like a State: How Certain Schemes to Improve the Human Condition Have Failed* (New Haven, CT: Yale University Press, 1998), pp. 4–5.
16. Cited in An Ansoms, "Re-engineering Rural Society: The Visions and Ambitions of the Rwandan Elite," *African Affairs* 108, 431 (2009), p. 307.
17. World Bank, "Rwanda: Population Density (people per sq. km. of land), 1961–2015," http://data.worldbank.org/indicator/EN.POP.DNST?locations=RW&name_desc=true, accessed December 15, 2016.
18. Andrea Purdeková, *Making Ubumwe: Power, State and Camps in Rwanda's Unity-Building Project* (New York and Oxford: Berghahn Books, 2015), pp. 100–1.
19. Purdeková, "'Mundane Sights' of Power," p. 62.

20. Ibid., p. 64.
21. Ministry of Finance and Economic Planning, *Participatory Poverty Assessment* (Kigali: National Poverty Reduction Program, MINÉCOFIN, 2001).
22. Gerard Howe and Andrew McKay, "Combining Quantitative and Qualitative Methods in Assessing Chronic Poverty: The Case of Rwanda," *World Development*, 35, 2 (2007), p. 200. World Bank, "Rwanda, Poverty Rates at International Poverty Lines' for 2010 data. The salaried poor person can generally afford daily basics, and may even own some land.
23. Adapted from Ansoms, "Re-Engineering Rural Society," pp. 289–309; Bert Ingelaere, "Peasants, Power and Ethnicity: A Bottom-up Perspective on Rwanda's Political Transition," *African Affairs*, 109, 435 (2010), pp. 273–92; Sommers, *Stuck*, pp. 31–3; Thomson, *Whispering Truth to Power*, pp. 16–17, 139–41.
24. On the perks and perils of being a *gacaca* judge, see Chakravarty, *Investing in Authoritarian Rule*, pp. 268–317.
25. The "rich with money" are so called as their wealth comes from employment, usually in government but increasingly in the private sector. They also own sizable tracts of land and multiple properties, whether in Kigali or the countryside. They often live in urban areas and will hire daily wage labor through local managers who generally come from the "rich without money" class. The rich with money are generally members of the elite political, military and economic class. The "rich without money" are relatively wealthy by Rwandan standards. Their wealth is expressed in non-monetary terms. They may own large tracts of land or herds of cattle and they can hire other peasants to work for them. The rich without money often live in urban areas in homes they either rent or have mortgaged. This distinguishes them from the largely rural "salaried poor." The salaried poor are generally those who make up the rural upper class as their wealth and status are tied to their control of land and the labor to work they land they own. They often lack the socio-political connections or educational status to become "rich without money."
26. Cited in Taylor Mayol, "Why One Country Banned Bare Feet," August 5, 2016, http://www.ozy.com/acumen/why-one-country-banned-bare-feet/70005, accessed September 1, 2016.
27. Jeannette Kagame does not own the Bata shoe factory. The company does not manufacture in Rwanda. I was unable to determine if she holds a Bata concession. Sunny's perception points to a lack of legitimacy for some government regulations, and to feelings of resentment for rules that seem arbitrary to those subject to them.
28. These reinvented traditions have their own websites, setting out the role and value of these "new" traditions. See the Rwandapedia website (modeled on Wikipedia) to learn about these practices (http://www.rwandapedia.rw/).
29. Philip Verwimp, "Development Ideology, the Peasantry and Genocide: Rwanda Represented in Habyarimana's Speeches," *Journal of Genocide Research*, 2, 2 (2000), p. 44.
30. Andrea Purdeková, " 'Even If I Am Not Here, There Are So Many Eyes': Surveillance and State Reach in Rwanda," *Journal of Modern African Studies*, 49, 3 (2011), p. 481.
31. Office of the President, *Report on the Reflection Meetings*, pp. 6–9.

32. Yolande Bouka, "*Nacibazo*, 'No Problem': Moving behind the Official Discourse of Post-genocide Rwanda," in *Emotional and Ethical Challenges for Field Research in Africa: The Story Behind the Findings*, edited by Susan Thomson, An Ansoms and Jude Murison (New York: Palgrave Macmillan, 2013), p. 116.

33. Christopher C. Taylor, "Kings or Presidents? War and State in Pre- and Post-Genocidal Rwanda," *Social Analysis*, 48, 1 (2004), pp. 138—40.

34. Vansina, "Polities," in *Antecedents to Modern Rwanda*, pp. 38—43.

35. Human Rights Watch, *Preparing for Elections: Tightening Control in the Name of National Unity* (New York: Human Rights Watch, May 2003), p. 3.

36. Aloys Ruzibiza, quoted in Reytnjens, *Political Governance*, p. 50, note 117.

37. Quoted in Sundberg, *Training for Model Citizenship*, p. 15.

38. Andrea Purdeková, "The Everyday Politics of Embodied Domination: Explaining the Production of Disempowerment in a Post-genocide Authoritarian System," paper presented at the Rwanda from Below conference, Institute of Development Policy and Management, University of Antwerp, June 29, 2012, p. 16.

39. Paul Kagame, "Preface," in *After Genocide: Transitional Justice, Post-Conflict Reconstruction and Reconciliation in Rwanda and Beyond*, edited by Phil Clark and Zachary D. Kaufman (New York: Columbia University Press, 2009), p. xxii.

40. For analysis, see Human Rights Watch, *Rwanda, Politically Closed Elections: A Chronology of Violations*, August 20, 2017, https://www.hrw.org/news/2017/08/18/rwanda-politically-closed-elections, accessed August 20, 2017.

41. Twagiramungu left Rwanda for Belgium immediately following the results of the 2003 election, fearing arrest.

42. Human Rights Watch, *Law and Reality: Progress in Judicial Reform in Rwanda* (New York: Human Rights Watch, 2008), pp. 34—43.

43. Chakravarty, "Navigating the Middle Ground," p. 233.

44. Constance Morrill, "Show Business and 'Lawfare' in Rwanda: Twelve Years after the Genocide," *Dissent*, 53, 3 (2006), pp. 17—18.

45. International Crisis Group, "*Consensual Democracy*," p. 4.

46. "Kagame Won, A Little Too Well," *The Economist*, August 28, 2003, http://www.economist.com/node/2023062, accessed October 13, 2014.

47. Jennie E. Burnet, "Gender Balance and the Meanings of Women in Governance in Post-Genocide Rwanda," *African Affairs*, 107, 428 (2008), pp. 361—86.

48. Timothy Longman, "Rwanda: Achieving Equality or Serving an Authoritarian State?," in *Women in African Parliaments*, edited by Gretchen Bauer and Hannah Britton (Boulder, CO: Lynne Rienner, 2006), pp. 133—50.

9 Good Citizens

1. Ministry of Finance and Economic Planning, *Poverty Reduction Strategy Paper* (Kigali: MINECOFIN, 2002).

2. Timothy Williams, Pamela Abbott and Alfred Mupenzi, "'Education at Our School Is Not Free': The Hidden Costs of Fee-free Schooling in Rwanda," *Compare: A Journal of Comparative and International Education*, 45, 6 (2014), pp. 931—52.

3. United Nations Fund for Children (UNICEF), "Rwanda: Statistics, Education," in *State of the World's Children 2015* (New York: UNICEF, 2015).
4. Tim Williams, "Why is Quality of Children's Education in Rwanda Surprisingly Low?," *Effective States and Inclusive Development* blog, 24 August 2016, http://www.effective-states.org/orientated-towards-action-but-low-on-quality-the-politics-of-childrens-education-in-rwanda/, accessed May 19, 2017.
5. Central Intelligence Agency, "Rwanda: People and Society," *CIA Factbook*, last updated November 19, 2015, https://www.cia.gov/library/publications/the-world-factbook/geos/rw.html, accessed November 24, 2015.
6. République Rwandaise, Direction de la statistique, *Enquête intégrale sur la conditions de vie des ménages au Rwanda 2000–2001* (Kigali: Directorate of Statistics, 2002), p. 12.
7. Ministry of Lands, Environment, Forestry, Water and Natural Resources (MINITERRE), *National Land Policy* (Kigali: MINITERRE, 2004), p. 9.
8. Freedom House, *Country Report: Rwanda* (2007), p. 19, https://freedomhouse.org/report/freedom-world/2007/rwanda, accessed December 19, 2015.
9. Quoted in Thomson, *Whispering Truth to Power*, p. 143.
10. World Bank, *World Development Indicators, 2013* (Washington, DC: The World Bank, 2013). For analysis, see An Ansoms and Daniela Rostagno, "Rwanda's Vision 2020 Halfway Through: What the Eye Does Not See," *Review of African Political Economy*, 39, 133 (2012), p. 430.
11. National Unity and Reconciliation Commission, *Nation-Wide Grassroots Consultations Report: Unity and Reconciliation Initiatives in Rwanda* (Kigali: NURC, 2000), p. 21.
12. An overview of NURC activities and programmes is online: http://nurc.gov.rw.
13. Susan Thomson, "Re-education for Reconciliation: Participant Observations on *Ingando*," in *Remaking Rwanda*, edited by Straus and Waldorf, pp. 331–9.
14. Anada Breed overviews the *ingando* syllabus in *Performing the Nation: Genocide, Justice, Reconciliation* (Calcutta: Seagull Books, 2014), pp. 206–12.
15. Efforts to disarm, demobilize and reintegrate soldiers in Rwanda involved five military forces: 1) the FAR, defeated in July 1994; 2) the RPF, the largely Tutsi rebel force that ended the genocide; 3) the postgenocide RPA, in 2002 renamed the Rwanda Defense Force (RDF); 4) the *abacegenzi* and ALiR insurgents who attacked the northwest in 1997–1999 and again in 2001; 5) armed groups, being a catch-all term for Hutu rebels fighting under various political and military groupings in the DRC. See Waldorf, *Transitional Justice and DDR*, pp. 8–9.
16. Quoted in Thomson, *Whispering Truth to Power*, p. 115.
17. For analysis of truth commissions in the Rwandan context and the RPF's postgenocide justice choices, see Waldorf, *Mass Justice for Mass Atrocity*, pp. 92–6, 167–9.
18. Waldorf wonders if there even was a precolonial equivalent to modern *gacaca*: see *Mass Justice for Mass Atrocity*, p. 113.
19. Bert Ingelaere, "From Model to Practice: Researching and Representing Rwanda's 'Modernized' *Gacaca* Courts," *Critique of Anthropology*, 32 (2012), pp. 400–3.

20. On the early concerns of donors, see Anuradha Chakravarty, "Gacaca Courts in Rwanda: Explaining Divisions within the Human Rights Community," *Yale Journal of International Affairs*, 1, 2 (2006), pp. 132–45.
21. Chakravarty, *Investing in Authoritarian Rule*, pp. 3–4.
22. These dates are estimates, as the courts functioned differently in each community, depending on local social and political realities.
23. For first-hand narratives, see the documentary films of director Annie Aghion, *My Neighbor My Killer* (2009) and *The* Gacaca *Trilogy:* Gacaca: *Living Together Again* (2002), *In Rwanda We Say . . .* (2004) and *The Notebooks of Memory* (2009).
24. Bert Ingelaere, *Inside Rwanda's* Gacaca *Courts: Seeking Justice after Genocide* (Madison, WI: University of Wisconsin Press, 2016), p. 5.
25. Quoted in Thomson, *Whispering Truth to Power*, p. 149.
26. FEWS/NET, *Rwanda: Food Insecurity Update December 2005*, http://www.fews.net/sites/default/files/documents/reports/Rwanda_200511en.pdf, accessed December 21, 2015.
27. Quoted in An Ansoms, "Rwanda's Post-Genocide Economic Reconstruction: The Mismatch Between Elite Ambitions and Rural Realities," in *Remaking Rwanda*, edited by Straus and Waldorf, p. 243.
28. Paul Kagame, "Rwanda and the New Lions of Africa," *Wall Street Journal*, May 19, 2013, https://www.wsj.com/articles/SB1000142412788732476700457848 5234078541160, accessed November 9, 2014.
29. Kirrily Pells, "Building a Rwanda 'Fit for Children,'" in *Remaking Rwanda*, edited by Straus and Waldorf, p. 79.

10 Conformity or Else

1. Human Rights Watch, *2008 World Report: Rwanda*, https://www.hrw.org/reports/2008/rwanda0708/7.htm, accessed July 12, 2016.
2. Burnet, *Genocide Lives in Us*, p. 21.
3. A good example is the work of Christian Davenport and Allan C. Stam, "What Really Happened in Rwanda?," October 6, 2009, http://www.thirdworldtraveler.com/East_Africa/Rwanda_WhatReallyHappened.html, accessed July 18, 2016.
4. Will Jones, "Victoire in Kigali, or Why Elections Are Not Won Transnationally in Rwanda," *Journal of Eastern African Studies*, 10, 2 (2016), p. 350.
5. The DGPR was allowed to register one week before the August elections. It did not field any candidates.
6. Jones, "Victoire in Kigali," p. 359.
7. Human Rights Watch, *Rwanda: Eight-Year Sentence for Opposition Leader*, October 30, 2012, https://www.hrw.org/news/2012/10/30/rwanda-eight-year-sentence-opposition-leader, accessed June 5, 2017.
8. Ivan R. Mugisha, "EU Renews Call for Review of Ingabire Trial," *The East African*, October 9, 2016, http://allafrica.com/stories/201610090237.html, accessed August 8, 2017.
9. Anjan Sundaram, "To Lionize Dictators like Paul Kagame is to Mock Those They Persecuted," *Guardian*, December 10, 2016, https://www.theguardian.

com/commentisfree/2016/dec/11/wrong-to-lionise-dictators-like-kagame, accessed December 19, 2016.

10. For an example of such exchanges, visit the Facebook group "Friends of Reason."

11. Quoted in Santoro and Thomson, "Why are Rwandans Disappearing?".

12. Cited in Purdeková, " 'Even If I Am Not Here, There Are So Many Eyes,'" p. 475.

13. Judi Rever and Geoffrey York, "Assassination in Africa: Inside the Plots to Kill Rwanda's Dissidents," *Globe and Mail* (Toronto), May 2, 2014, https://beta. theglobeandmail.com/news/world/secret-recording-says-former-rwandan-army-major-proves-government-hires-assassins-to-kill-critics-abroad/article18396349/?ref=http://www.theglobeandmail.com&, accessed August 18, 2017.

14. Harry Verhoeven, "Nurturing Democracy or Into the Danger Zone? The Rwandan Patriotic Front, Elite Fragmentation and Post-liberation Politics," in *Rwanda Fast Forward*, edited by Campioni and Noack, pp. 265–80.

15. Marie E. Berry, "When 'Bright Futures' Fade: Paradoxes of Women's Empowerment in Rwanda," *Signs: Journal of Women in Culture and Society*, 41, 1 (2015), p. 2.

16. Villia Jefremovas, *Brickyards to Graveyards: From Production to Genocide in Rwanda* (Albany: State University of New York Press, 2002), pp. 97–108.

17. Aili Mari Tripp, *Women and Power in Post-Conflict Africa* (Cambridge: Cambridge University Press, 2015).

18. Gregory Warner, "It's the No 1 Country for Women in Politics, but Not in Daily Life," *NPR Radio, Goats and Soda: Stories of Life in a Changing World*, July 29, 2016.

19. Justine Uvuza, *Hidden Inequalities: Rwandan Female Politicians' Experiences of Balancing Family and Political Responsibilities*, PhD dissertation, School of Geography, Politics and Sociology, Newcastle University, April 2014.

20. Cited in Nishtha Chugh, "The Drive to Beat Rwanda's Gender-based Violence," *Guardian*, November 22, 2013, https://www.theguardian.com/global-development-professionals-network/2013/nov/22/rwanda-gender-based-violence, accessed July 3, 2017.

21. Burnet, "Gender Balance and the Meanings of Women in Governance in Post-genocide Rwanda," p. 386.

22. Cited in "President Paul Kagame under Scrutiny," *The Economist*, August 5, 2010, http://www.economist.com/node/16750119, accessed November 9, 2014.

23. Burnet, "Women Have Found Respect," p. 310.

24. Ibid., p. 309.

25. Mann and Berry, "Understanding the Motivations that Shape Rwanda's Emergent Developmental State," p. 2.

26. Author's interview with a NURC official, Kigali, August 2006. A resource guide to assist teachers is available online: *The Teaching of History of Rwanda: A Participatory Approach* (2006), https://www.law.berkeley.edu/files/HRC/Rwanda_resource_book_for_teachers_version_10._rwandan_history_book. pdf, accessed August 2, 2016. For analysis of the politics of teaching history,

see Sarah Warshauer Freedman, Harvey M. Weinstein, K.L. Murphy and Timothy Longman, "Teaching History in Post-Genocide Rwanda," in *Remaking Rwanda*, edited by Straus and Waldorf, pp. 302–3.

27. King's *From Classrooms to Conflict* (2013) analyzes classroom content and context before and after the genocide in the only study of its kind.

28. Angie went on to say that a small group of American and European teachers had started a monthly study group in 2011 to brainstorm how best to teach the genocide to their high schoolers. When David Newbury's article "Understanding Genocide" (*African Studies Review*, 41, 1 (1998), pp. 73–97) was assigned, military police visited their group meeting, asking why they were teaching the genocide with instructions prepared by a foreigner. Newbury's paper addresses the historical causes of the 1994 genocide, noting that genocide is not unique to Rwanda but rather the result of a variety of social, economic, historical, political and cultural factors. It was written with high-school teachers in mind.

29. Chakravarty, "Navigating the Middle Ground," p. 2.

30. Chris Huggins, "Land Grabbing and Land Tenure Security in Post-Genocide Rwanda," in *Losing Your Land: Dispossession in the Great Lakes*, edited by An Ansoms and Thea Hilhorst (London: James Currey, 2014), pp. 141–62.

31. The government published four reports between 2003 and 2008: République Rwandaise, Assemblée nationale, "*Rapport de la Commission Parlementaire de controle mise en place le 27 décembre 2002 pour enquêter sur les problèmes du MDR*"; Assemblée nationale, "*Rapport de la Commission Parlementaire ad hoc crée en date du 20 janvier 2004 par le Parlement, Chambre des Députés, chargée d'examiner les tueries perpétrées dans la province de Gikongoro, l'idéologie génocidaire et ceux qui la propagent partout au Rwanda*"; Assemblée nationale, "*Rapport d'analyse sur le problème d'idéologie du génocide evoquée au sein des établissements scolaires,*" December 2007; Rwandan Senate, "Genocide Ideology and Strategies for Its Eradication," 2006.

32. Email correspondence with a representative of the Netherlands Embassy in Kigali, June 12, 2009.

33. I reached out to the CNLG official named by my Dutch informant for comment. She did not reply.

34. UNOHCHR, "Report of the Mapping Exercise Documenting the Most Serious Violations of Human Rights and International Humanitarian Law Committed within the Territory of the Democratic Republic of the Congo between March 1993 and June 2003," http://www.ohchr.org/EN/Countries/AfricaRegion/Pages/RDCProjetMapping.aspx, accessed August 20, 2016.

35. Human Rights Watch, "Rwanda: Spate of Enforced Disappearances," May 16, 2014, https://www.hrw.org/news/2014/05/16/rwanda-spate-enforced-disappearances, accessed August 22, 2016.

36. National Unity and Reconciliation Commission, "Rwanda Reconciliation Barometer," October 2010, available online: http://www.nurc.gov.rw/file-admin/Documents/RWANDA_RECONCILIATION_BAROMETER.pdf, accessed December 19, 2016.

37. Bert Ingelaere, "Do We Understand Life After Genocide? Center and Periphery in the Construction of Knowledge in Postgenocide Rwanda,"

African Studies Review, 53, 1 (2010), p. 47, pp. 49–50; and Eduard Jordaan, "Inadequately Self-Critical: Rwanda's Self-Assessment for the African Peer Review Mechanism," *African Affairs*, 105, 420 (2006), pp. 333–51.

38. See press releases from the National Unity and Reconciliation Commission, the Governance Board, the Electoral Commission, and the Ministry of Justice.

39. Rodrigue Rwirahira, "At Least 92% of Rwandans Reconciled, Says New Survey," *New Times*, January 28, 2016, http://www.newtimes.co.rw/section/read/196536/, accessed July 10, 2016.

40. Edward Kagire, "Mo Ibrahim Index Full of Discrepancies—Official," *New Times*, October 8, 2010, http://www.newtimes.co.rw/section/read/24771/, accessed July 9, 2016.

41. Chakravarty found the same: see "Navigating the Middle Ground," p. 21.

11 Rules, Rules and More Rules

1. Purdeková, "'Even If I Am Not Here, There Are So Many Eyes,'" p. 477.
2. Benjamin Chemouni, "Explaining the Design of the Rwandan Decentralization: Elite Vulnerability and the Territorial Repartition of Power," *Journal of Eastern African Studies*, 8, 2 (2016), p. 246.
3. On the origins and duties of *nyumbakumi*, see Purdeková, "'Mundane Sights' of Power," pp. 67–9.
4. Quoted in Thomson, *Whispering Truth to Power*, p. 121.
5. Purdeková, "'Mundane Sights' of Power," p. 68.
6. Purdeková, "'Even If I Am Not Here, There Are So Many Eyes,'" p. 479.
7. Quoted in Chemouni, "Explaining the Design of the Rwandan Decentralization," p. 250.
8. Malin Hasselskog, "Participation or What? Local Experiences and Perceptions of Household Performance Contracting in Rwanda," *Forum for Development Studies*, 43 (2015), pp. 1–23.
9. Bugingo Silver, "Reporters Notebook: Rwanda," *Global Integrity Report 2009*, http://report.globalintegrity.org/Rwanda/2009/notebookComments#1, accessed December 20, 2013.
10. Chemouni, "Explaining the Design of the Rwandan Decentralization," p. 251.
11. "Paul Kagame: You Cannot Build Democracy on Sand," *New Times*, July 1, 2012, http://www.newtimes.co.rw/section/read/52484/, accessed June 20, 2016.
12. Longman, "Limitations to Political Reform," p. 41.
13. Patricia Crisafulli and Andrea Redmond, *Rwanda, Inc.: How a Devastated Nation Became an Economic Model for the Developing World* (New York: St. Martin's Griffins, 2014).
14. Ingelaere, "'The Ruler's Drum and the People's Shout': Accountability and Representation on Rwanda's Hill," in *Remaking Rwanda*, edited by Straus and Waldorf, p. 74; Sommers, *Stuck*, pp. 245–9.
15. A good example of the provision of government services to reward the population is the Burera hospital. Located in northern Rwanda in Butaro sector next

to Lake Bulera (see Map 2), the hospital offers the best cancer treatment in East and Central Africa as well as a respected school of public health. Butaro sector in Burera district was the RPF's base of military operation from 1992 to 1993. The hospital also acts as a reminder of the importance of the RPF's role in transforming Rwanda, bringing development to rural areas in exchange for political quiescence.

16. Central Intelligence Agency, "Rwanda: People and Society," *CIA Factbook*, last updated November 19, 2015, https://www.cia.gov/library/publications/the-world-factbook/geos/rw.html, accessed November 24, 2015.

17. Pritish Behuria and Tom Goodfellow, "The Political Settlement and 'Deals' Environment in Rwanda: Unpacking Two Decades of Economic Growth," Effective States and Inclusive Development Research Centre Working Paper No. 57, 2016, pp. 5–6; Ministry of Finance and Economic Planning, *Economic Development and Poverty Reduction Strategy: 2013–2018* (Kigali: MINECOFIN, 2013).

18. Pritish Beharia, "Countering Threats, Stabilising Politics and Selling Hope: Examining the *Agaciro* Concept as a Response to a Critical Juncture in Rwanda," *Journal of Eastern African Studies*, 10, 3 (2016), p. 3.

19. Information on the household poverty surveys (known by their French-language acronym EICV) are online at the National Institute of Statistics website, http://statistics.gov.rw/datasource/integrated-household-living-conditions-survey-eicv, accessed July 9, 2016. The surveys have been conducted since 2000. The next survey is scheduled for 2018.

20. An Ansoms, Esther Marijnen, Giuseppe Cioffo and Jude Murison, "Statistics versus Livelihoods: Questioning Rwanda's Pathway out of Poverty," *Review of African Political Economy*, 43, 151 (2016), pp. 1–19.

21. Gaudiose Mujawamariya, Marijke D'Haese and Stign Speelman, "Exploring Double Sided-Selling in Cooperatives, Case Study of Four Coffee Cooperatives in Rwanda," *Food Policy*, 39 (2013), pp. 72–83.

22. Mann and Berry, "Political Motivations in Rwanda," p. 18.

23. For analysis, see Sophie Pilgrim, "Smugglers Work on the Dark Side of Rwanda's Plastic Bag Ban," Al-Jazeera America, February 25, 2016, http://america.aljazeera.com/articles/2016/2/25/rwanda-plastic-bag-ban.html, accessed April 19, 2017.

24. Katherine Klein, "Reinventing Rwanda—A Conversation with President Paul Kagame," *Knowledge@Wharton* podcast, October 22, 2015, http://knowledge.wharton.upenn.edu/article/president-paul-kagame-on-rwandas-reinvention/, accessed November 9, 2015; Waldorf, " 'Thinking Big.' "

25. Frank Kanyesigye, "Agaciro Fund: Sign of Dignity," *New Times*, September 2, 2012, http://www.newtimes.co.rw/section/read/90190/, accessed June 19, 2016.

26. Olivia Umurerwa Rutazibwa, "Studying Acagiro: Moving Beyond Wilsonian Interventionist Knowledge Production on Rwanda," *Journal of Intervention and Statebuilding*, 8, 4 (2014), p. 298.

27. In 2013, property tax collected in Rwanda amounted to 0.018 percent of GDP: Tom Goodfellow, *Property Taxation and Economic Development: Lessons from*

Rwanda and Ethiopia, SPERI Global Political Economy Brief No. 4, September 2016, p. 3.

28. Kirrily Pells, Kirsten Pontalti and Timothy P. Williams, "Promising Developments? Children, Youth and Post-genocide Reconstruction under the Rwandan Patriotic Front (RPF)," *Journal of Eastern African Studies*, 8, 2 (2014), p. 304.

29. Official Gazette of the Republic of Rwanda, "Law 16/2008 Establishing Rwanda Cooperative Agency (RCA) and Determining Responsibilities, Organisation and Functioning," http://www.rca.gov.rw/spip.php?article94, accessed August 21, 2016.

30. Leegwater, *Sharing Scarcity*, p. 140.

31. Multiple ministries and government agencies were tasked with promoting self-employment among Rwandans. United Nations in Rwanda and the Government of Rwanda, *Youth and Women Employment* (Kigali: UN, 2014); Ministry of Public Service and Labour, "National Employment Policy," November 2007, http://www.mifotra.gov.rw/fileadmin/templates/downloads/National%20Employment%20Policy.pdf, accessed July 4, 2015.

32. Eramian, *Peaceful Selves*.

33. "Americans Were Rwanda's Top Tourists in 2014, Reports KT Press," *KT Press*, April 15, 2015, http://ktpress.rw/2015/02/over-a-million-tourists-help-rwandas-tourism-revenue-cross-us-300m/, accessed November 6, 2016.

34. Rwanda Development Board, "Tourism," n.d., http://www.rdb.rw/rdb/tourism.html, accessed October 6, 2016.

35. "Kigali City Hotels Risk Closure over Poor Hygiene," *East African*, November 9, 2013, http://www.theeastafrican.co.ke/Rwanda/News/Kigali-city-hotels-risk-closure-over-poor-hygiene-/1433218-2066486-513alnz/index.html, accessed December 2, 2016.

36. On the relationship between agricultural zones and rural livelihoods, see United States Agency for International Development, Famine Early Warning Systems Network (FEWS), *Rwanda: Livelihood Zones and Descriptions* (Kigali: USAID, 2012).

37. Rwandan Ministry of Agriculture with the World Food Programme, *Comprehensive Food Security and Vulnerability Analysis and Nutrition Survey* (Kigali: MINAGRI, 2012), p. 4.

38. For analysis, see Malin Hasselskog, "Rwandan Developmental 'Social Engineering': What Does It Imply and How Is It Displayed?," *Progress in Development Studies*, 15, 2 (2015), pp. 154–69.

39. Kagame made this promise in his September 2010 inauguration speech.

40. Minister of Finance and Economic Planning Claver Gatete, *Budget Speech 2014/2015*, http://www.minecofin.gov.rw/fileadmin/templates/documents/BUdget_Management_and_Reporting_Unit/Budget_Speeches/2014-2015_Budget_Speech.pdf, accessed August 21, 2017.

12 Friends Only

1. United Nation Group of Experts on the Democratic Republic of Congo, "Final Report of the Group of Experts on the DRC Submitted in Accordance with Paragraph 4 of the Security Council Resolution 2021," November 15,

2012, http://www.un.org/ga/search/view_doc.asp?symbol=S/2012/843, accessed August 22, 2016.

2. Duncan Miriri, "Rwanda Demands Respect from the West after Aid Cuts," *Reuters World News*, July 29, 2012, http://www.reuters.com/article/us-congo-democratic-rwanda-idUSBRE86R10W20120728, accessed August 19, 2017.

3. Danielle Beswick, "Peacekeeping, Regime Security and 'African Solutions to African Problems': Exploring Motivations for Rwanda's Involvement in Darfur," *Third World Quarterly*, 31, 5 (2010), pp. 739–54.

4. Jennifer Gandhi and Adam Przeworski, "Cooperation, Cooptation and Rebellion under Dictatorships," *Economics and Politics*, 18, 3 (2006), p. 21.

5. Cited in Chris McGreal, "Is Kagame Africa's Lincoln or a Tyrant Exploiting Rwanda's History?," *Guardian*, May 26, 2013, https://www.theguardian .com/world/2013/may/19/kagame-africa-rwanda, accessed November 14, 2015.

6. Ibid.

7. General Nyamwasa Kayumba, Colonel Patrick Karegeya, Dr. Theogene Rudasingwa and Gerald Gahima, "Rwanda Briefing," August 2010, p. 4 (NB: the document was released without page numbers), https://docs.google.com/file/d/0BzL0v-ZpWCAIMGM1MWVkMTQtMWY0Zi00NjNmLT-gxZDgtOTI3NWNkZDhmYTMy/edit?pli=1, accessed December 23, 2015.

8. Ibid.

9. "Response to Allegations by Four Renegades," October 2010, http://mod.gov.rw/news-detail/?tx_ttnews%5Btt_news%5D=423&cHash=d2fc10d48571daa 8de4685d55de02523, accessed July 9, 2015.

10. For analysis of the political uses of *Hotel Rwanda*, see: Mohamed Adkikari, "Hotel Rwanda—The Challenges of Historicising and Commercializing Genocide," *Development Dialogues*, 50 (2008), pp. 173–96; Lars Waldorf, "Revisiting Hotel Rwanda: Genocide, Ideology, Reconciliation, and Rescuers," *Journal of Genocide Research*, 11, 1 (2009), pp. 101–25.

11. Edouard Kayihura with Kerry Zukus, *Inside the Hotel Rwanda: The Surprising True Story and Why it Matters Today* (Dallas, TX: BenBella Books, 2014).

12. For analysis of the ideological goals and differences of the opposition in exile, see Jones, "Victoire in Kigali."

13. Rwandan National Congress, "Rwanda: Pathway to Peaceful Change, Declaration of Core Values, Goals and Agenda for a New Rwanda," December 2010, http://www.rwandanationalcongress.info/RNC_Interim%20policy.pdf, accessed July 19, 2015.

14. When asked why her government continued to support the RPF, the donor said on the condition of anonymity: "I'm only in Rwanda for another year. I'm trying to get posted to [names prestigious locale]. The best way to be considered for such positions is to make sure [my government's] funds are used well. Rwanda is a very good country for such projects. The RPF knows how to make people commit to development projects and that makes us look good with our superiors." Email exchange with the author, August 19 and 21, 2014.

15. Rice's speech, titled "Building a New Nation: Rwanda's Potential and Progress," is online: http://usun.state.gov/briefing/statements/2011/177743.htm, accessed July 15, 2013.

16. Email exchange with the author, November 24, 2011.
17. See Julius Adekunle, *Culture and Customs of Rwanda* (Westport, CT: Greenwood Publishing, 2007), particularly pp. 54–5; Pierre Crépeau and Simon Bizimana, *Proverbes du Rwanda* (Tervuren: Musée Royal de l'Afrique Centrale, 1979); and Aimable Twagilimana, *Hutu and Tutsi* (New York: Rosen Publishing Group, 1998), particularly pp. 23–8.
18. Ingelaere, "Do We Understand Life After Genocide?," p. 54.
19. Twagiramungu, "The Anatomy of Leadership," p. 5.
20. René Lemarchand, "Power and Stratification in Rwanda: A Reconsideration," *Cahiers d'Études Africaines*, 6, 24 (1969), pp. 592–610, esp. p. 598.
21. Rever and York, "Assassination in Africa."
22. Reyntjens, *Political Governance in Post-Genocide Rwanda*, pp. 1–18.
23. Human Rights Watch, "Repression Across Borders: Attacks and Threats Against Critics at Home and Abroad," January 28, 2014, https://www.hrw.org/news/2014/01/28/rwanda-repression-across-borders, accessed August 12, 2017.
24. News of Rwanda, "Gen Kabarebe on Karegeya: 'When You Choose to be a Dog, You Die like a Dog,'" January 11, 2014, http://www.newsofrwanda.com/featured1/21824/gen-kabarebe-on-karegeya-when-you-choose-to-be-dog-you-die-like-dog/, accessed August 12, 2017.
25. To view the full performance, see Kwibuka Rwanda Channel, *Kwibuka 20 Play: Shadows of Memory*, https://youtu.be/I2ioiQ6brfk, accessed October 19, 2016.
26. Paul Kagame, "Speech at the 20th Commemoration of the Genocide against the Tutsi," April 7, 2014, http://www.kwibuka.rw/speech, accessed October 21, 2016.
27. In 2008, Kigali won the United Nations' Habitat Scroll of Honour Award: UN Habitat, "The 2008 Scroll of Honour Winners," n.d., http://mirror.unhabitat.org/content.asp?typeid=19&catid=827&cid=6586, accessed October 7, 2015.
28. Bert Ingelaere, "What's on a Peasant's Mind? Experiencing RPF State Reach and Overreach in Postgenocide Rwanda (2000–2010)," *Journal of Eastern African Studies*, 8, 2 (2014), p. 215.
29. Guichaoua, *From War to Genocide*, p. 346.
30. An English subtitled version of the song is available online: https://www.youtube.com/watch?v=S2n8hTQl2lI&feature=player_detailpage&app=desktop, accessed October 19, 2016.
31. Edmund Kagire, "Singer Kizito Mihigo Jailed for 10 Years," *The East African*, February 28, 2015, http://www.theeastafrican.co.ke/news/Singer-Kizito-Mihigo-jailed-for-10-years/2558-2638664-7bp3eaz/index.html, accessed March 9, 2015.

Epilogue

1. See, for example, "Remarks by Minister of State in Charge of Cooperation, Eugene-Richard Gasana, at the 22nd Commemoration of the Genocide Against the Tutsi," April 12, 2016, http://rwandaun.org/site/2016/04/12/remarks-by-minister-of-state-in-charge-of-cooperation-eugene-richard-

gasana-at-the-22nd-commemoration-of-the-genocide-against-the-tutsi/, accessed November 9, 2016.

2. Kagame's 2017 inauguration speech, delivered on August 18, 2017, alludes to his intent to one day lead the Organisation of African Unity: https://www.scribd.com/document/356661212/Inaugural-Address-by-Rwanda-President-Paul-Kagame, accessed August 21, 2017.

3. Straus' review of academic arguments about preventing and responding to genocide is excellent. See his chapter "Escalation and Restraint," in *Making and Unmaking Nations*, pp. 34–53.

4. Uvin's *Aiding Violence* documents the role foreign donors played in creating the conditions for the 1994 genocide.

5. *Stuck* is the title of Sommers' book on Rwandan youth.

6. Three key texts teach the history before 1900, analyzing the kingdom that would come to form the modern Rwanda state: Jean-Pierre Chrétien, *The Great Lakes of Africa: Two Thousand Years of History* (New York: Zone Books, 2003); Des Forges, *Defeat is the Only Bad News*; and Vansina, *Antecedents to Modern Rwanda*. See also René Lemarchand, *Rwanda and Burundi* (New York: Praeger Publishers, 1970), especially pp. 13–89; and David Newbury, *Land Beyond the Mists: Essays on Identity and Authority in Precolonial Rwanda and Congo* (Athens, OH: Ohio University Press, 2009), pp. 189–277.

7. For analysis of this strategy in action, see Dan Magaziner, "#MindYourOwnBusiness," September 21, 2016, *Africa is a Country*, http://africasacountry.com/2016/09/mindyourownbusiness/, accessed October 9, 2016.

8. Learn more at http://rwandaday.org/2016/, and "President Kagame Speaks at Rwanda Day," https://www.youtube.com/watch?v=PH5ld-GV95U, September 24, 2016, accessed December 16, 2016.

9. Pritish Behuria, "Centralising Rents and Dispersing Power while Pursuing Development? Exploring the Strategic Uses of Military Firms in Rwanda," *Review of African Political Economy*, 43, 150 (2016), pp. 630–47.

10. Times Reporters, "Rwigara Case was Handled Professionally, Police, City Officials Say," *New Times*, August 11, 2015, http://www.newtimes.co.rw/section/read/191462/, accessed August 25, 2015.

11. Chad Kitungu, "Nude Photos of Rwanda's Female Presidential Candidate Leaked," *Nairobi News,* May 7, 2017, http://nairobinews.nation.co.ke/news/nude-photos-of-rwandas-female-presidential-candidate-leaked/, accessed May 20, 2017.

12. Diane Shima Rwigara's campaign ended before it started. She was not eligible to stand as a presidential candidate, following the rejection of her nomination by Rwanda's National Election Commission. Voice of America, "Three Rwandan Presidential Candidates Disqualified Amid Criticism," July 7, 2017, https://www.voanews.com/a/three-rwandan-presidential-candidates-disqualified/3933118.html, accessed July 10, 2017.

13. Rodrigue Rwirahira, "Byabagamba, Rusagara Get Lengthy Jail Terms," *New Times*, April 1, 2016, http://www.newtimes.co.rw/section/read/198556/, accessed May 6, 2016.

14. Eugene Kwibuka, "Umushyikirano Mulls Vision 2050," *New Times*, December 23, 2016, http://allafrica.com/stories/201512230502.html, accessed January 9, 2017.
15. World Bank, "Rwanda: Data," http://data.worldbank.org/country/rwanda, accessed November 31, 2016.
16. Ansoms et al., "Statistics versus Livelihoods"; and Sam Desiere, "The Evidence Mounts: Poverty, Inflation and Rwanda," *Review of African Political Economy Blog*, June 28, 2017, http://roape.net/2017/06/28/evidence-mounts-poverty-inflation-rwanda/, accessed July 9, 2017.
17. Magaziner, "#MindYourOwnBusiness."

GLOSSARY

Kinyarwanda

abacengezi	infiltrators; commonly used to refer to the Hutu insurgents who fought to overthrow the RPF-led government in the late 1990s and early 2000s
abakada	RPF civilian cadres
abakene (pl.)	poor
abakene wifashije (pl.)	salaried poor
abakire (pl.)	rich, wealthy
abakungu (pl.)	rich without money
abaryi	"eaters," a pejorative term used to describe those in positions of power
abatindi (pl.)	destitute
abatindi nyakujya (pl.)	abject poor
abazungu	foreigners, usually refers to those with white skin
abiru	royal ritualists, royal advisors
agaciro	dignity
akazi	forced labor requirement introduced by the Belgians
amarorerwa yo muri 94	the turbulent events of 1994
Banyamulenge	people of the Mulenge region of DRC/Zaire; perceived to be Tutsi
gacaca	a traditional dispute resolution mechanism appropriated and modified by the RPF to try genocide crimes at the community level; literally means "grass"

289

gatunga agatoki	finger-pointing
Girinka	"one cow, one family" economic development program
gupfa uhagaze	living dead
ibipinga	literally, "people with deep-rooted principles"; since 2011, RPF cadres have modified the meaning to name and shame whoever tries to oppose the RPF ideology and programs; also used pejoratively to mean Hutu opponents or critics
Ibuka	literally, "remember"; the name of the main civil society organization catering to Tutsi survivors of the 1994 genocide
ibyitso	accomplices; used by members of the Habyarimana regime during the civil war and genocide to describe citizens who supported or collaborated with the then rebel RPF
igihirahiro	a period of political uncertainty
Igisobanuro Cy'urupfu	"The Meaning of Death," a gospel song released by Kizito Mihigo in 2014
igitero	a mob attack
imidugudu (pl.)	villages
imihigo	performance contracts signed by local government officials and other government employees, including university professors and ministers
imirenge	sector level of government
ingabo	army
ingando	literally, camp; since the 1994 genocide, used to mean either political indoctrination/solidarity camps or citizenship reeducation camps intended to provide civic education to released prisoners and demobilized combatants as well as government officials and matriculating university students
ingengabitekerezo ya jenoside	genocide ideology; literally means the ideas that lead to genocide
Inkotanyi	the RPF's name for its armed wing, later becoming the official name of the political party around 2000
intambara	civil war and genocide, 1990–94; fell out of popular usage around 2008 as the RPF leadership intensified its monitoring of language to weed out those presumed to hold genocide ideology
intara	provincial level of government
interahamwe	those who work together, or those who attack together

intore	a person who has been chosen to participate or undergone the training of *itorero*, citizen with military values
Intsinzi bana b'Urwanda	"Victory to the Children of Rwanda," a liberation song written and sung by Maria Yohana Mukankuranga to honor the RPF's liberation struggle
inyangamugayo	community-appointed *gacaca* court judges, literally, those who detest disgrace, or a person of irreproachable conduct
itorero	civic leadership-training to learn Rwandan values and gain a sense of patriotism
itsembabwoko	genocide; a neologism created in 1994 from two compound words: *gutsemba* (to kill) and *bwoko* (ethnicity)
jenoside yakorewe abatutsi	genocide against the Tutsi; replaced *itsembabwoko* as the term for the genocide by constitutional amendment in 2008
Kinyarwanda	the language or culture of Rwanda
Kwibohora	Liberation Day
Kwibuka!	a political slogan introduced by the RPF in 2009 to describe the annual commemoration of the genocide against Tutsi
muri '94	in 1994
mwami	king
Ndi Umunyarwanda	"I am Rwandan" initiative designed to produce ethnic unity, instituted in 2013
nyakatsi	homes made of mud and thatch
nyumbakumi	unit of ten households, also refers to an appointed informal local official
shambas	personal gardens, plots
ubudehe	community mobilization for poverty reduction
ubwenge	clever, bright or brilliant, in reference to the speaker
umudugudu (sing.)	village
umugabo	male
umuganda	work for the public good
umukene (sing.)	poor
umukene wifashije (sing.)	salaried poor
umukire (sing.)	rich
umukungu (sing.)	rich without money
umukuru	four-person village-level committees, instituted in 2006; also refers to an appointed local official known as *umukuru w'umudugudu*, meaning "the head of *umudugudu* [village]"; an elected local government official who oversees all

	activities in a village, formally replacing the *nyumbakumi*
umurenge	sector
Umurenge SACCO	sector-level cooperative savings scheme
umuryango	family; since the genocide, also refers to the RPF
umushyikirano	national leadership summits
umutindi (sing.)	destitute
umutindi nyakujya (sing.)	abject poor
urugerero	national service
Urugwiro	presidential compound
urwagwa	banana beer
utugari	cell level of government
uturere	district level of government

French

bourgmestre	mayor
cellule	cell
conseiller	councilor
génocidaires	the term describing those accused of acts of genocide
Hutu de service	token Hutu
Opération Turquoise	a French-led military operation in Rwanda in 1994 under the mandate of the United Nations
préfectures	provinces
République Rwandaise	Republic of Rwanda
responsable	responsible
secteur	sector
Zone Turquoise	the humanitarian zone monitored by French troops covering the provinces of Gikongoro, Kibuye and Cyangugu

INDEX

Figures and tables are indicated by page numbers in italics; plates found in the center of the book are indicated by "pl." in italics. References such as the civil war that took place between 1990–94 are written "1990–94 civil war" and indexed as if written "nineteen ninety–nineteen ninety-four."

DMI (Department of Military Intelligence), 37, 184, 185, 194

double genocide, 161, 181–2

doublespeak (*ubwenge*; clever, bright or brilliant speaker), 231–4

DRC (Democratic Republic of Congo; Congo; Zaire). *See* Democratic Republic of Congo (DRC; Congo; Zaire)

Dusaidi, Claude, 117

eaters (*abaryi*), 154

economic development: AgDF and, 214–15; citizens/citizenship and, 9, 180; communal labor (*umuganda*) and, 158; cooperatives and, 51, 134, 164, 213, 215, 216–17; entrepreneurship and, 178, 180, 211, 213, 217–18, 219; Habyarimana and, 49, 62, 63–5; human rights abuses versus, 38, 147, 250; *imidugudu* (villages) policy and, 110; information management and, 195; international aid/community and, 147, 285n14; justice during postgenocide period versus, 8, 80, 108; Kagame and, 3, 48–9, 180, 200, 249; Kayibanda and, 48–9; in Kigali, 11, 12, *pl. 14*; manufacturing industry and, 147, 211; "one cow, one family" (Girinka) program and, 219; political power and, 48–9; during postgenocide period, 2, 3, 8, 9, 48–9; private sector investors in, 12, 147, 178, 249; in rural communities, 2, 10, 11, 63, 168–9; self-employment and, 217–18, 284n31; shame or shaming and, 211; tourism and, 1, 12–13, 37–8, 173, 218, 251; transition period and, 83; for Tutsi, 150–1, 180; for Twa, 180; twentieth anniversary of 1994 genocide and, 235; urban area and, 2; Vision 2020 and, 122, 146, 147; Vision 2050 and, 254. *See also* infrastructure

economics: Habyarimana and, 63–4; income inequality and, 168, 169–70, 212; informal sector and, 213–14; mass violence and, 251; middle-income country and, 122, 146, 254; modernization goal and, 146; national unity and, 3–4; natural resources/minerals trade and, 121, 146–7, 193; and prosperity, image of, 2, 172, 221, 236, 253–4; sector-level cooperative savings scheme (*Umurenge Sacco*) and, 216–17. *See also* economic development

education: civil rights versus, 179; class status and, 156; curriculum on 1994 genocide, 190, 281n28; during Habyarimana regime, 191; higher education, 1–2, 12, 151, 167; Hutu extremists/hardliners and, 191; of old-caseload returnees, 98–9; poor/poverty and, 156; primary education, 9, 12, 41, 98, 99, 167, 269n1, *pl. 13*; reconciliation and, 41; refugees and refugee camps and, 55, 98; in rural communities, 167–8; Rwandan history and, 113–14; secondary education, 8, 10, 12, 41, 83, 113–14, 167, 190; statistics, 167; for women, 167. *See also* reeducation, citizen

elections, and Habyarimana, 64, 65, 71

elections during postgenocide period: coercion and, 164; criticism of RPF and, 123, 161, 182, 222–3; ethnic identity (ethnicity), *pl. 12*; genocide denial and, 182–4; Hutu during postgenocide period, 162; information management and, 161, 162, 183; international aid/community and, 161, 183, 222; loyalty to RPF and, 134, 164; MDR and, 162, 277n41; multi-party politics in, 64, 162, 182, 186, 279n5; national security and, 161; for parliament, 123, 161, 162, 164, 186, 222; political power and, 161; for president, 123, 161, 162, 164, 182,

forgiveness and apology, 177, 197, 238–9, 240

Forum of Political Organizations (National Consultative Forum of Political Organizations), 133–4, 189

France: 1990–94 civil war and, 62, 66, 70; Opération Turquoise and, 35, 88; political exiles in, 62, 124; postgenocide period and, 34, 80, 85; universal jurisdiction in, 124; Zone Turquoise as monitored by, 34, 35, 85

free speech, 162, 163

French, Howard, 86

friends or enemies of RPF. *See* enemies or friends of RPF

future of Rwanda: external threats against RPF and, 244, 250; Kagame and, 253–4; mass violence in, 8–9, 168, 243; RPF and, 253–4; women's role in, 168; youth's role in, 168, 247. *See also* Rwanda

gacaca (community-based) courts: about history of, 124, 145, 174, 178, 197, 278n18, 279n22, *pl. 12*; amnesty for crimes versus, 173–4; apology and forgiveness in, 177, 197, 239; democracy and, 175; divisionists and, 198; forgiveness and, 176, 177; *gacaca* judges (*inyangamugayo*, "people of integrity") and, 174, 176; human rights abuses and, 175–6; Hutu and, 177–8, 197–8; institutional mobilization and, 158; international aid/community and, 176–7; justice and, 173–4, 175, 178, 197; national unity and, 173, 175, 176–7; poor/poverty and, 177; reconciliation and, 173–4, 176–7; RPF and, 174, 175, 176; secrecy and silence code and, 173, 175; statistics, 176; surveillance and, 205; truth and, 176, 177, 178, 197; truth commissions versus, 174;

women's role in, 177. *See also* court system; trials

Gahima, Gerald, 84, 224, 226, 227

Gasana, Anastase, 128

gatunga agatoki (finger-pointing), 31, 89

gender equality/inequality, 186–9, 249

gender norms: patriarchal, 98, 100–1, 108–9, 152–3, 159, 187–8; proverbs and, 232; violence and, 19. *See also* gender equality/inequality

Geneva Conventions, 124

génocidaires (those accused of acts of genocide), 22, 89, 90, 92, 107, 136–7, 210, 211, *pl. 8*

genocide: definition of, 4, 257n8; double genocide and, 161, 181–2; rape as crime of, 126; RPA policy and, 20–1, 125; RPF policy and, 20–1, 46, 125. *See also* 1994 genocide

genocide against Tutsi (*jenoside yakorewe abatutsi*), 181–2

genocide denial (deniers): criticism of RPF and, 123, 129, 161–2, 193, 228; elections and, 182–4; ethnic unity and, 129; Hutu and, 163, 181, 182–3, 192; Hutu extremists/hardliners and, 181; reports on, 195; shame or shaming and, 181; trials and, 126; trials for, 183–4

genocide ideology (*ingengabitekerezo ya jenoside*): citizen with military values (*intore*) and, 149; CNLG and, 190; Constitution and, 163; free speech versus accusations of believing, 163; Hutu and, 162, 163, 192–3, 245; Hutu extremists/hardliners and, 193; "I am Rwandan" (Ndi Umunyarwanda) initiative and, 238; Ingabire Umuhoza as presidential candidate and, 183; international aid/community on, 192–3; national symbols versus, 172; national unity and, 194; "never again" mantra and, 242; prisons and prisoners and, 198; reports on, 192, 195, 281n31; shame